Youth in Crisis?
'Gangs', territoriality and violence

Few issues attract greater concern and censure than those that surround youth 'gangs'. Paradoxically, youth researchers have conventionally been reluctant to even use the term 'gang' but, more recently, such reluctance has receded. Indeed, it is increasingly claimed that – in particular urban 'territories' – youth gangs are commonplace, some young people are deeply immersed in violence and the carrying and use of weapons (particularly knives and firearms) is routine.

Comprising a series of essays from leading national and international researchers, this book subjects such claims to rigorous critical scrutiny. It provides a challenging and authoritative account of complex questions pertaining to urban youth identities, crime and social order.

This book:

- Locates the question of 'gangs' in both historical and contemporary contexts;
- Engages a spectrum of theoretical perspectives and analytical positions;
- Presents and analyses cutting-edge empirical research;
- Addresses a range of previously neglected questions, including those pertaining to girls, young women and 'gangs'.

The volume provides a vital resource for researchers, educators, policy-makers and practitioners with an interest in key questions facing criminology, sociology and social policy.

Barry Goldson holds the Charles Booth Chair of Social Science at the University of Liverpool where he was previously Professor of Criminology and Social Policy. He is the founding editor of *Youth Justice: An International Journal*.

Youth in Crisis?
'Gangs', territoriality and violence

Edited by Barry Goldson

Routledge
Taylor & Francis Group

LONDON AND NEW YORK

First published 2011 by Routledge
2 Park Square, Milton Park, Abingdon, Oxon, OX14 4RN

Simultaneously published in the USA and Canada
by Routledge
270 Madison Avenue, New York, NY 10016

Routledge is an imprint of the Taylor & Francis Group, an informa business

Typeset in Times New Roman
by Keystroke, Station Road, Codsall, Wolverhampton
Printed and bound in Great Britain
by CPI Antony Rowe, Chippenham, Wiltshire

British Library Cataloguing in Publication Data
A catalogue record for this book is available from the British Library

Library of Congress Cataloging in Publication Data
Youth in crisis? : 'gangs', territoriality and violence / edited by Barry Goldson.
   p. cm.
1. Gangs–Great Britain–History. 2. Urban youth–Great Britain–History.
3. Weapons–Great Britain. 4. Human territoriality–Great Britain.
I. Goldson, Barry.
HV6439.G7Y68 2011
364.1'0660941–dc22
2010031306

ISBN 13: 978–1–84392–752–5 hbk
ISBN 13: 978–1–84392–751–8 pbk
ISBN 13: 978–0–203–83200–4 ebook

Contents

List of figures

List of figures

Contributors

Judith Aldridge is Senior Lecturer in the School of Law at the University of Manchester. Her research on gangs, recreational drug use and drug dealing has been widely published including: the best-selling *Illegal Leisure: The Normalisation of Adolescent Recreational Drug Use* (with Measham and Parker, Routledge, 1998); *Dancing on Drugs: Risk, Health and Hedonism in the British Club Scene* (with Measham and Parker, Free Association Books, 2001) and *Illegal Leisure Revisited* (with Measham, Parker and Williams, Routledge, 2010). She was Principal Investigator on the ESRC-funded ethnographic study *Youth Gangs in an English City* from which the findings reported in this volume emerge.

Jon Bannister is Senior Lecturer in Urban Studies and Network Leader of the Scottish Centre for Crime and Justice Research in the School of Social and Political Sciences, University of Glasgow. His research primarily focuses on the forces that impact upon the quality (and the perception) of social interaction. He has recently completed research exploring youth gangs and knife carrying in Scotland together with the factors governing perceptions of anti-social behaviour. He is currently working on an ESRC-funded Knowledge Exchange project on community safety.

Susan A. Batchelor is Lecturer in Criminology in the Department of Sociology at the University of Glasgow. She has worked on a wide range of research projects relating to young people and violence including: girls' views and experiences of violence; young people and sexual violence; persistent young offenders; young women in custody; domestic violence and abuse and, most recently, gangs and knife carrying. Her current projects include: an oral history of growing up in Glasgow in the 1960s; a visual methods project on young people's use of public space and the evaluation of an intensive support service for girls at risk of involvement in the criminal justice system.

Andrew Davies is Senior Lecturer in the School of History at the University of Liverpool. He is the author of *Leisure, Gender and Poverty: Working-Class Culture in Salford and Manchester, 1900–1939* (Open University Press, 1992) and *The Gangs of Manchester* (Milo Books, 2008). He is currently writing a book, provisionally entitled *The Scottish Chicago*, on street gangs, crime and sectarianism in Glasgow during the 1920s and 1930s. In 2008–9, he worked with MaD Theatre Company on an original stage play, *Angels with Manky Faces*, which explored the lives of gang members and their families in late Victorian Manchester.

Barry Goldson holds the Charles Booth Chair of Social Science at the University of Liverpool where he was previously Professor of Criminology and Social Policy. During 2010–12 he is also Visiting Professorial Research Fellow at the University of New South Wales, Sydney, Australia. He has researched and published extensively and his most recent books include: *Youth Crime and Justice* (with Muncie, Sage, 2006); *Comparative Youth Justice* (with Muncie, Sage, 2006); *Dictionary of Youth Justice* (Willan, 2008) and *Youth Crime and Juvenile Justice*, a three-volume set of international 'major works' (with Muncie, Sage, 2009). He is the founding editor of *Youth Justice: An International Journal* (Sage).

Simon Hallsworth is Professor of Social Research at London Metropolitan University where he is also Director of the Centre for Social and Evaluation Research. He has written extensively on urban street violence and is an acknowledged expert on street organisations such as gangs. He has also written on contemporary penal change and development. Publications in these two substantive areas of his research include: *Street Crime* (Willan, 2005) and *The New Punitiveness: Issues, Themes and Perspectives* (with Pratt, Brown, Brown and Morrison, Willan, 2005). He is currently exploring (with John Lea) the emerging contours of what they term the 'security state'.

Deena Haydon is Postgraduate Researcher within the Childhood, Transition and Social Justice Initiative at Queen's University, Belfast and an Independent Research Consultant. Formerly she was Senior Lecturer and Head of Research in the School of Education at Edge Hill University and Principal Officer for Research and Development at Barnardo's. Her publications include: *The Illusions of Post-Feminism* (with Coppock and Richter, Taylor & Francis, 1995); *Northern Ireland NGO Alternative Report: Submission to the United Nations Committee on the Rights of the Child* (Save the Children and Children's Law Centre, 2008); *Developing a Manifesto for Youth Justice in Northern Ireland* (Include Youth, 2008) and *Childhood in Transition: Experiencing Marginalisation and Conflict in Northern Ireland* (with McAlister and Scraton, Save the Children/The Prince's Trust, 2009).

Keith Kintrea is Senior Lecturer in Urban Studies in the School of Social and Political Sciences, University of Glasgow, where he teaches on housing and planning programmes. His research mainly focuses on neighbourhood policy, and on the impact on life chances of living in disadvantaged neighbourhoods. He is currently leading a longitudinal study that aims to understand how young people's aspirations in relation to education and work are shaped by the contexts of parents, place and poverty.

Siobhán McAlister is Research Fellow within the 'Childhood, Transition and Social Justice Initiative' at Queen's University, Belfast. She has worked as a researcher in both the education and voluntary sectors in Northern Ireland and has authored several major research reports including: *Still Waiting: The Stories Behind the Statistics of Young Women Growing up in Northern Ireland* (with Gray and Neill, YouthAction Northern Ireland, 2007); *Childhood in Transition: Experiencing Marginalisation and Conflict in Northern Ireland* (with Haydon and Scraton, Save the Children/The Prince's Trust, 2009) and *An Independent Analysis of Responses to the Department of Education's 'Priorities for Youth' Consultation* (with Haydon, Department of Education Northern Ireland, 2009).

Juanjo Medina is Senior Lecturer in Criminology at the University of Manchester. He has previously held positions at the Violence Institute of New Jersey, USA and the University of Seville, Spain. His research focuses on gangs, violence against women and crime reduction policy and politics and he is particularly interested in comparative analysis.

Geoffrey Pearson is Emeritus Professor of Criminology at Goldsmiths College, University of London. His research interests concern crime, drugs, drug markets, youth studies and historical criminology. He is the author of numerous books and articles, including: *The Deviant Imagination* (Macmillan, 1975); *Working Class Youth Culture* (with Mungham, Routledge, 1976); *Hooligan: A History of Respectable Fears* (Macmillan, 1983); *Young People and Heroin* (with Gilman and McIvor, Health Education Council and Gower, 1985); *The New Heroin Users* (Blackwell, 1987); *Young People, Drugs and Community Safety* (Russell House, 1999) and *Middle Market Drug Distribution* (with Hobbs, Home Office, 2001). From 1998 to 2006 he was Editor-in-Chief of the *British Journal of Criminology*.

Jon Pickering is Lecturer in Public Policy at the Department of Urban Studies in the School of Social and Political Sciences, University of Glasgow. His principal research interests include: territoriality; youth gangs; community development; community health; voluntary sector activity; social exclusion and evaluation methodologies. He was the main researcher on 'Youth Gangs and Knife Carrying in Scotland', a project funded by the Scottish Government, and he is currently working on a study utilising visual methods to develop a greater understanding of how young people perceive the areas in which they live. Further, he is a Research Associate of the Scottish Centre for Criminal Justice Research.

John Pitts is Vauxhall Professor of Socio-Legal Studies at the University of Bedfordshire. He has acted as a consultant on violent youth gangs to local authorities, police forces and 'think tanks'. His recent publications include: *The*

New Politics of Youth Crime: Discipline or Solidarity (Macmillan, 2001); *Crime Disorder and Community Safety* (with Matthews, Routledge, 2001); *The Russell House Companion to Working with Young People* (with Factor and Chauhan, Russell House, 2001); *The Russell House Companion to Youth Justice* (with Bateman, Russell House, 2005) and *Reluctant Gangsters: The Changing Face of Youth Crime* (Willan, 2008). He is Editor of the journal *Safer Communities*.

Robert Ralphs is Lecturer in Criminology at Manchester Metropolitan University. He has over a decade of research experience with a particular focus on drug users and youth crime. In recent years he has contributed to several studies across the UK centred on youth gangs, gun and knife crime. He was the lead ethnographer on the three-year ESRC-funded study *Youth Gangs in an English City* based at the University of Manchester. Rob is also a Trustee of the voluntary group Mothers Against Violence.

Phil Scraton is Professor of Criminology at Queen's University, Belfast and Director of the 'Childhood, Transition and Social Justice Initiative'. His most recent books include: *Power, Conflict and Criminalisation* (Routledge, 2007) and *The Violence of Incarceration* (with McCulloch, Routledge, 2009). He has also co-authored a number of recent research reports including: *The Hurt Inside: The Imprisonment of Women and Girls in Northern Ireland* and *The Prison Within* (both NI Human Rights Commission); *Children's Rights in Northern Ireland* (NI Commissioner for Children and Young People) and *Childhood in Transition: Experiencing Marginalisation and Conflict in Northern Ireland* (Save the Children). He works closely with community-based initiatives and is Chair of the Board of 'Include Youth'.

Peter Squires is Professor of Criminology and Public Policy at the University of Brighton. His main research interests include: youth crime; anti-social behaviour; violence; gangs; weapon-related offending and policing. He has published in each of these areas including: *Rougher Justice: Anti-social Behaviour and Young People* (with Stephen, Willan, 2005); *Community Safety: Critical Perspectives on Policy and Practice* (Policy Press, 2006) and *ASBO Nation: The Criminalisation of Nuisance* (Policy Press, 2008). His most recent book – *Shooting to Kill? Policing, Firearms and Armed Response* (with Kennison, Wiley Blackwell, 2010) – critically explores the development of armed response policy and practice within the British police.

Rob White is Professor of Criminology in the School of Sociology and Social Work at the University of Tasmania, Australia. He is extensively published and has particular research interests in juvenile justice and environmental crime. His most recent books include: *Juvenile Justice: Youth and Crime in Australia* (with Cunneen, Oxford University Press, 2002); *Crimes Against Nature: Environmental Criminology and Ecological Justice* (Willan, 2008); *Crime, Criminality and Criminal Justice* (with Perrone, Oxford University Press,

2010) and *Global Environmental Harm: Criminological Perspectives* (Willan, 2010).

Tara Young is Senior Research Fellow at the Centre for Social and Evaluation Research at London Metropolitan University. She has expertise in qualitative and evaluation research and has worked on a number of research projects, focusing on group delinquency and gang membership. She has authored and co-authored several journal articles on street-based youth groups and her primary research on gangs in the UK (with Hallsworth) has influenced policy at local and national levels.

Acknowledgements

The origins of this book can be traced back to a British Society of Criminology (BSC) Youth Criminology/Youth Justice Network (YC/YJN) conference that was held at the University of Liverpool in April 2009. Several, but not all, of the essays that are published in this volume began life at that conference. Thanks are due to colleagues from the BSC, to each of the speakers and to all of the delegates who not only made the conference such an intellectually stimulating and memorable meeting, but also laid the foundations for what we have here. Particular gratitude is owed to Willan Publishing for sponsoring the conference and to Dianne Webb and Mike Jones from the University of Liverpool for their invaluable practical support in making it happen.

I am, of course, especially grateful to each of the authors and to both Willan Publishing and Routledge for having faith in, and realising, this collaborative project.

The chapters that follow build upon and present different lines of argument and analysis but, taken as a whole, they define the contours for serious reflection, debate and critical analysis. Collectively, we offer the book in the hope that it will, at least, serve two primary purposes. First, to clarify and contextualise a range of questions pertaining to urban youth identities and social order(ing). Second, to provoke further theoretical and empirical inquiry into the complex worlds inhabited by identifiable constituencies of (working-class) young people, the formidable challenges they encounter and the negotiations they engage with during the processes of 'growing up'.

Barry Goldson,
Liverpool, 2010

Youth in crisis?

Barry Goldson

Crisis? What crisis?

> Gangs are not new in Britain, but the nature and scale of current gang culture is fundamentally different from that of previous generations ... in certain communities ... young people have created their own alternative society – the gang – and they live by the gang's rules: the 'code of the street'. As gangs have become more common over the past decade, territory has become increasingly important. For many gangs, defending a geographical territory – often a postcode – has become part of their raison d'être, an integral part of their identity. This, together with the declining age of gang members, has contributed to the increasingly chaotic nature of gang violence.
>
> (Centre for Social Justice, 2009: 25–26)

> The modern gang is perhaps the best illustration of how broken Britain's society is.
>
> (Rt. Hon. Iain Duncan Smith, MP, 2009: 9)

> There are certain sensitive parts of the social structure and there are others that are definite trigger points for the crystallization of feelings of unfairness and despair ... And the triggers? As always it is youth ... They are the triggers and they are the targets in their supposed ... violence, their drug use, their dress ... They have played this role throughout history ... and do so today.
>
> (Young, 2009: 12)

> [C]onstructing the problem of street violence as essentially a problem of gangs is an exercise flawed on empirical, theoretical and methodological grounds ... there appears to be little evidence to suggest a pervasive and growing gang problem ... 'gang talk', as we label this garrulous discourse, runs the risk of misrepresenting what it claims to represent ... while sanctioning 'solutions' that might be as misdirected as they are misguided.
>
> (Hallsworth and Young, 2008: 177)

Within social science, critical analyses both of the symbolic purchase of 'childhood' and 'youth' and the means by which children and young people – or at least identifiable constituencies of children and young people – are governed, are reasonably well-established. Phil Cohen (1997: 9), for example, observes that 'young people . . . carry a peculiar burden of representation; everything they do, say, think, or feel, is scrutinised by an army of professional commentators for signs of the times'. Equally, according to Rose (1989: 121), children and young people belong to 'the most intensively governed sector of personal existence'. In this sense, an almost totemic status is ascribed whereby the 'state of youth' is taken to signify the moral wellbeing (or otherwise) of wider social relations; a barometer signalling the composure or agitation, the equilibrium or instability of the social order. It is within this context, as Muncie (2009: 13) notes, that 'young people tend to be a perennial source of anxiety' and, through political discourse, we are persistently reminded of '"new" delinquent syndromes in which youth seems to delight in crudity, cruelty and violence'. The past two decades have served as stark exemplars of such phenomena.

In the early 1990s widely proclaimed assumptions about the demise of 'child-hood', the ill-discipline of children and the lawlessness of youth, consolidated in popular and political discourse. According to some commentators, this gave rise to 'pervasive negativity' (Haines and Drakeford, 1999: 1); a 'widespread belief' that children and young people 'are in some way turning feral' (Jeffs and Smith, 1996). Concentrated (and often distorted/exaggerated) media coverage of civil unrest (within which children and young people appeared to be prominent players), juvenile crime (particularly car crime) and the social construction of the 'bail bandit' and 'persistent young offender' (children apparently beyond the reach and/or control of the law) inevitably stoked such 'negativity'. As Newburn (1996: 70) observed: 'it was open season in the press':

Mini-gangster is beyond control.

(Daily Express, 9 September 1992)

One Boy Crime Wave
He was only eleven when his life of crime began with the theft of chocolate bars from a corner shop . . . within two years he had become a one boy crime wave.

(Daily Mail, 10 September 1992)

We've got too soft. Children are supposed to be little innocents not crooks in short trousers. But much of Britain is now facing a truly frightening explosion of kiddie crime. As we reveal today too many youngsters are turning into hardened hoods almost as soon as they've climbed out of their prams.

(Daily Star, 30 November 1992)

During this period there was minimal objective analysis, nor any sustained attempt to provide discrete accounts for separate – and quite different – strands of child deviance and transgression. Rather, a reductionist assimilation of widely disparate behaviours was peddled crudely by an assembly of 'red top' journalists, moral entrepreneurs, self-serving 'experts' (with a penchant for sound bites) and cynical political opportunists (for a fuller discussion see Scraton, 1997).

The apogee (or nadir) of this angst-ridden period was reached in February 1993 when the mutilated body of a 2-year-old child, James Bulger, was discovered on a railway siding in Bootle, to the north of Liverpool, and two 10-year-old boys were subsequently charged with, and convicted of, his murder. The media coverage – nationally and internationally – was unprecedented (Hay, 1995; Franklin and Petley, 1996; Davis and Bourhill, 1997; Morrison, 1997). This tragic and exceptional case of child murder was presented as the ultimate expression of 'crisis'. Identifiable constituencies of children and young people came to be conceptualised as both the *cause* and the *product* of wider social problems and moral malaise: the 'disintegration' of the family; inadequate parenting; 'fatherless' households; indiscipline in schools; 'softness' in the courts; a corrosive 'excuse culture'; the clamour for rights without associated responsibilities; and, ultimately, the 'out of control' progeny of an amoral and utterly dysfunctional 'underclass' – a 'lost generation'. As Marina Warner asserted in her 1994 'Reith Lectures':

> The child has never been seen as such a menacing enemy as today. Never before have children been so saturated with all the power of projected monstrousness to excite repulsion – and even terror.
>
> (cited in Franklin and Petley, 1996: 134)

Inevitably, classic processes of deviance amplification, moral panic and symbolic demonisation soon translated into intitutionalised 'clampdown', paving the way for a flurry of 'tough' legislative activity (Goldson, 1997; 2001).

Spool forward a decade and it was as if the 'memories and cognitive deposits' (Ben-Yehuda, 2009: 3) of the 1990s were reawakened (if ever they lay dormant) via a second-wave 'crisis'. If the 'crisis' of the 1990s centred on 'childhood', the emphasis – in many respects – turned to 'youth' during the first decade of the twenty-first century. Striking similarities and parallel processes were at work: a burgeoning sense of unease; concentrated media attention; intense and repeated coverage of exceptional 'cases'; claims that the control apparatus was failing; and, finally, the institutionalisation of a spectrum of new powers, interventions, sanctions and punishments. It is not practical to track the detail here but key milestones are instructive.

In March 2002, ostensibly 'in response to sustained and accelerating increases in annual levels of robbery' (Tilley et al., 2004: 3), the New Labour Government launched a major 'Street Crime Initiative' which introduced a broad range of measures underpinned by 'zero tolerance' imperatives and operationalised through 'fast track' 'justice' processes. Whether or not British cities were witnessing accelerating levels of 'street crime' is open to debate, but the 'initiative' clearly targeted young people and (re)focused attention on 'youth'. Mirroring the 1990s, widely disparate behaviours were conflated and served to facilitate crude and deeply problematic slippages between violence, drugs, 'street crime', robbery and, ultimately, 'gangs', weapons, stabbings, shootings and youth fatalities. If concern had been invoked in November 2000 by the death of 10-year-old schoolboy Damilola Taylor, killed whilst he walked home from school in Peckham, London, it was reactivated and bolstered further by the seemingly random, but fatal, 'drive by' shooting of 18-year-old Charlene Ellis and 17-year-old Latisha Shakespear in Aston, Birmingham, in January 2003. Perhaps more than any other single case, however, the death of 11-year-old Rhys Jones in Liverpool in August 2007, the victim of a 'stray bullet' dispensed from a handgun by an 18-year-old youth, set the agenda.

Above all else, it is the question of the contemporary youth 'gang' that both captures and tortures the collective imagination fuelled, as ever, by distorted and exaggerated media presentation: 'media coverage has . . . been suggestive of an epidemic of gang-related youth violence'; a 'media frenzy [surrounds] the development of a supposedly American-style gang culture in Britain' (Centre for Social Justice, 2009: 19 and 35). As Ben-Yehuda (2009: 2) notes: 'such imaginary and highly overstated fears have typically focused on gang activites [and] youth' and, 'following the newsroom slogan of "if it bleeds it leads"', individual cases, such as those mentioned above, in all their tragedy and gore, become potent 'mechanisms for creating and sustaining cultures of fear'. Moreover, such cases are often read as graphic illustrations of defective and deficient control systems: 'the inadequacy of central and local government responses' (Duncan Smith, 2009: 9); 'the lack of leadership shown by central and local government . . . [and a failure] to understand and act on the growing problem of street gangs' (Centre for Social Justice, 2009: 27); and the absence of a 'clear and integrated joint national strategy to support criminal justice and community agencies in tackling the causes as well as the effects of gang activity' (HM Chief Inspector of Prisons et al., 2010: 4). With mundane predictability and almost without exception, such complaints are followed by calls for more sophisticated intelligence gathering, closer monitoring and surveillance, greater and less inhibited flows of inter-agency information exchange, system expansion, additional powers, more rigorous enforcement and tougher penalties, sanctions and sentences.

There is a far more significant problem at play here, however. It is not so much that the control apparatus has 'failed' in checking and suppressing the youth 'gang' and/or managing and regulating the youth 'crisis', but rather the precise nature of such phenomena are unknown; they are, in essence, imaginaries. Marshall et al. (2005: 6) refer to a 'dearth of research looking at the specific problems of gangs in the UK', Smith and Bradshaw (2005: 5) observe that 'over the past 20 years there have been very few studies of youth gangs in Britain' and Duncan Smith (2009: 9) claims that 'it is unthinkable that a full and proper study of such a devastating problem has not been undertaken prior to setting policy'. Whilst some gaps in knowledge have certainly been closed since 2005 when Marshall and his colleagues and Smith and Bradshaw lamented the under-researched nature of 'gang' questions, and although Conservative MP Duncan Smith's indignant tone has to be understood and interpreted with reference to the political context from which it derives, it remains the case that the knowledge base is both substantially incomplete and far from settled (Young et al., 2007). This should not be taken to imply that the street worlds in which young people live and operate are unproblematic (for themselves and for others), but the realities of such worlds express a far greater sense of historical continuity and are profoundly more disorganised, localised, nuanced and complex than 'crisis' discourses – underpinned by notions of unique temporal specificity, aberration and national uniformity – seem to assert.

Quantifying 'crisis'

[T]he prevalence of gangs, their membership and the extent of their criminal activity – including violence – is largely unknown.

(Centre for Social Justice, 2009: 20)

Indeed, it has been noted that in some cases intelligence reports create a cycle of misinformation causing gangs to be created by police that may not actually exist. This, along with the liberal use of the word 'gang', may lead to events which may not be gang-related at all . . . being redefined as gangland conflicts.

(Marshall et al., 2005: 7)

In December 2007, BBC News concluded it had been the worst year on record for fatal street violence among young people. Twenty-eight people under 20 were murdered in 'gang related' incidents in the capital alone. The figure grew to 29 in 2008, most of whom were victims of stabbing.

(HM Chief Inspector of Prisons et al., 2010: 12)

In the USA, gang research is well-established. Originating with studies such as Herbert Asbury's *The Gangs of New York* (1927) and Frederic Thrasher's seminal work, *The* Gang*: A Study of 1313* Gangs *in Chicago* (1927), the body of American gang research comprises a wide range of classic observational and ethnographic inquiries and, more recently, large-scale surveys (see, for example, Esbensen and Huizinga, 1993; Thornberry, 1998; Esbensen et al., 2001). This is not to suggest that such research is entirely free of problems associated with methodological design, data analysis and interpretation, but at least there is a substantive body of work from which to draw. As stated above, despite burgeoning interest and some important recent additions – including the various contributions to this volume – the research base in the UK, in comparison with the USA, is severely limited, rendering incautious interpretation of data especially hazardous. With this in mind, the existing hard data speaks – at least in part – to three key issues: first, 'gang' prevalence and patterns of 'gang' affiliation/membership; second, the relations and correlations between 'gangs' and youth offending; and third, the extent and nature of weapon carrying/use amongst young people.

Reporting the findings from a major 'offending, crime and justice survey' in England and Wales, Sharp et al. (2006: v, emphasis added) state: 'overall, an estimated six per cent of young people aged 10–19 were classified as belonging to a *delinquent youth group'*, whereas Bennett and Holloway (2004: 312–13) have perhaps come closest to estimating a total national (England and Wales) *gang membership*. By using 'New English and Welsh Arrestee Drug Abuse Monitoring' (NEW-ADAM) data, they have estimated – with a confidence range of plus or minus 5,000 – that there are 20,000 gang members aged 17 and over but caution that, owing to the limitations of their principal data source, this is likely to be a significant underestimation. As Young et al. (2007: 54) explain, 'no such estimate exists for juvenile gangs in the UK'. At a more localised level, Smith and Bradshaw (2005), drawing on longitudinal data collected for the 'Edinburgh Study of Youth Transitions and Crime', report that a staggering twenty per cent of 13-year-olds surveyed claimed to belong to 'gangs', falling to five per cent amongst 17-year-olds. The Centre for Social Justice (2009: 19) reports that 'police in London and Strathclyde have each identified 171 and 170 gangs respectively' and Pitts (2007) claims that between 600 and 700 young people aged between 10 and 29 were directly 'gang involved' (in the autumn of 2006) in one or more of eighteen gangs operating in a single London borough – Waltham Forest.

Turning to the reported relations between 'gang' membership and youth offending, a number of studies in the USA claim to provide evidence that 'gang' membership itself increases both the incidence and gravity of youth crime (see Howell, 1998, for an overview), and similar claims have been made in the UK (Bennett and Holloway, 2004). The Centre for Social Justice (2009: 24) asserts:

> Research shows that gang members tend to be engaged in a wide range of criminal activities: drug dealing to robbery, assault to rape. They are also prolific in their offending . . . Furthermore gang membership itself has a direct impact on an individual's offending, over and above the impact of affiliating with delinquent peers.

Similarly, Sharp et al. (2006: 24), in summarising the 'first set of nationally representative results', report:

> Sixty three per cent of those belonging to delinquent youth groups have, themselves, committed at least one 'core offence'[1] in the last year. This is significantly higher than for non-members (26%). The pattern remains when examining individual offence types . . . Only a minority of group members had committed a serious offence (34%) or had offended on a frequent basis (committed six or more offences in the last year) (28%) and seven per cent had committed a serious offence on six or more occasions. However, these figures are significantly higher compared with the equivalent in young people not classed as members (13, 7 and 2% respectively). Consequently, the six per cent of individuals who were members of delinquent youth groups were responsible for around a fifth (21%) of all core offences committed by this

age group (ten to 19 years) . . . Offending in those who were members of delinquent youth groups was significantly higher than for non-members who had 'delinquent friends' (measured by whether the respondent had friends who had been in trouble with the police) . . . This pattern also held for serious and frequent offending and drug use.

(Sharp et al., 2006: vi)

Finally, the extent and nature of weapon carrying/use amongst young people. By distilling the findings from twelve research studies, Marshall et al. (2005: 3) report: 'there is . . . evidence of the emergence of a weapon carrying culture among young people with nearly one in four 15- to 16-year-old boys admitting to having carried a knife or other weapon in the past year'. Furthermore, the Centre for Social Justice (2009: 64) claims that 'in the past five years there has been an 89 per cent increase in the number of under-16s admitted to hospital with serious stab wounds, and a 75 per cent increase amongst older teenagers' (also, see Squires, this volume). Marshall and his colleagues also refer to a 'general perception' that the possession of firearms is increasing, stating:

The prime age of gun-related offending is between 17 and 24 . . . Of those carrying firearms, [Metropolitan Police Service] figures suggest that 17–24 year olds were five times more likely to be carrying lethal weapons than those aged 10–16 who more often carry non-lethal firearms such as airguns.

(Marshall et al., 2005: 13)

Whilst there is nothing to suggest that *all* young people who carry knives and/or guns are necessarily 'gang' affiliated, the Centre for Social Justice (2009: 20) states: 'in both Manchester and Liverpool around 60% of shootings are gang related [and] at least half of the 27 murders of young people perpetuated by young people in London [in 2007] were gang-related'.

Taken at face value such quantitative data appear to articulate a series of troubling messages but, as noted, particular care is required with regard to data analysis and interpretation. To begin, the 'delinquent youth groups' to which Sharp et al. (2006) refer, are not necessarily 'gangs' in the way in which the term is commonly understood, thus exposing complex questions of definition, to which we shall return. Much of the available data is drawn from studies underpinned by self-reporting and self-nomination methods and, despite the value of such methodological approaches, they suffer obvious limitations regarding validity and reliability. Equally, it would be erroneous to draw over-hasty conclusions from reported temporal shifts in the incidence and/or gravity of youth crime. It is well known that the task of identifying and analysing crime trends over time is notoriously difficult and, for a multitude of reasons, the coterminous relations between the categories of 'reported', 'recorded' and 'actual' crime are limited. Police statistics, victimisation surveys and/or data drawn from other sources need to be interpreted with great care and sophistication. Comparing youth crime statistics over time can indeed be misleading owing to, for example: fluctuations in the definition of particular 'offences'; the partial and/or incomplete nature of (police) recorded data; the problems associated with documenting 'victimless crimes'; the difficulties in attributing (and thus recording) responsibility in cases where no 'offender' is apprehended/known and the tendency for statistical variability to reveal as much, if not more, about phenomena other than actual crime trends – for example, revised methods of recording, modified system behaviour and/or changes in legislation, policy and practice. In addition, the processes of publicly reporting and/or applying crime statistics can be distorted by ulterior motives and political interests (Booth, 2008; Goldson, 2010; Hope, 2004; Walters, 2003; 2008) and this may be particularly salient with regard to the highly charged questions of youth 'gangs', violence, guns and knives.

Qualifying 'crisis'

There is little, if any, consensus as to what constitutes a gang and who is a gang member, let alone what gangs do either inside or outside the law.

(Esbensen et al., 2001: 106)

There now appears a tendency to apply the word 'gang' to any and all groups of young people . . . This knee-jerk response . . . is profoundly unhelpful. The vast majority of groups of young people are *not* gangs, and the labelling of them as such has negative consequences for all involved.

(Centre for Social Justice, 2009: 39, original emphasis)

There is no evidence either way of any change over time in the extent of group related offending by young people, although there has been a significant increase in recent years in public perceptions of groups of young people on the streets as posing problems associated with crime . . . this occurred in a context which had in any case, turned the spotlight on young people's offending more generally, not least with major reforms of the youth justice system.

(Young et al., 2007: 55)

The issue of gangs . . . is an emotive and difficult one. There is a considerable risk of over-reaction . . . [to] criminal activity carried out by groups of young people – a pattern of offending that is neither new nor surprising . . . However, the opposite extreme – ignoring or failing to recognize the existence of genuinely gang-related activity among young people – is . . . dangerous.

(HM Chief Inspector of Prisons et al., 2010: 3)

[I]t is not simply the availability of licit and illicit [weapons] that escalate routine conflicts into lethal encounters . . . but the cultural, economic and political conditions that place a premium on recourse to lethal violence to resolve disputes in 'fast time' through extra-judicial action on the streets . . . the relationship . . . is mediated by particular social orders.

(Sheptyki and Edwards, 2009: 260)

In order to develop a rounded understanding of contemporary youth 'gangs' – together with an appreciation of the meanings that identifiable constituencies of young people attach to specific territorial spaces and their terms of engagement with violence – it is, as noted, necessary to locate the present within a broader sense of historical context. This necessitates tracing *continuities* as well as *changes* pertaining to youth cultures and subcultures over time, analysing various constructions and reconstructions of 'problematic youth' and 'youth problems', and subjecting multiple discourses – academic, policy, political, populist – to detailed critical scrutiny. We shall return to the significance of socio-historical inquiry shortly, but first a more immediate 'qualifying' aspect merits attention: the question of definition.

It is quite extraordinary that despite the contemporary preoccupation with youth 'gangs' in the UK and elsewhere, the existing literature reveals little consensus about precisely what constitutes a 'gang', how and why 'gangs' originate and/or the purpose and function that 'gangs' are thought to serve. Many researchers in the UK, for example, have traditionally been reluctant to even apply the term 'gang' and, although such reluctance has receded in recent years, the question of definition remains. Indeed, semantic slippages between terms such as 'peer group', 'informal peer group network', 'fluid and transitional youth group formation', 'street-based group', 'delinquent peer group', 'delinquent youth group', 'gang', 'criminal gang', 'organised criminal group', 'organised crime network' and 'crime firm' obfuscate meaning, create confusion, produce contrasting and contradictory findings and impede coherent analysis. At its most fundamental, accounts of the nature and extent of 'gang' activity – at any given place and time – will be contingent and heavily dependent on the adopted definitions. Given the breadth of descriptors applied to youth group formations and the widely varying 'definitions' employed, attempts at temporal and/or spatial comparative 'gang' analysis are often akin to comparing apples with oranges. There can be no guarantee of like-with-like pairings. Unsurprisingly, therefore, the literature is replete with lengthy debates pertaining to 'gang' criteria and discursive discussions on the various meanings attributed to the term 'gang' (for useful summaries see Young et al., 2007: 23–48 and Centre for Social Justice, 2009: 39–49).

There are signs, however, that the spectrum of definitions is narrowing, assisted, at least in part, by the 'Eurogang Network' – a collective of American and European researchers. Klein (2001) has produced a five-point 'gang' typology comprising: 'traditional'; 'neo-traditional'; 'compressed'; 'collective'; and 'speciality' 'gangs'. Similarly, Pitts (2007) has formulated a conceptual schema consisting of six categories: 'the articulated super gang'; 'the street gang'; 'the compressed street gang'; 'the criminal youth group'; 'the wannabees'; and the 'middle level international criminal business organisation'. Whilst such typologies might succeed in narrowing the definitional field, they are certainly not beyond critique. Questions remain pertaining to the conceptual legitimacy of the typologies and their constituent elements, their durability over time, the validity of their application beyond the immediate locales within which 'gangs' normally operate and, consequently, their value in terms of meaningful regional, national and/or transnational comparative analysis (White, this volume).

Beyond definitional problematics, the demographics of youth 'gangs' also require clarification. Perhaps differences and uncertainties regarding the question of age best exemplify further incoherence and conceptual dissonance. In their attempt to 'rationalise' current research Marshall et al. (2005: 9, emphasis added) note:

> The literature *suggests* most street gang members are under 18 years of age, 25 *appears to be* the oldest. Young people become involved with street gangs between the ages of 12 and 14, although *sometimes this can be* as young as 9. There are also *suggestions* that age of involvement is decreasing. It is *generally accepted* that gang members belonging to higher level collectives are older and are involved with more serious offending.

The statement exudes hesitancy and ambiguity. Similar imprecision and variance is evident amongst the most cited recent studies in the UK. The age range of 'gang' members in Bullock and Tilley's (2002) study in Manchester, for example, was 17–24 years whereas Mares' (2001) research in the *same city* found different age profiles within and across the three principal 'gangs' studied, ranging from 10–30 years, 10–25 years and 14–18 years. Pitts (2007) notes that in the London Borough of Waltham Forest 'gang' members range in age from 10–40 years or, in some cases, up to 50. The 'delinquent youth groups' identified by the national study led by Sharp et al. (2006) were significantly younger, 10–19 years, with male involvement peaking amongst 14–17-year-olds and female involvement being highest amongst the 14–15 age group. The Metropolitan Police Service's *Pan-London Gang Profile* (2006) suggests that most young people join 'gangs' between the ages of 12 and 14 and that the majority of members are under the age of 18, whereas Smith and Bradshaw (2005) found that 13 was the peak age at which young people in Edinburgh claimed to be in a 'gang'.

With regard to gender, 'gangs' have conventionally been seen as a male pre-serve, with females accounting for no more than between 5 per cent (Bennett and Holloway, 2004) and 11 per cent (Bullock and Tilley, 2002) of members. Moreover, and with a few notable exceptions – see, for example, Batchelor, this volume; Young, this volume – girls and young women have been largely over-looked by 'gang' researchers beyond their supportive ancillary roles and/or their status as sex objects and victims of sexual violation – including 'gang' rape – within male 'gang culture'. Indeed, the specific relations of girls and young women both to, and within, youth 'gangs' and, more specifically, 'the impact of guns and knives on girls has not been thoroughly explored' (Silvestri et al., 2009: 12). The literature, and accordingly the knowledge base, remains largely 'malestream'.

It is not uncommon for 'gang' discourses to be played through implicit or explicit racialised – and racist – frames, both recalling earlier constructions of 'crisis' (Hall et al., 1977) and implying that black and minoritised youth are particularly 'gang-prone'. As Silvestri et al. (2009: 12) observe:

A significant amount of research (especially around guns) tends to concentrate on young people from minority ethnic backgrounds. Likewise, a number of interventions aiming at reducing use of weapons or gang membership focus on such groups, thereby treating race as an almost independent variable in the relationship between young people, weapons and violence.

This is both deeply problematic and conceptually skewed. In fact, as more nuanced analysts have explained, ethnicity is, at most, a secondary variable located within a complex context in which spatialised socio-economic conditions are key (Esbensen and Weerman, 2005; Hagedorn, 2007; 2008, Kramer, 2000). In other words, 'gangs' primarily derive from the most distressed and disadvantaged neighbourhoods and communities characterised by structural neglect, poverty, poor housing and severely circumscribed labour market opportunities. Whilst it is true that black and minoritised youth are overrepresented in such localities, place rather than 'race' is the principal 'variable': 'the degree to which gangs are mono-ethnic [is] more to do with local resident demographics than the deliberate congregation of individuals from the same ethnic group though living in different areas' (Marshall et al., 2005: 8). In short, class-based social injustice, as distinct from ethnicity, is the primary determining context.

Even a cursory 'qualifying' discussion such as this, reveals the profound inadequacy of much that passes for 'gang' discourse and 'crisis' talk. Indeed, any serious attempt to comprehend the myriad youth group formations that we have seemingly learnt to call 'gangs', to understand the spaces in which they emerge and develop and, at the 'heavy end', to conceptualise youth violence must be both theoretically rigorous and empirically robust. Theoretical questions – within which the constructs of place, opportunity, power, identity and masculinity are key – must be foregrounded. Placed-based attachments, postcode identities and group-centred bonds assume, perhaps as they always have, profound significance for young people whose opportunities, aspirations and horizons are stultified and thwarted by structural disadvantage. For identifiable constituencies of the young, power, identity and 'social capital' are closely indexed with reference to street-level 'respect', credibility ('cred') and reputation ('rep'), although the gendered nature of such phenomena and, in particular, the specific agency of girls and young women, is largely unknown. 'Beefs' deriving from territorial trespass and/or any expression of 'disrespect' – and intensified by particular constructions of masculinity (machismo) – are often the motors of violent exchange. Weapons symbolise anxiety, fear and insecurity, they are the tools of precautionary personal 'protection' as much as, if not more than, the instruments of calculated 'gangstas' and purposeful 'street soldiers'. Ill-defined, historically decontextualised and hyperbolic constructions of 'crisis' offer little by way of understanding such complexity; of determining whether or not the incidence, gravity and nature of street violence has changed over time; or in appreciating complex intersecting tendencies that can produce problematic street worlds for young people and the mediating contingencies that impact upon such worlds, at specific moments and within particular social orders. More detailed, sophisticated and nuanced analyses are imperative.

'Gangs', territoriality and violence: contestation and critical debate

It is the *real* crisis of knowledge deficit and the misappropriation of complex social phenomena, rather than the *imagined* crisis of youth, that this book aims to address. The chapters that follow comprise a series of essays from leading national and international researchers and, together, they subject the concepts of 'gangs', 'territoriality' and 'violence' to critical scrutiny by: opening up and engaging with key debates; identifying and addressing major sites of conceptual contestation; locating the question of 'gangs' in both historical and contemporary contexts; interacting with a spectrum of theoretical perspectives and analytical positions; presenting and evaluating cutting-edge empirical research and integrating a range of previously neglected questions, including those pertaining to girls and young women.

In Chapter 1, Geoffrey Pearson contends that the recurring tendency to negate historical context and antecedent – 'historical amnesia' – is profoundly problematic. He exposes the means by which an obsession with the present and a peculiar sense of 'perpetual novelty' gives rise to conceptual myopia whereby 'street crime and violence . . . are unhesitatingly seen as entirely new and unprecedented'. In contrast, and by gazing back in time across a spectrum of youthful 'disorderly conduct' – from the 'Teddy Boys' and the 'Mods' of the 1950s and 1960s, the 'juvenile delinquents' of the inter-war years, the 'Hooligans' and 'scuttlers' of the late Victorian and Edwardian eras and, finally, to the transgressive youth of the early-modern and pre-industrial periods – Pearson identifies and traces the longevity and historical embeddedness of youth 'gangs', their attachment to territoriality and their engagement with violence.

In Chapter 2, Andrew Davies narrows and deepens the analytical focus by surveying the historical literature on youth 'gangs' and street violence in major English cities during the late nineteenth century. It is both striking and prescient that Birmingham, Liverpool, London and Manchester attracted most attention and concern during the Victorian period. Indeed, more than a century later the very same cities comprise the *loci sigilli* for contemporary anxieties pertaining to 'gangs' and youth violence (at least in England). More specifically, Davies presents selected findings from a meticulously researched case-study of youth 'gangs' – known as 'scuttlers' – in Manchester and Salford where, between 1870 and 1900, there were more than 300 reported outbreaks of often violent, territorially-based exchanges. Described by the press as a 'reign of terror', more than 800 young people were formally prosecuted during this period.

Both Pearson and Davies disrupt and unsettle the ahistorical notion that the youth 'gang' is a peculiarly modern phenomenon; a twenty-first-century aberration. As noted earlier, such analyses are vital in tracing both historical *continuity* and *change*: the long-enduring and recurring presence of youth 'gangs' – or youth groupings/subcultures popularly, if erroneously, labelled 'gangs' – their multiple forms, diverse characteristics, principal rationales and core activities. They reveal the persistent, if uneven, importance attributed to 'territory' by identifiable groups of young people at particular moments and in specific circumstances, together with their preparedness to mobilise violence in representing and/or defending circumscribed spaces. Perhaps most significantly, historical contextualisation exposes the socio-economic conditions and social–structural relations within which youth 'gang' formations typically emerge and form, the disparate and contested range of domain assumptions expressed through various forms of discourse and, ultimately, the nature of the state's favoured 'remedies' repeatedly, if paradoxically, packaged as uniquely 'modern' and 'new'.

In this way, history bears witness to a catalogue of pathologising and distorting processes including: moral panic; folk-devilling; demonisation; othering; conflation, exaggeration and amplification, and it testifies to the extraordinary symbolic power exerted by such phenomena. Regarding the domain assumptions characteristic of various media, populist, political and (some) academic discourses, historical analyses unveil a routine emphasis on notions of moral breakdown including the supposed fragmentation, dissolution and/or malfunctioning of the 'family', the 'community', state institutions and 'civic society'. In short, such discourses express an obsessive attachment to constructions of the diminishing and disintegrating hold of 'authority' – however it is configured and imagined – over the young. In turn, and with mundane inevitability, they persistently give rise to flurries of legislative activity and multiple 'new' initiatives, experiments and interventions. In all such senses, the echoes of the past reverberate loudly in the present.

In Chapter 3, Keith Kintrea, Jon Banister and Jon Pickering – by drawing on their research in six cities in Scotland and England (Bradford, Bristol, Glasgow, London, Peterborough and Sunderland) – provide an engaging analytical account of the importance of place for working-class young people. As Kearns and Forrest (1998: 13) have observed, 'residents of poor neighbourhoods spend more time in their local areas than do residents of wealthier neighbourhoods' and, as such, the immediate locality assumes particular significance in working-class communities. Kintrea, Banister and Pickering trace the historical and cross-generational contexts within which young people 'learn' territorial affiliations and place-based identities, sometimes to the point of 'hyper place attachment'. In circumstances where young people's prospects are severely circumscribed 'their estates or inner urban areas are the places that they feel they belong to and, in turn, belong to them, and they are ultimately prepared to defend them'. The authors note that numerous 'problematic youth groups' form in such areas, varying in age, gendered divisions of labour and levels of violent and criminal activity. But such groups, together with 'territorial "gang" conflict', are not 'new', nor are they necessarily 'problematic' seen from the perspectives of their 'members'. Rather, the youth groups and their activities represent historically and culturally embedded social relations and, as one interviewee explains, they provide 'a sense of belonging that no-one can take away from you'.

In Chapter 4, Judith Aldridge, Robert Ralphs and Juanjo Medina provide a challenging and sophisticated analysis of the meaning of 'territory' for both 'gang affiliated' and 'non-gang-affiliated' young people. The chapter derives from in-depth fieldwork in 'Research City' within which, over a 30-year period, two 'gangs' had developed notorious reputations as 'highly criminal; highly likely to use firearms; highly territorial and permanently warring'. Aldridge and her colleagues question typical constructions of youth 'gangs' as street-based entities both operating, and living within, clearly defined and demarcated territories. Rather they argue – on the basis of apparent contradictions between gang members' use and negotiation of space and the methods of policing them – that 'territory-focused responses are based on outdated and/or stereotypical assumptions of gang membership'. The researchers discovered 'gang' members residing outside 'territorial' boundaries, beyond city boundaries, in 'rival gang territory' and 'some even had members of rival gangs in their immediate families'. The chapter unsettles conventional readings of rigid territorially-based 'gang' formation and raises important questions for policing practices and emergent policy developments.

In Chapter 5, Siobhán McAlister, Phil Scraton and Deena Haydon engage explicitly with the social, cultural and material contexts that provide the analytical framework within which their research with children and young people in Northern Ireland is located. In a society in transition following three decades of intense political conflict, the authors foreground questions of power, authority, legitimacy, the structural inequalities of class and the social dynamics of communities. They shed analytical light on the significance of place in the formation of young people's identities. In particular, McAlister and her colleagues explore the issue of territoriality in a 'new' Northern Ireland where some symbolic markings of space have been removed and 'outsiders' have arrived into previously closed and insular communities. The chapter centres on the social, historical and local contexts of territoriality, not least the significance of inter- and intra-community violence. By illuminating the agency of young people and the impact of such phenomena on their everyday lives and experiences, McAlister, Scraton and Haydon provide a powerful antidote to the dominant negative emphases characteristic of popular – and some academic – discourses on contemporary youth 'gangs'.

As a counterbalance to the hegemony of 'malestream' analyses, Chapters 6 and 7 each focus explicitly on girls' and young women's experiences of youth 'gangs'.

In Chapter 6, Susan A. Batchelor develops an analysis that reaches beyond the conventional dichotomy characteristic of dominant discourses, whereby 'girl gangstas' are typically presented either as hapless sexually exploited victims or as 'one of the lads' – deviant masculinised 'tomboys'. Batchelor laments the failure of many commentators to fully incorporate gender analyses into examinations of UK 'gangs'. She argues that, together with the relative absence of critical theory, this has led to constructions that are 'partial, superficial and naïve . . . perpetuating unquestioned stereotypes about street-orientated young women'. By building upon feminist theorisation – largely drawn from a US literature – and applying it to primary research conducted in Scotland, Batchelor explores the complex and contradictory constitution of gender identity among girls and young women in violent street 'gangs'.

In Chapter 7, Tara Young also engages critically with dichotomous forms of conceptualisation. On one hand, 'Lombrosian women, atavistic throwbacks, out of control and capable of gratuitous brutality'. On the other hand, 'victims . . . propelled towards a gang as a result of neglect, brutality and trauma . . . [but] often considered more dangerous owing to the combination of chronic low self-esteem and shame and a hyper-inflated sense of self-respect forming a retaliative fighter capable of giving and receiving "man licks"'. Situating her analysis within a context in which a claimed increase in violent behaviour amongst girls and young women is coupled with their apparently growing involvement in 'gangs', Young critiques the means by which the 'shemale gangster' has (re)entered contemporary public consciousness. She argues that dominant representations of 'gang'- affiliated girls and young women ultimately comprise crude caricatures, and the question at the core of her chapter is: why, despite the absence of empirical evidence, does the search for the 'shemale gangster' continue?

In Chapter 8, attention focuses more sharply on questions of youth violence and, in particular, processes of 'weaponisation'. Within a context in which reports of stabbings and shootings feature within the print and broadcast media on an almost daily basis, Peter Squires engages critically with key questions relating to young people and weapons (knives and guns). Squires traces statistical patterns of weapon use and injury, before surveying the nature of Government response. He analyses major reports from the Home Affairs Select Committee and particular national interventions – including the 'Tackling Gangs Action Programme' and the 'Tackling Knives Action Programme' – together with more localised variants of 'Operation Blunt', intensive area-based police stop and search initiatives. Whilst acknowledging some merits of both 'moral panic' modes of analysis and more 'realist' approaches, Squires argues compellingly that criminal justice interventions have become heavily implicated in sustaining and consolidating the predicament of marginalised youth in the UK, as they have in the USA.

In Chapter 9, John Pitts contends that in specific urban neighbourhoods in England 'violent, armed, youth gangs' are established. For Pitts such formations mark the culmination of patterns of social, economic and cultural estrangement that have deepened over two decades or more. By drawing on substantial empirical research in London, Pitts presents a left realist vision. He sternly repudiates analytical accounts of youth 'gangs' that appeal to 'moral panic' discourses. Instead Pitts argues that identifiable neighbourhoods are witnessing 'new' forms of illicit activity within which the distinctions between adult and youth offending are dissolving, organised youth 'gangs' are consolidating and violence is becoming more serious, more entrenched and more commonplace.

In Chapter 10, Simon Hallsworth also draws on substantial empirical research undertaken in London and elsewhere, but he develops a fundamentally different theoretical and interpretive narrative to the one presented by Pitts. For Hallsworth, problematic street violence is historically embedded within urban locales and it principally derives from long-established patterns of social disorganisation. The notion that organised youth 'gangs' are proliferating in the contemporary period is, in essence, an illusion. Developing lines of argument and analysis that are directly informed by notions of 'moral panic', Hallsworth argues that it is the 'gang control industry', rather than the 'gang' itself, that comprises the principal source of concern. The 'industry' includes: academics (including various American gang 'gurus'); commissioners of research; politicians and specialist government 'task forces'; self-professed 'gang experts'; policymakers with dedicated 'gang suppression' portfolios; 'gang busting' enforcement agencies and law and order lobbies; journalists and documentary film makers; a range of practitioners offering 'gang suppression programmes'; various 'consultants' and even some young people themselves who have learned the value of playing-up to the 'gang' label. The 'industry' has a vested interest in maintaining precisely the very object – the violent youth 'gang' – it otherwise aspires to suppress. This being so, according to Hallsworth, the problem of the 'gang' is likely to deepen, the control net will widen as gang suppression programmes multiply and researchers will continue to find as many, or as few 'gangs', as are required by the industry that 'feeds' them. To address the problems of violent street worlds, the chapter concludes, it is necessary to suppress the very 'industry' that produces and sustains them.

In Chapter 11, Rob White widens the focus beyond Britain and Ireland and engages with extremely complex questions relating to 'gangs' at the transnational level. White distils common and convergent elements among 'gangs' from many national contexts alongside an analytical discussion of principal points of differ-ence and divergence. He presents an overview of the burgeoning international literature on youth 'gangs' – particularly in Europe – and synthesises the key propositions, tensions and disagreements that emerge. White then presents a more detailed discussion of key themes that illuminate understanding of the core similarities and differences in 'gang' formations around the world.

Taken together the chapters open up debates, expose controversies, identify key points of theoretical contestation, present some of the latest empirical research and engage a breadth of critical analysis. There is also an implicit – and sometimes explicit – commitment to interventionist social science running through the book. This raises its own challenges of course (Goldson and Hughes, 2010). Whilst it is not practical to consider the detail here, suffice it to note that if the academy is to retain analytical integrity and counter the 'annihilation of meaning' (Cohen, 1971), it must simultaneously resist becoming the 'handmaidens of administration' (Young, 2009) whilst striving to convert 'private troubles' into 'public concerns' (Wright Mills, 1959). Whatever theoretical standpoints are preferred and/or practical interventions are taken in the contested terrain surrounding youth 'gangs', territoriality and violence, therefore, perhaps what is needed more than anything is:

> greater reflexivity among social scientists over the implication of their work in the very social problems they study; social scientists are implicated in the weaponisation of civil society through their representations of the problem and this needs careful management if they are to control better the political manipulation of their work in this and other criminological disputes.
>
> (Sheptyki and Edwards, 2009: 261)

Note

1   The 'core' offences covered by the survey include robbery, assault, burglary, criminal damage, theft of and from vehicles, other miscellaneous thefts and selling drugs.

References

Asbury, H. (1927) *The Gangs of New York: An Informal History of the Underworld*. New York: Thunder's Mouth Press.

Ben-Yehuda, N. (2009) 'Foreword: Moral Panics – 36 Years On', *British Journal of Criminology*, 49(1): 1–3.

Bennett, T. and Holloway, K. (2004) 'Gang Membership, Drugs and Crime in the UK', *British Journal of Criminology*, 44(3): 305–23.

Booth, R. (2008) 'Home Office Accused of Releasing Selective Knife Crime Figures: Chief Statistician Did Not Want Details Published; Data Could Have Falsified Effect of Stop and Search', *The Guardian*, 13 December.

Bullock, K. and Tilley, N. (2002) *Shootings, Gangs and Violent Incidents in Manchester: Developing a Crime Reduction Strategy*. London: Home Office.

Centre for Social Justice (2009) *Dying to Belong: An In-depth Review of Street Gangs in Britain*. London: Centre for Social Justice.

Cohen, P. (1997) 'The Same Old Generation Game', *Criminal Justice Matters*, 28(1): 8–9.

Cohen, S. (ed.) (1971) *Images of Deviance*. Harmondsworth: Penguin.

Davis, H. and Bourhill, M. (1997) '"Crisis": The Demonization of Children and Young People', in P. Scraton (ed.) *'Childhood' in 'Crisis'?* London: UCL Press.

Duncan Smith, I. (2009) 'Preface', in Centre for Social Justice *Dying to Belong: An In-depth Review of Street Gangs in Britain*. London: Centre for Social Justice.

Esbensen, F-A. and Huizinga, D. (1993) 'Gangs, Drugs and Delinquency in a Survey of Urban Youth', *Criminology*, 31(4): 565–89.

Esbensen, F-A. and Weerman, F. (2005) 'Youth Gangs and Troublesome Youth Groups in the United States and the Netherlands: A Cross-National Comparison', *European Journal of Criminology*, 2(1): 5–37.

Esbensen, F-A., Winfree, L.T., He, N. and Taylor, T.J. (2001) 'Youth Gangs and Definitional Issues: When Is a Gang a Gang and Why Does It Matter?', *Crime and Delinquency*, 47(1): 105–30.

Franklin, B. and Petley, J. (1996) 'Killing the Age of Innocence: Newspaper Reporting of the Death of James Bulger', in J. Pilcher and S. Wagg (eds) *Thatcher's Children. Politics, Childhood and Society in the 1980s and 1990s*. London: Falmer Press.

Goldson, B. (1997) 'Children in Trouble: State Responses to Juvenile Crime', in P. Scraton (ed.) *'Childhood' in 'Crisis'?* London: UCL Press.

—— (2001) 'The Demonisation of Children: From the Symbolic to the Institutional', in P. Foley, J. Roche and S. Tucker (eds) *Children in Society: Contemporary Theory, Policy and Practice*. Basingstoke: Palgrave.

—— (2010) 'The Sleep of (Criminological) Reason: Knowledge–Policy Rupture and New Labour's Youth Justice Legacy', *Criminology and Criminal Justice*, 10(2): 155–78.

Goldson, B. and Hughes, G. (2010) 'Sociological Criminology and Youth Justice: Comparative Policy Analysis and Academic Intervention', *Criminology and Criminal Justice*, 10(2): 211–30.

Hagedorn, J. (ed.) (2007) *Gangs in the Global City: Alternatives to Traditional Criminology*. Urbana and Chicago: University of Illinois Press.

—— (2008) *A World of Gangs: Armed Young Men and Gangsta Culture*. Minneapolis: University of Minnesota Press.

Haines, K. and Drakeford, M. (1999) *Young People and Youth Justice*. London: Macmillan.

Hall, S., Critcher, C., Jefferson, T., Clarke, J. and Roberts, B. (1977) *Policing the Crisis: Mugging, the State and Law and Order*. London: Macmillan.

Hallsworth, S. and Young, T. (2008) 'Gang Talk and Gang Talkers: A Critique', *Crime, Media, Culture*, 4(2): 175–95.

Hay, C. (1995) 'Mobilisation Through Interpellation: James Bulger, Juvenile Crime and the Construction of a Moral Panic', *Social and Legal Studies*, 4(2):197–223.

HM Chief Inspector of Prisons, HM Chief Inspector of Probation and HM Chief Inspector of Constabulary (2010) *The Management of Gang Issues Among Children and Young People in Prison Custody and the Community: A Joint Thematic Review*. London: HM Inspectorate of Prisons.

Hope, T. (2004) 'Pretend It Works: Evidence and Governance in the Evaluation of the Reducing Burglary Initiative', *Criminal Justice*, 4(3): 287–308.

Howell, J. (1998) *Youth Gangs: An Overview*. Washington DC: US Department of Justice, Office of Juvenile Justice and Delinquency Prevention.

Jeffs, T. and Smith, M. (1996) '"Getting the Dirt-Bags off the Street": Curfews and Other Solutions to Juvenile Crime', *Youth and Policy*, 53: 1–14.

Kearns, A. and Forrest, R. (1998) 'Social Cohesion, Neighbourhoods and Cities', *Housing Studies Spring Conference*, 15–16 April. York: University of York.

Klein, M. (2001) 'Resolving the Eurogang Paradox', in M. Klein, H-J Kerner, C. Maxon and E. Weitekamp (eds) *The Eurogang Paradox: Street Gangs and Youth Groups in the U.S. and Europe*. Dordrecht: Kluwer Academic Publishers.

Kramer, R. (2000) 'Poverty, Inequality and Youth Violence', *The Annals of the American Academy of Political and Social Science*, 567: 123–39.

Mares, D. (2001) 'Gangstas or Lager Louts? Working Class Gangs in Manchester', in M. Klein, H-J. Kerner, C. Maxon and E. Weitekamp (eds) *The Eurogang Paradox: Street Gangs and Youth Groups in the U.S. and Europe*. Dordrecht: Kluwer Academic Publishers.

Marshall, B., Webb, B. and Tilley, N. (2005) *Rationalisation of Current Research on Guns, Gangs and Other Weapons: Phase 1*. London: Jill Dando Institute of Crime Science, University College London.

Metropolitan Police Service (2006) *Pan-London Gang Profile*. London: Metropolitan Police Service.

Morrison, B. (1997) *As If.* London: Granta Books.

Muncie, J. (2009) *Youth and Crime*, 3rd edition. London: Sage.

Newburn, T. (1996) 'Back to the Future? Youth Crime, Youth Justice and the Rediscovery of "Authoritarian Populism"', in J. Pilcher and S. Wagg (eds) *Thatcher's Children: Politics, Childhood and Society in the 1980s and 1990s.* London: Falmer Press.

Pitts, J. (2007) *Reluctant Gangsters: Youth Gangs in Waltham Forest.* Luton: University of Bedfordshire.

Rose, N. (1989) *Governing the Soul: The Shaping of the Private Self.* London: Routledge.

Scraton, P. (ed.) (1997) *'Childhood' in 'Crisis'?* London: UCL Press.

Sharp, C., Aldridge, J. and Medina, J. (2006) *Delinquent Youth Groups and Offending Behaviour: Findings from the 2004 Offending, Crime and Justice Survey.* London: Home Office.

Sheptyki, J. and Edwards, A. (2009) 'Guns, Crime and Social Order', *Criminology & Criminal Justice*, 9(3): 259–64.

Silvestri, A., Oldfield, M., Squires, P. and Grimshaw, R. (2009) *Young People, Knives and Guns.* London: Centre for Crime and Justice Studies, King's College London.

Smith, D. and Bradshaw, P. (2005) *Gang Membership and Teenage Offending.* Edinburgh: Centre for Law and Society, University of Edinburgh.

Thrasher, F. (1927) *The Gang: A Study of 1313 Gangs in Chicago.* Illinois: University of Chicago Press.

Thornberry, T.P. (1998) 'Membership in Youth Gangs and Involvement in Serious and Violent Offending', in R. Loeber and D. Farrington (eds) *Serious and Violent Juvenile Offenders: Risk Factors and Successful Interventions.* Thousand Oaks: Sage.

Tilley, N., Smith, J., Finer, S., Erol, R., Corrine, C. and Dobby, J. (2004) *Problem-solving Street Crime: Practical Lessons From the Street Crime Initiative.* London: Home Office.

Walters, R. (2003) *Deviant Knowledge: Criminology, Politics and Policy.* Cullompton: Willan.

—— (2008) 'Government Manipulation of Criminological Knowledge and Policies of Deceit', in T. Hope and R. Walters *Critical Thinking About the Uses of Research.* London: Centre for Crime and Justice Studies.

Wright Mills, C. (1959) *The Sociological Imagination.* New York: Oxford University Press.

Young, J. (2009) 'Moral Panic: Its Origins in Resistance, Ressentiment and the Translation of Fantasy into Reality', *British Journal of Criminology*, 49(1): 4–16.

Young, T., Fitzgerald, M., Hallsworth, M. and Joseph, I. (2007) *Groups, Gangs and Weapons.* London: Youth Justice Board.

Chapter 1

Perpetual novelty

Youth, modernity and historical amnesia

Geoffrey Pearson

The analysis of generational conflicts in Britain is bedevilled by a peculiar kind of difficulty in that it is widely regarded as a problem without a history. Street crime and violence, 'gangs' and stabbings, are unhesitatingly seen as entirely new and unprecedented, involving some kind of radical discontinuity with the past, which is fondly 'remembered' as a time of peace and tranquillity. Against this, I will argue in this chapter that youth crime and disorder are better understood as persistent, if somewhat intermittent, features of the social landscape, and that in this respect we suffer from a profound historical amnesia.

It may be remembered that long before the notion of the so-called 'broken society' was foisted on us by David Cameron in the wake of the shooting of 11-year-old Rhys Jones in Liverpool (*Daily Telegraph*, 24 August 2007), Prime Minister John Major in 1993 had launched his 'back to basics' moral crusade at the Conservative Party conference in October. Earlier that year, in April, Major had characterized England in the following way in a speech to the Conservative Group for Europe: 'The country of long shadows on cricket grounds, warm beer, invincible green suburbs, dog lovers'. It is deeply evocative of the English culture to characterize the nation as the countryside rather than the town, rural rather than urban (Weiner, 1981). And in his 'back to basics' speech, Major was equally evocative. 'Let me tell you what I believe', he said, 'for two generations too many people have been belittling things that made this country: it is time to return to core values, time to get back to basics, to self-discipline and respect for the law, to consideration for others, to accepting responsibility for yourself and for your family' (*Guardian*, 9 October 1993).

The time-scale is generational – 'thirty or forty years' – although that would take us back not to 'Old England' and warm beer, but to 'mixed-up teenagers' and to allegations of lawlessness, indiscipline and faltering family values. It was in the late 1950s that the British Medical Association had decided to inaugurate a discussion amongst its membership on a 'Subject of the Year'. It had chosen the adolescent:

> The society in which today's adolescents find themselves is one of bewil-
> dering change . . . the whole face of society has changed in the last 20 years

... a decrease in moral safeguards, and the advent of the welfare state has provided a national cushion against responsibility and adversity ... Looked at in his worst light the adolescent can take on an alarming aspect: he has learned no definite moral standards from his parents, is contemptuous of the law, easily bored ... vulnerable to the influence of TV programmes of a deplorably low standard ... Reading matter for teenagers was roundly condemned as 'full of sex and violence'.

(British Medical Association, 1961: 5–6)

We can only hope, given the disparaging tone of this review of the nation's youth, that these good doctors were talking about someone else's children. As indeed they were. Nor were they talking about 'adolescents'; they were talking about 'Teddy Boys'. Young working-class boys and men, dressed to the nines in their velvet-collar jackets, drainpipe trousers, 'duck's arse' haircuts and blue suede 'brothel creeper' shoes.

The 'Teds' might be thought of as the first rush of blood to the head among Britain's post-war youth. And they certainly caused a rush of blood in the British press. Following disturbances at cinemas showing the Bill Haley film *Rock Around the Clock*, in a front-page editorial, 'Rock 'n Roll Babies', the *Daily Mail* (5 September 1956) described the new music as 'a communicable disease' and 'the music of delinquents'. Issuing a hollow prophecy on the future of rock-and-roll – 'It will pass' – it went on to condemn 'this sudden "musical" phenomenon which has led to outbreaks of rowdyism'. Stoutly defending compulsory national service, 'to knock the rock 'n roll out of these babies, and to knock a bit of sense into them', it then revealed the awful unblemished 'truth' about the musical force that was rocking the nation. Having already said in the previous day's edition that 'rock, roll and riot is sexy music. It can make the blood race. It has something of the African tomtom and voodoo dance', the front-page editorial continued in this vein: 'It is deplorable. It is tribal. And it is from America. It follows rag-time, blues, Dixie, jazz, hot cha-cha and the boogie-woogie, which surely originated in the jungle. We sometimes wonder whether this is the negro's revenge'.

Since the war: which war was that?

In an essay on 'The Teddy Boy', Paul Rock and Stanley Cohen (1970: 289) later described how, 'We have had our Beats, Mods and Rockers, and Hippies – all in their turn inevitably labelled problems. The first and greatest of this sequence was the Ted'. And the thing about the 'Ted' was, he was indisputably 'new'. He dressed in outlandish clothes, and through his attachment to rock-and-roll he was 'Americanized', where 'Americanization' acts as a signifier for modernity and a portent for the dreadful future. In Richard Hoggart's (1958: 248) characterization in *The Uses of Literacy*, the 'juke box boys' were 'boys between fifteen and twenty, with drape-suits, picture ties, and an American slouch'. The Teddy Boy was picture perfect for the post-war lament that began to organize itself around the youth question, describing how everything in Britain was going to the dogs 'since the war', or in John Major's 'Back to Basics' speech in 'two generations'.

The lament had perhaps first been fully rehearsed in the post-war years by the Conservative Party publication, *Crime Knows No Boundaries* in the mid-1960s:

> We live in times of unprecedented change – change which often produces stress and social breakdown. Indeed the growth in the crime rate may be attributed in part to the breakdown of certain spontaneous agencies of social control which worked in the past. These controls operated through the family, the Church, through personal and local loyalties, and through a stable life in a stable society.
>
> (Conservative Party, 1966: 11)

We know this sorry post-war blues well enough. It runs in the veins of the British people, it is part of our DNA. Here it is again:

> That's the way we're going nowadays. Everything slick and streamlined, everything made out of something else. Celluloid, rubber, chromium-steel everywhere . . . radios all playing the same tune, no vegetation left, everything cemented over . . . There's something that's gone out of us in these twenty years since the war.

And again:

> The passing of parental authority, defiance of pre-war conventions, the absence of restraint, the wildness of extremes, the confusion of unrelated liberties, the wholesale drift away from churches, are but a few characteristics of after-war conditions.

And yet the immediate, complicating difficulty is that these last two complaints about what has gone wrong 'since the war' were both written *before* the war. The first is from George Orwell's pre-war novel *Coming Up for Air* as the main character, grumpy old George Bowling, searches around for signs of his lost childhood (Orwell, 1939: 27, 168). The second is from Christian youth worker James Butterworth's *Clubland* (1932: 22) reflecting on his experiences in the boys' club movement in the Elephant and Castle area of working-class London.

This 'postwar' malaise was a general current of feeling in the 1920s and 1930s. One active focus of discontent was F.R. Leavis's 'Scrutiny' group at Cambridge, repeatedly thundering against 'this vast and terrifying disintegration' of social life (Leavis and Thompson, 1933: 87). Cheap literature, popular music, cinema-going, the newly acquired habit of listening to the radio, advertising gimmicks, educational bankruptcy and 'Americanization' were all targeted as symptoms of decline. Because it was not only literary and artistic values that were alleged to be threatened, but also personal identity, family life and community. 'Change has been so catastrophic', wrote Leavis in 1930, that:

> [it] has, in a few years, radically affected religion, broken up the family, and revolutionized social custom. Change has been so catastrophic that the generations find it hard to adjust themselves to each other, and parents are helpless to deal with their children . . . It is a breach of continuity that threatens . . . It is a commonplace that we are being Americanised.
>
> (Leavis, 1930: 6–7)

T.S. Eliot's writings were drenched in the same anxieties. 'We have arrived', he thought, 'at a stage of civilisation at which the family is irresponsible, or incompetent, or helpless; at which parents cannot be expected to train their children properly . . . the moral restraints so weak . . . the institution of the family is no longer respected' (Eliot, 1948: 104).

Then as now, these sentiments were linked directly to problems of crime and criminal justice, particularly the question of juvenile crime. In addition to common allegations that the family, community and authority were in disrepair, a key cause of crime was seen as American movies that had a disorienting effect and offered encouragements towards immorality among the young. As early as 1913 in a commentary on 'Cinematography and the Child', *The Times* had spotted the first flickering danger signs from the silent movies:

> Before these children's greedy eyes with heartless discrimination horrors unimaginable are . . . presented night after night . . . Terrific massacres, horrible catastrophes, motor-car smashes, public hangings, lynchings . . . All who care for the moral well-being and education of the child will set their faces like flint against this new form of excitement.
>
> (*The Times*, 12 April 1913)

The silent movies, and then later the 'talkies', also invited the more specific charge that they encouraged imitative 'copy cat' crime among the young – *The Times* had alleged that many children 'actually begin their downward course of crime by reason of the burglary and pickpocket scenes they have witnessed' – a complaint we usually think of as belonging to the television age and the era of 'video nasties', but which had been scrutinized with great thoroughness in the monumental report of the National Council of Public Morals on *The Cinema* as early as 1917. More generally, however, the Hollywood cinema was understood to have had an unbalancing effect on the morals of the younger generation. As described by A.E. Morgan in his King George's Jubilee Trust report on *The Needs of Youth* in 1939, here on the silver screen was:

> A Never-never land of material values expressed in terms of gorgeous living, a plethora of high-powered cars and revolvers, and unlimited control of power

> ... of unbridled desire, of love crudely sentimental or fleshly, of vast possessions, of ruthless acquisition, of reckless violence ... It is an utterly selfish world ... It is a school of false values and its scholars cannot go unscathed.
>
> (Morgan, 1939: 242)

Accompanying these fears of a newly demoralizing form of popular entertainment, other accusations were thrown against the nation's youth in the 1930s that were understood to be associated with a galloping 'crime wave'. Morgan, once again, recited a catalogue of complaint that is uncannily familiar:

> Relaxation of parental control, decay of religious influence, and the transplantation of masses of young persons to housing estates where there is little scope for recreation and plenty for mischief ... a growing contempt by the young person for the procedure of juvenile courts ... The problem is a serious challenge, the difficulty of which is intensified by the extension of freedom which, for better or worse, has been given to youth in the last generation.
>
> (Morgan, 1939: 166, 191)

There had indeed been a sharp increase in recorded juvenile crime in the 1930s that in some quarters was blamed on the 'namby pamby methods' of 'our drawing room courts' (cited by Elkin, 1938: 288) resulting from the legislative reforms of the Children and Young Persons Act 1933, which had moved the juvenile courts towards a welfare model of justice, allegedly weakening their influence. Indeed, a correspondent in *The Times* could sum up the mood of the nation concerning mounting crime and dwindling authority in the following terms:

> There has been a tendency of late to paint a rather alarming picture of the depravity of the youth of the nation ... Headlines scream the menace of 'boy gangsters'. Elderly magistrates deplore the abandonment of their panacea, the birch ... by gloomy forebodings in the Press of the inevitably disastrous results of the leniency and weakness of the present day.
>
> (*The Times*, 4 January 1937)

Queen Victoria's 'Hooligans': gangs and territoriality in late nineteenth-century London

In so many ways these inter-war complaints seem like a carbon copy of our own, and those who voiced them were often to be found looking back to happier times 'before the war'. Indeed, even today the late Victorian and Edwardian years are often regarded as the gold standard of moral worth, remembered as a time of unrivalled domestic harmony. The cosy fug of the music hall. The rattle of clogs on cobbled streets. The unhurried pace of a horse-drawn civilization. Here, perhaps, is the true home of 'Old England' and unfettered tradition. This was not, however, a picture of itself that late Victorian and Edwardian England would always have found recognizable.

There were already gloomy rumblings in the editorial pages of *The Times* (6 February 1899; 16 August 1899; 17 August 1898) about 'the break-up or weakening of family life', no less than 'the break-up or impairment of the old ideas of discipline or order' in the cities, where there was 'something like organized terrorism in the streets'. Nor would we find much reassurance from Robert Baden-Powell as he boomed off in the first edition of *Scouting for Boys* against football as a 'vicious game when it draws crowds of lads away from playing themselves to be mere onlookers at a few paid performers':

> Thousands of boys and young men, pale, narrow-chested, hunched up, miserable specimens, smoking endless cigarettes, numbers of them betting, all of them learning to be hysterical as they groan or cheer in panic unison with their neighbours – the worst sound of all being the hysterical scream of laughter that greets any little trip or fall of a player. One wonders whether this can be the same nation which had gained for itself the reputation of a stolid, pipe-sucking manhood, unmoved by panic or excitement, and reliable in the tightest of places.
>
> (Baden-Powell, 1908: 338)

It is once again perceived as a generational shift. This was picked up elsewhere, as when Mr. C.G. Heathcote, the Stipendiary Magistrate for Brighton, noted in 1898 the disorienting effects of 'modernity', although that is not a word that he would have recognized. 'The tendencies of modern life', he wrote, 'incline more and more to ignore or disparage social distinctions, which formerly did much to encourage respect for others and habits of obedience and discipline.' Submitting evidence to the Howard Association on the subject of juvenile offenders, Mr Heathcote was in no doubt that 'the manners of children are deteriorating' and that 'the child of today is coarser, more vulgar, less refined than his parents were' (Howard Association, 1898: 22).

The most authoritative account of this generational discontinuity was provided by the young Liberal Charles Masterman in *The Heart of the Empire*, where he thundered out his warning of inevitable decline as the result of 'a perpetual lowering in the vitality of the Imperial Race in the great cities of the Kingdom through over-crowding in room and in area':

> Turbulent rioting over military successes, Hooliganism, and a certain temper of fickle excitability has revealed to observers during the past few months that a new race, hitherto unreckoned and of incalculable action, is entering the sphere of practical importance – the 'City type' of the coming years; the 'street-bred' people of the twentieth century; the 'new generation knocking at our doors' . . . The result is the production of a characteristic physical

type of town dweller: stunted, narrow-chested, easily wearied; yet voluble, excitable, with little ballast, stamina or endurance.

(Masterman, 1902: 7–8)

The mention of 'Hooliganism' brings us immediately to the point. The word 'Hooligan' had been catapulted into the English language in the immediate aftermath of an extremely hot and rowdy August Bank Holiday celebration in working-class London in 1898 which resulted in hundreds of people being brought before the Police Courts on charges of drunkenness, disorderly conduct, assault, and assaults on police officers.

One aspect of this turbulent street life was the fierce tradition of hostility to the police in many working-class neighbourhoods. Policemen attempting to make arrests in the open streets would commonly be set upon by a large crowd of bystanders, sometimes numbered in hundreds, to the battle-cry of 'Rescue! Rescue!' and 'Boot 'im!' As one example of this, at the height of the Bank Holiday outrages in 1898, various newspapers picked up on what one described as a 'Midnight Riot' in the vicinity of Euston Road when policemen attempted to deal with a disorderly woman who 'began to shriek, and . . . screamed that she was being choked'. Surrounded by a hostile crowd that began to hiss and hoot, one officer swept a semi-circle with his truncheon to make space while another blew his whistle for assistance. 'Unfortunately for the constable', we were told, 'this only had the effect of bringing reinforcements to the mob'. A roar went up of 'Rescue! Rescue!' and among those alerted to the commotion were the notorious 'Somers Town Boys' (*Daily Mail*, 15 August 1898; *News of the World*, 14 August 1898; *Evening News*, 13 August 1898; *The Sun*, 13 August 1898).

More typically, perhaps, 'Hooligan' gangs were to be found engaging in territorial battles with neighbouring gangs – Chapel Street versus Margaret Street, or Cable Street against Brook Street. In one pitched battle that obtained considerable publicity, a gang of about twenty youths were described, said to be known as the 'Chelsea Boys', who, 'armed with sticks and stones were fighting a contingent of similar young ruffians from Battersea' at Cheyne Walk by the River Thames (*The Daily Graphic*, 18 August 1898). Cheyne Walk was then, as it is now, a most desirable residence – George Eliot, Henry James, Elizabeth Gaskell, Dante Gabriel Rossetti and Isambard Kingdom Brunel were among the people who had lived there – and one can imagine that the neighbours were not pleased.

During the following weeks and months, there were any number of reports in the press of similar gangs – as well as the 'Somers Town Boys', who were said to be the pests of Gower Street and Euston Square station; there were the 'Lion Boys' from the Lion and Lamb in Clerkenwell; the so-called 'Clerkenwell "Pistol Gang"'; the 'Girdle Gang' from South London, which took its name from Thomas, alias 'Tuxy' Girdle; the 'Drury Lane Boys'; the 'Fulham Boys'; the 'Pinus Gang', who occupied Leather Lane and Clerkenwell; the notorious 'Waterloo Road Gang'; the 'Pickett Gang'; 'McNab's'; the 'Rest Gang'; the 'Fulham Ruffians' from Land's End; the 'Velvet Cap Gang' from Battersea; the 'Plaid-Cap Brigade' from Poplar; and a band of youngsters who had adopted the dare-devil title of the 'Dick Turpin Gang'. Whereas in Hammersmith *The Sun* (6 August 1898) described how 'the King Street larrikins do just as they like', the gangs who romped about Great Church Lane were said to be 'NOT "HOOLIGANS" BUT WORSE'.

One thing that quickly became apparent was that the 'Hooligans' had adopted a uniform dress-style (Pearson, 1983: 50, 92–101). The main features were bell-bottom narrow-go-wide trousers, cut tight at the knee and flared at the bottom, often pictured with a buttoned side-vent in the leg; a peaked cap and neck scarf; heavy leather belts, often worked with ornamental designs using metal studs; and heavy boots, which according to *The Sun* (7 August 1898) in one part of South London were said to be 'toe-plated in iron and calculated to kill easily'. Gang members also had identical hairstyles, the hair clipped close to the scalp, except for a tuft on the crown that was pulled forward to form a 'donkey fringe'. Similar gangs were known and feared in other cities by other names – 'Peaky Blinders' in Birmingham, and 'scuttlers' in Manchester and Salford who fought fierce territorial battles – with almost completely identical styles of dress, with pointed clogs substituted for boots, for example, among Manchester's 'scuttlers' who also sometimes wore 'billycock' hats as well as peaked caps. How this dress-fashion was diffused and adopted by youths in these far-flung cities is not known, but the fashion had almost certainly originated among the 'scuttlers', whose reign of terror went back to the 1870s (Davies, 2008; this volume).

Apart from attacks on police officers and rival gang fights, newspaper reports frequently depicted the London 'Hooligans' cluttering up the streets in noisy gatherings, swearing at passers-by, spitting on them, and sometimes assaulting and robbing them. *The Daily Graphic* (15 August 1898) described the antics of one gang from Battersea: 'Some dozen boys, all armed with sticks and belts, wearing velvet caps, and known as the "Velvet Cap Gang", walking along . . . pushing people off the pavement, knocking at shop doors, and using filthy language'. And then, a few days later, a similar story from another part of London: 'A gang of roughs, who were parading the roadway, shouting obscene language, playing mouth organs, and pushing respectable people down. The young ruffians were all armed with thick leather belts, on which there were heavy brass buckles' (*The Daily Graphic*, 25 August 1898).

The frequent reports of people being hustled, or pushed off the pavement, probably derived from the practice among working-class youths known as 'holding the street'. This violent ritual of territorial supremacy was described by Walter Besant in 1901 in his book *East London*: 'The boys gather together and hold the street; if anyone ventures to pass through it they rush upon him, knock him down, and kick him savagely about the head; they rob him as well . . . the boys regard holding the street with pride' (Besant, 1901: 177). Besant provided other details of these violent street gangs, describing how the boys of Cable Street would 'constitute themselves, without asking the permission of the War Office, into a small regiment':

They arm themselves with clubs, with iron bars, with leather belts to which buckles belong, with knotted handkerchiefs containing stones – a lethal weapon – with sling and stones, with knives even, with revolvers of the 'toy' kind, and they go forth to fight the lads of Brook Street. It is a real fight (Besant, 1901: 176–7).

The mention of pistols – the 'Hooligans' were sometimes known as 'Belt and Pistol gangs' – alerts us to another worrying dimension of the 'Hooligan' gangs. Cases of pistol shootings were not uncommon. Reporting one case under the headline 'PISTOL GANGS IN LONDON. A SCHOOLBOY COMMITTED', *The Daily Graphic* (15 February 1898) had described the case of a 13-year-old boy, John Bird from Camden, who had appeared before Marylebone magistrates court. The magistrate had described it as 'an extraordinary tale of life in London', saying that 'these pistol cases are getting much too frequent'. The young teenager had shot at an 18-year-old greengrocer's son, shouting, 'You won't touch me when I have this. I'll put daylight into you'. In a case reported by the *Illustrated Police News* (5 November 1898) another 13-year-old boy, without provocation, had shot an 18-year-old in the leg on a canal tow-path; whereas a month earlier the *News of the World* (16 October 1898) had described how a 14-year-old boy, Henry Green from Westminster, had been charged with shooting his 2-year-old brother Edwin with a 'toy pistol' and a box of cartridges. The magistrate in this case commented on the ease with which 'these dangerous toys' could be bought.

A few months before the 'Hooligan' was officially christened by the news media, the *London Echo* (7 February 1898) had already remarked that 'No one can have read the London, Liverpool, Birmingham, Manchester and Leeds papers and not know that the young street ruffian and prowler, with his heavy belt, treacherous knife and dangerous pistol, is amongst us'. In a discussion of 'Those Pistol Cases' as its chosen 'Topic of the Day', *The Daily Graphic* (15 February 1898) had agreed that they 'are getting much too frequent' and that 'the latest pistol cases have almost all been of boys, hardly in their teens, deliberately using pistols as weapons of aggression . . . those "gangs" of young ruffians . . . seem to think little more of discharging them than they would of throwing stones. It is a practice that will have to be suppressed; and if birching and short sentences will not stop it, then more birching and longer sentences will have to be tried.' A couple of years later, *The Graphic* (16 November 1900) would even assert that 'the pistol is the ideal weapon of the Hooligan . . . his love for it can be traced directly to the influence of the "penny dreadfuls"'.

With this accusation, which was also levelled against the 'scuttlers' in Manchester, 'Hooliganism' is reconnected to that long, weary catalogue of complaint that blames youth crime and disorder on demoralizing popular entertainments – whether the cinema, television violence, video-nasties, gangsta rap, or the music halls. The 'Hooligans', when all is said and done, were the children, the grandchildren and the great-grandchildren of those who earlier in the nineteenth century had attended cheap theatres, penny gaffs and twopenny hop dancing saloons which had been held up as incitements to crime and immorality among the young. In his thesis *On the Treatment of the Dangerous and Perishing Classes of Society* of 1853, 'The corruption of youth from spectacles, songs, etc., of an indecent nature' had excited C.F. Cornwallis, no less than others who described how the daring enactments of the outrages of Jack Sheppard, Dick Turpin and Claude Duval 'inculcate the same lesson, exhibit to admiration noted examples of successful crime' and thereby 'attract the attention and the ambition of these boys, and each one endeavours to emulate the conduct of his favourite hero' (Cornwallis, 1853: 41; Worsley, 1849: 78, 94; Beggs, 1849: 97). In her book *Artful Dodgers*, Heather Shore also describes how in early nineteenth-century London the public houses or 'flash-houses', where young delinquents gathered to share their spoils and to divide themselves into 'companies' or thieving teams, were inevitably accused of being 'nurseries of crime' (Shore, 1999: 24–6).

So, in the first decade of Queen Victoria's long reign, there was already considerable disquiet about the nation's youth. Edwin Chadwick, in his ground-breaking report of 1842, *Sanitary Conditions of the Labouring Population of Great Britain*, had passed shuddering judgement on the British people, finding 'a population that is young, inexperienced, ignorant, credulous, irritable, passionate, and dangerous', and that during the riots of Manchester, Bristol and elsewhere 'the great havoc . . . was committed by mere boys' (Chadwick, 1965: 267–8). In the following year, Lord Ashley, Earl of Shaftesbury, rose before the House of Commons to urge the necessity of a system of elementary education for the children of the 'dangerous classes'. Brooding repeatedly on 'a fearful multitude of untutored savages' in the manufacturing districts, 'children of the tenderest years . . . suffered to roam at large through the streets . . . contracting the most idle and profligate habits', lads 'with dogs at their heels and other evidence of dissolute habits', girls who 'drive coal-carts, ride astride upon horses, drink, swear, fight, smoke, whistle, and care for nobody', and the great acquaintance of young people with the exploits of Dick Turpin and Jack Sheppard, 'not to mention the preposterous epidemic of a hybrid negro song', Lord Ashley arrived at a tumultuous conclusion: 'The morals of the children are tenfold worse than formerly' (Hansard, 28 February 1843).

The unruly apprentice: maypoles, misrule and mischief

The profound historical amnesia surrounding the youth question can be measured by the fact that at the dawn of the Industrial Revolution, we find a minister of the National Scotch Church issuing a remarkable sermon on the coming of *The Last Days*:

> From this relaxation of parental discipline . . . doth it come to pass that children who have been brought up within these thirty years, have nothing like the same reverence and submission to their parents . . . This is the cause of juvenile

depredation: this is a chief cause of the increase of crime, especially amongst children . . . Hence, also, the trustlessness of apprentices and of domestic servants . . . the domestication of man's wild spirit is gone . . . Oh, oh! what a burden hath the Lord laid upon his ministers, to stand amidst the wreck of a dissolving society, and, like Canute, to preach unto the surging waves!

(Irving, 1829: 79, 84, 86–7)

The judgement is once more generational, and it was commonplace in the first decades of the nineteenth century to assert that the factory system had caused the breakdown of what were seen as the old patrician and paternal disciplines and brought about moral havoc. And yet, fully 150 years before this, Richard Baxter in *A Christian Dictionary* of 1678 was to be found lamenting the morals of 'Voluptuous Youths that run after Wakes, and May-games, and Dancings, and Revellings, and are carried by the Love of sports and pleasure . . . into idleness, riotousness and disobedience to their Superiors' (cited by Malcolmson, 1973: 7).

In the pre-industrial era, where the young were concerned, the main focus of anxiety was on apprenticeship. In the most general terms, a voluminous literature described apprentices as idle, violent and profligate. In London, apprentices were so numerous that they formed an identifiable 'subculture', with its own standards, codes of honour, literature and heroes (Smith, 1973). There were also pitched battles between rival groups of apprentices, as when Elizabeth George (1966: 272) describes a case from the *London Sessions Papers* of 1722: 'It was usual for the boys of St. Anne's parish to fight those of St. Giles armed with sticks for "a week or two before the holidays"'. 'This fact survives', she continues, 'because in 1722 the captain of the boys of St. Giles, a chimney-sweep aged twenty-one was killed by another boy aged sixteen'.

It is probably equally likely that these violent conflicts were arranged not so much around neighbourhoods or parishes, but where apprentices were concerned, around trades and occupations – just as some of the 'scuttling' conflicts in late nineteenth-century Manchester and Salford were between different occupations or between 'scuttlers' working in different factories (Davies, 2008; this volume). We hear from Dijon in France, for example, in the years between 1440 and 1490 that:

These groups of young males who disturbed the nightly peace of Dijon showed some very clearly defined characteristics, the first of which is a relative homogeneity in age . . . Two-thirds of these groups had marked socio-occupational affinities . . . who were connected with a specific trade or related occupations or else were lads of the same social standing. An equal proportion of groups was formed 'on the street corner' . . . In more than 80 per cent of the cases . . . these groups had no previous record of group delinquency. In other words, the *juvenes* of closed cities, from sheer boredom, spontaneously set out in search of nightly adventure and fighting, defying patrols, chasing girls, and engaging in rape.

(Rossiaud, 1978: 11–12)

There was a close association also between English apprentices and bawdy-houses and ale houses and, writing of seventeenth-century London, Smith (1973: 161) states that London's prostitutes 'were frequent targets of apprentice riots throughout the century'. It was also sometimes alleged that on Shrove Tuesday London apprentices were accustomed to work off their energies by wrecking bawdy houses – according to the gallows humour, to preserve themselves from temptation during Lent – and apprentices had thrown themselves into the thick of it during London's 'evil May Day' in 1517, which turned into a riot against foreigners (Burke, 1978: 204).

The evidence in early modern and pre-industrial England is necessarily fragmented and enigmatic, since these were matters concerning humble people who did not have a voice in public affairs, except when anonymous threatening letters were pinned to the doors of magistrates or employers during times of popular unrest (Thompson, 1975; Hobsbawm and Rudé, 1970; Charlesworth, 1983: 169). We can nevertheless glimpse the more specific anxieties that surrounded apprentices by looking at some of the statutes and regulations brought in to control and constrain them.

The strict enforcement of the 'indoor' apprentice system prohibited apprentices from contracting marriage, or from owning personal possessions without the master's express approval. Various regulations banned apprentices from public houses and brothels, from playing dice and card games, and even the playing of music was sometimes forbidden. In Manchester in 1609 football rowdyism was frowned upon, and in other trades and localities, football games were outlawed. The 'Merchant Adventurers' had a rule of curfew which forbade apprentices to 'knock or ring at men's doors or to beat at windows', and, by a regulation of 1697 in Newcastle, they were not allowed 'to get to fencing or dancing schools, nor to music houses, lotteries or playhouses, neither to keep any sort of horses, dogs for hunting, or fighting cocks'. Regulations controlled what fashions apprentices might (or might not) wear, including a prohibition on 'silke garters', lace and embroidery. In one area it was said that, 'those whose dress was not sufficiently sober were brought into the court, stripped of superfluous ribbons, and sent to prison' (Dunlop, 1912: 189–90). The length of hair was another area of widespread prohibition. An order of 1603 that they should not 'weare their haire long nor locks in their ears like ruffians' provoked a long drawn-out battle in Newcastle in which the apprentices were eventually triumphant – but only after 40 years of struggle during which many recalcitrant youths were committed to prison with shaven heads; so many that the courts complained they were being overworked and the regulation was annulled. 'At the close of the seventeenth century', we learn, 'there was a new difficulty: the attraction of ruffles, ribbons and curls faded before the glory of wigs, and new regulations had to be devised'. 'Noe apprentice shall weare long wigs nor any short wigs, above the price of fifteene shillings' (Dunlop, 1912: 191–3). In 1692 apprentices were included in a Parliamentary Act that prohibited hunting. Another statute in 1757 banned 'cards, dice, shuffle-board, mississipi or billiards, skittles and nine-pins'. Apprentices were, therefore, embroiled in a series of controversies of far too long a duration to be thought of as a moral panic.

Indeed, the popular culture of early modern Europe was more generally unruly and transgressive, as evidenced by not only the multitude of subversive and satirical tracts, pamphlets and images of the 'Lords of Misrule' and a world turned upside down, but also by the village rituals of public disgrace such as the 'Skimmington' and 'rough music' (Davis, 1975; Underdown, 1985; Thompson, 1991; Pierce, 2008). Youths were invariably at the centre of these carnivals of disorder, whether in the ceremonial mockery of 'boy bishops' or in the more vulgar displays of 'Skimmington', which held various forms of domestic disgrace – illegitimacy, adultery, wife beating, cuckoldry – up to public shame by means of processions of local people banging improvised drums and kitchen implements, and blowing crude forms of horn. Edward Thompson on more than one occasion remarks on such processions 'got up by the village lads' or 'a procession got up by the Blacksmiths' apprentices, attended by a large Mob . . . carrying torches . . . discharging fireworks in great abundance in the most reckless manner' (Thompson, 1991: 471–5). As Samuel Butler described the 'Skimmington' in his satirical burlesque verse *Hudibras*, written between 1660 and 1680:

> And now the cause of all their fear
> By slow degree approach'd so near
> They might distinguish diff'rent noyse
> Of horns, and *pans*, and *dogs*, and *boyse*

(Butler, 1967: 143)

Similar customs to 'Skimmington' and 'rough music' were known throughout Europe by different names, sometimes involving other forms of elaborate ritual such as requiring the victim to ride backwards on a donkey or on a wooden pole, and could also be turned to political purposes as during the Rebecca disturbances in Wales in the 1830s and 1840s when the *ceffyl pren* (or wooden horse) was often carried by the rioters (Pearson, 1983: 197–201; Williams, 1955). Natalie Zemon Davis reports that in France these disturbances, where they were known as 'charivari' and were equivalent to the 'Skimmington', were most frequent and could also be particularly vexing if they targeted an older widower who had re-married a much younger bride: 'Then the masked youths with their pots, tambourines, bells, rattles, and horns might make their clamour for a week outside the house of their victims, unless they settled and paid a fine. Others in the village might join them, but it was the young men who took the initiative.' Davis (1975: 105–6) also notes the 'fines collected from lads from another village who came to court local girls and the fights that sometimes broke out on these occasions'.

We are back in the realm of territoriality and territorial conflict, the 'postcode' rivalries of early modern Europe. In England one thing that exemplified these territorial embodiments of locality and prestige as well as any other was football.

Underdown (1985: 75) describes the structure and functions of the early modern 'game' in the following terms:

> A more or less ritualised combat between communities, often represented by virtually the entire young male population of whole parishes, it was an appropriate expression of parochial loyalty against outsiders, in which the identity of the individual was almost totally submerged in that of the group . . . Its collective character made it an appropriate game for communities with strong habits of cooperation.

He adds that 'its disorderly violence made it an inevitable target of moral reformers'. Football was not the codified game as we know it now. Douglas Reid (1982: 126) in a Bakhtinian interpretation of the festival calendar of wakes and fairs describes football matches as 'often ritual battles rather than true sport'. It was played across open terrain, criss-crossed by many obstacles such as ditches, brooks, hedges and fences, and both Underdown (1985) and Malcolmson (1973) describe many different local and regional variations both in how it was played, and the names by which it was known, such as 'camp ball' in the eastern counties or 'bottle-kicking' in Leicestershire.

A favourite time in the festival calendar for arranging football matches was Shrove Tuesday, thus associating it with the 'carnivalesque', although it was played at other times of the year as well. Games arranged at these holidays could be gargantuan affairs, and Malcolmson (1973: 37) describes one Shrovetide match between two parishes in Derby as being an open invitation match to the people of the surrounding town and county with between 500 and 1,000 a side. Football matches could also be staged as political or 'industrial relations' events. In the *Northampton Mercury* in 1765, it was reported that:

> We hear from West-Haddon, in this County, that on Thursday and Friday last a great Number of People being assembled there, in order to play a Foot-Ball Match . . . formed themselves into a tumultuous Mob, and pulled up and burnt the Fences designed for the Inclosure of that Field, and did other considerable Damage.
>
> (Malcolmson, 1973: 40)

Thompson (1991: 234) also describes how during the food riots of 1740, an informant from Northamptonshire announced to the Secretary of State that 'a Mach of Futtball was Cried at Ketring of five Hundred Men of a side but the design was to Pull Down Lady Betey Jesmains Mills'.

Apart from its association with popular unrest, it is the link of football with fairs and feasts that reminds us of the youthfulness of so much of this restive popular culture in pre-industrial England. At fairs and feasts, as Robert Malcolmson (1973: 53) observes, 'the most active participants, as one might expect, were men and women in their teens and early twenties'. One reason is that recreations such as this offered opportunities for courtship and sexual encounters, and one of Malcolmson's sources noticed that 'towards evening each lad seeks his lass, and they hurry off to spend the night at the public houses', while another recounted how in the evening with 'fiddlers tuning their fiddles in public houses, the girls begin to file off, and gently pace the streets, with a view to gaining admirers; while the young men . . . follow after, and having eyed the lasses, pick up each a sweetheart, whom they conduct to a dancing room, and treat with punch and cake' (1973: 54). May Day was a particularly popular festival for young people, where in some localities at midnight young people of both sexes would go into the woods, playing music and blowing horns, playing games (of which kind it is not difficult to imagine), breaking branches and gathering garlands, and returning home at sunrise when they might dance around a large pole – the Maypole of 'Merrie England' (Malcolmson, 1973: 30). However, Maypoles were often frowned upon and much contested (Underdown, 1985; Thompson, 1991: 75), possibly viewed as a relic of pagan sexual symbolism.

From the sixteenth century there had been moral opposition to these popular customs. The Elizabethan Puritan, Philip Stubbes, in his *Anatomy of Abuses* (1583) regarded feast days as the source of all kinds of moral ruin: dancing was denounced as 'filthy groping and unclean handling'; whereas football was attacked as 'a friendly kind of fight' and 'a murthering play'; and from many quarters it was alleged that 'popular songs too often presented criminals as heroes' (Stubbes, 1877: 145, 155, 184; Burke, 1978: 212). 'Are not unlawful games, plays, interludes and the like everywhere frequented?', asked Stubbes, 'Was there ever seen less obedience in youth of all sorts, both menkind and womenkind, towards their superiors, parents, masters and governors?' (cited by Underdown, 1985: 48).

We must be careful in interpreting these kinds of commentary, however, since Stubbes was a Puritan reformer who was deeply hostile to popular culture and may have misunderstood, misrepresented and exaggerated this kind of behaviour. Although that, too, offers its own kind of continuity, in that New Labour ideologues with their catalogue of ASBOS, parenting orders and exclusion zones may have misunderstood, exaggerated and misrepresented 'chavs', 'hoodies' and 'gangsta rap'.

Conclusion: stop press

Some of the claims for the novelty of youth crime are quite preposterous. 'We face new causes of crime', said the then Prime Minister Gordon Brown when launching one of New Labour's numerous crime prevention initiatives, 'and we need new ways of responding'. Among these 'new causes' of crime, he listed 'binge-drinking, youth gangs and problem families' (*Guardian*, 12 May 2009). Here we witness the shallow profundity of modern politics, eliminating many self-evident aspects of human self-understanding in the search for news headlines and sound-bites. Because, there have been 'problem families' as long as there have been families. The demon drink has been with us probably as long, at least since humankind stumbled across the fermentation process, and certainly since Pharaonic and Biblical times (Dodson and Ikram, 2008: 96, 97–8; Bierbrier, 1982: 77; Manniche, 1987: 45, 62, 118; Genesis, 9: 20–5; Proverbs, 23: 20–1; Isaiah 5: 11). And as we have seen in this chapter, youth gangs are certainly not a 'new' cause of crime, and might even be rooted in sociobiological aspects of human sociality (Wilson, 1975; Ardrey, 1969; Davis, 1962). Whatever arguments there might be against biological reductionism (Montagu, 1976; Midgley, 1979), we cannot exempt ourselves from the animal kingdom. Even so, this longstanding preoccupation with youthful misconduct and its novelty invariably fixes on working-class 'hooliganism' rather than the 'rowdyism' and high spirits of upper-class young gentlemen (Pearson, 1983: 153–5).

This profound historical amnesia blots out even the most recent past. The violence of the Teddy Boys that rocked the nation in the 1950s is now forgotten, wrapped in a nostalgic embrace of the music of Buddy Holly and the young Cliff Richard. The memory of the juvenile crime wave of the inter-war years, together with anguished complaints against the decline of family life, is entirely suppressed. As for the 'Hooligan' gangs of late Victorian London, they are completely dead and buried. Indeed, when the word 'hooligan' was put to work again in the 1970s to describe violence at football matches, 'football hooliganism' was itself seen as an entirely novel departure from the British traditions of 'fair play' and sports-manship, although violence at football matches had been quite common both in the inter-war years and in the late Victorian epoch (Pearson, 1983: 29–31, 64–5; Mason, 1980, 161–6; Ensor, 1898).

We are faced with a paradox. On the one hand, a relentless vocabulary of complaint against modernity and social change. On the other hand, a lament against young people – invoking family decline, increasing irresponsibility, increasing disrespect, the influence of demoralizing popular entertainments – that itself seems immune to change. This long, connected history of complaint against the deteriorated present, in which the past is lovingly remembered (but hopelessly falsified) as a time of generational harmony and social tranquilly, requires us to make a number of readjustments to our ways of thinking about youth crime and 'crime waves'. It is not that the world does not change – the vast, historical alterations of the social landscape are undeniable – but that this immovable vocabulary of complaints is somehow unable to keep pace with a moving world.

Youth and modernity are inescapably twinned. Moreover, the preoccupation with youth has often acted as a convenient metaphor for social change (Smith, 1975: 242). We can hardly begin to guess at the guiding forces within the extraordinary historical amnesia that cancels out all signs of trouble in even the most recent past. What we can say with certainty is that the long pedigree of the social preoccupation with the novelty of youthful misconduct guarantees it against any immediate demise. Given its proven immunization against changing social and historical circumstances, what kind of social alteration would there have to be for the metaphor itself to change? While a sense of urgency governs our attention, the pale shadow of time is no match for the instant photo-flash of the present. But if we wish to combat the dreadful cultural pessimism that haunts the youth question, we must begin to learn to re-possess the past in all its forms, if we are to face the present and build the future.

References

Ardrey, R. (1969) *The Territorial Imperative*. Glasgow: Fontana/Collins.

Baden-Powell, R. (1908) *Scouting for Boys*. London: Horace Cox.

Beggs, T. (1849) *An Inquiry into the Extent and Causes of Juvenile Depravity*. London: Gilpin.

Besant, W. (1901) *East London*. London: Chatto & Windus.

Bierbrier, M. (1982) *The Tomb-Builders of the Pharaohs*. Cairo: The American University in Cairo Press.

British Medical Association (1961) *The Adolescent*. London: British Medical Association.

Burke, P. (1978) *Popular Culture in Early Modern Europe*. London: Temple Smith.

Butler, S. (1967) *Hudibras*. Ed. by J. Wilders. Oxford: Oxford University Press.

Butterworth, J. (1932) *Clubland*. London: Epworth.

Chadwick, E. (1965) *Report on the Sanitary Condition of the Labouring Population of Great Britain*. Edited by M.W. Flinn. Edinburgh: Edinburgh University Press.

Charlesworth, A. (ed.) (1983) *An Atlas of Rural Protest in Britain 1548–1900*. London: Croom Helm.

Conservative Party (1966) *Crime Knows No Boundaries*. London: Conservative Political Centre.

Cornwallis, C.F. (1853) *On the Treatment of the Dangerous and Perishing Classes of Society*. London: Smith, Elder & Co.

Davies, A. (2008) *The Gangs of Manchester: The Story of the Scuttlers, Britain's First Youth Cult*. Preston: Milo Books.

Davis, D.E. (1962) 'An Inquiry into the Philogeny of Gangs', in E.L. Bliss (ed.) *Roots of Behavior: Genetics, Instinct and Socialisation in Animal Behavior*. New York: Harper & Row, pp. 316–20.

Davis, N.Z. (1975) 'The Reasons of Misrule', in N.Z. Davis (ed.) *Society and Culture in Early Modern France*. London: Duckworth, pp. 97–123.

Dodson, A. and Ikram, S. (2008) *The Tomb in Ancient Egypt*. Cairo: The American University in Cairo Press.

Dunlop, O.J. (1912) *English Apprenticeship and Child Labour: A History*. London: Fisher Unwin.

Eliot, T.S. (1948) *Notes Towards the Definition of Culture*. 1962 edn. London: Faber & Faber.

Elkin, W. (1938) *English Juvenile Courts*. London: Kegan Paul.

Ensor, E. (1898) 'The Football Madness', *Contemporary Review*, 74: 751–60.

George, M.D. (1966) *London Life in the Eighteenth Century*. Harmondsworth: Penguin.

Hobsbawm, E.J. and Rudé, G. (1970) *Captain Swing*. London: Readers Union.

Hoggart, R. (1958) *The Uses of Literacy*. Harmondsworth: Penguin.

Howard Association (1898) *Juvenile Offenders*. London: Howard Association.

Irving, E. (1829) *The Last Days: A Discourse on the Evil Character of these Our Times*. London: Seeley & Burnside.

Leavis, F.R. (1930) *Mass Civilisation and Minority Culture*. Cambridge: Minority Press.

Leavis, F.R. and Thompson, D. (1933) *Culture and Environment*. London: Chatto & Windus.

Malcolmson, R.W. (1973) *Popular Recreations in English Society: 1700–1850*. Cambridge: Cambridge University Press.

Manniche, L. (1987) *The Tombs of the the Nobles at Luxor*. Cairo: The American University in Cairo Press.

Mason, T. (1980) *Association Football and English Society 1863–1915*. Brighton: Harvester Press.

Masterman, C.F.G. (1902) *The Heart of the Empire*. London: Fisher Unwin.

Midgley, M. (1979) *Beast and Man: The Roots of Human Nature*. Brighton: Harvester Press.

Montagu, A. (1976) *The Nature of Human Aggression*. Oxford: Oxford University Press.

Morgan, A.E. (1939) *The Needs of Youth*. Oxford: Oxford University Press.

National Council of Public Morals (1917) *The Cinema*. London: Williams & Norgate.

Orwell, G. (1939) *Coming Up for Air*. 1962 edn. Harmondsworth: Penguin.

Pearson, G. (1983) *Hooligan: A History of Respectable Fears*. London: Macmillan.

Pierce, H. (2008) *Unseemly Pictures: Graphic Satire and Politics in Early Modern England*. New Haven: Yale University Press.

Reid, D.A. (1982) 'Interpreting the Festival Calendar: Wakes and Fairs as Carnivals', in R.D. Storch (ed.) *Popular Culture and Custom in Nineteenth Century England*. London: Croom Helm, pp. 125–53.

Rock, P. and Cohen, S. (1970) 'The Teddy Boy', in V. Bogdanor and R. Skidelsky (eds) *The Age of Affluence*. London: Macmillan, pp. 288–320.

Rossiaud, J. (1978) 'Prostitution, Youth, and Society in the Towns of Southeastern France in the Fifteenth Century', in R. Forster and O. Ranum (eds) *Deviants and the Abandoned in French Society: Selections from the Annales Economies, Sociétés Civilisations, vol. 4*. Baltimore: Johns Hopkins University Press, pp. 1–46.

Shore, H. (1999) *Artful Dodgers: Youth Crime in Early Nineetenth-Century London*. London: The Royal Historical Society and Boydell Press.

Smith, A.C.H. (1975) *Paper Voices: The Popular Press and Social Change, 1935–1965*. London: Chatto & Windus.

Smith, S.R. (1973) 'The London Apprentices as Seventeenth Century Adolescents', *Past and Present*, 61: 149–61.

Stubbes, P. (1583) *Anatomy of Abuses in England*. London: New Shakespeare Society, 1877 edn.

Thompson, E.P. (1975) 'The Crime of Anonymity', in D. Hay, P. Linebaugh and E.P. Thompson (eds) *Albion's Fatal Tree: Crime and Society in Eighteenth-Century England*. London: Allen Lane, pp. 255–344.

—— (1991) *Customs in Common*. London: Merlin Press.

Underdown, D. (1985) *Revel, Riot and Rebellion: Popular Politics and Culture in England*. Oxford: Oxford University Press.

Weiner, M. (1981) *English Culture and the Decline of the Industrial Spirit 1850–1980*. Cambridge: Cambridge University Press.

Williams, D. (1955) *The Rebecca Riots*. Cardiff: University of Wales Press.

Wilson, E.O. (1975) *Sociobiology: The New Synthesis*. Cambridge, MA: Harvard University Press.

Worsley, H. (1849) *Juvenile Depravity*. London: Gilpin.

Chapter 2

Youth gangs and late Victorian society

Andrew Davies

The growth of 'gang culture' in major British cities and the associated 'epidemics' of gun- and knife-crime have been widely identified as some of the most pressing social problems of recent years. In media coverage and political discourse alike these trends are firmly stated to be unprecedented: gangs are more widespread than ever before, their members younger and more violent.[1] In fact, as Geoffrey Pearson (1983; this volume) reminds us, such anxieties are themselves nothing new. The late Victorian period witnessed strikingly similar concerns: a reported proliferation of youth gangs, a 'growing' resort to weapons and allegations of a 'reign of terror' in London, Manchester, Birmingham and Liverpool.[2] As Pearson (this volume) points out, present debates on youth and crime are underpinned by a profound amnesia. With historical antecedents buried under media sensationalism and political opportunism, gangs become a by-product of 'Broken Britain' – of family breakdown, the loss of community cohesion, or the malign influence of American 'gangsta' rap.[3]

Historical research challenges many of our assumptions about the novelty of gang formation and conflict in British cities. This chapter provides an overview of existing studies of youth gangs in the late Victorian period, before presenting some findings from a case-study of the Manchester conurbation during the period from 1870 to 1900.

Histories of hooliganism

The first historical accounts of youth gangs in late Victorian society were published in the 1980s. In *Hooligans or Rebels?* (1981), Stephen Humphries argued that gang membership provided 'an inarticulate and immediate solution to the problems of disadvantage that confronted working-class youth in all spheres of life' (Humphries, 1981: 176). Humphries identified two types of street gang: 'delinquent' and 'semi-delinquent'.

The majority of working-class boys joined semi-delinquent gangs between the ages of 10 and 13. These informal 'cliques' were loosely structured friendship groups with no recognized leaders and no connections with the criminal 'underworld'. They defined themselves in opposition to their counterparts from rival streets and their members commonly 'drifted' into delinquency through their attempts to transcend boredom: vandalism and conflicts with the police yielded action and excitement (Humphries, 1981: 178–9). Humphries downplayed the extent of violence in late Victorian gang conflicts, claiming that fights between semi-delinquent gangs were 'to a large extent ritualized and involved customary constraints that prevented serious injury' (ibid. 189). In his account, membership of a semi-delinquent gang served as a youthful rite of passage. Most youths gave up gang membership by their late teens in tandem with courtship and marriage (ibid. 179). Alternatively, 'delinquent' gangs – concentrated in 'inner city areas of deprivation and high unemployment' (ibid. 179–80) – were distinguished by their deeper immersion in both petty crime and territorial battles. Gang members carried weapons 'largely as symbols of defiance and resistance', generally reserving 'serious' violence for members of newly arrived immigrant communities: 'in these circumstances, territorial divisions were deepened and reinforced by racial divisions'. Severe injuries and even fatalities were the occasional result (ibid. 192–3).

Humphries' account was followed by Geoffrey Pearson's *Hooligan: A History of Respectable Fears*, published in 1983. Whereas Humphries had sought to identify structural explanations for gang formation, Pearson was principally concerned with the rapidity with which a new label for youthful disorder – 'hooliganism' – was adopted by the London press following a rowdy Bank Holiday weekend in August 1898 (Pearson, 1983: 74–83). As Pearson pointed out, this new label was used to depict customary forms of behaviour as both unprecedented and un-English (ibid. 75–6), yet, 'if Hooliganism was an entirely novel outburst as was usually supposed, then a tropical growth of gang life must have sprouted overnight' (ibid. 82).[4] Pearson identified some of the provincial counterparts of London's hooligans, including the 'scuttlers' of Manchester and Salford, Birmingham's 'peaky blinders', and the 'High Rip' gangs of Liverpool, pointing out that they shared a common 'uniform' (ibid. 94–8). Pearson located gang fights within the unruly street life of the Victorian city, noting that 'in many working-class neighbourhoods hostility towards the police was a remarkably cohesive force' (1983: 86). Pearson's assessment of the level of violence in gang conflicts differed from Humphries'. To Pearson, there was no doubt that late Victorian youth gangs routinely fought with weapons such as knives and belts (1983: 101–2).

The role of the press in orchestrating fears of juvenile crime and disorder was further examined by Rob Sindall in his study of *Street Violence in the Nineteenth Century*, published in 1990. Sindall applied Stanley Cohen's (1987) concept of 'moral panic' to a series of episodes in the period from the 1850s to the 1880s, showing how the expanding popular press identified a series of 'folk devils' in the figures of 'garrotters', 'roughs', and 'cornermen' (Sindall, 1990: 45–75). Such people were typically drawn from the ranks of the urban poor; they were often – although not always – young males, and they were frequently believed to form gangs. Sensational press coverage fuelled public anxieties, prompting police clampdowns which in turn were taken as evidence of crime waves (ibid. 110).

Magistrates and judges responded by imposing exemplary sentences and, whilst most 'panics' subsided before Parliament intervened, the furore over garrotting in 1862–3 led to the introduction of longer, harsher prison sentences, and to the re-introduction of flogging as a punishment for those convicted of robbery with violence (ibid. 136–43).

Humphries, Pearson and Sindall all drew examples from across the major British cities. The first local case-study, however – of youth gangs in Birmingham during the 1870s – was published by Barbara Weinberger in 1991. Weinberger (1991: 408–9) argued that territorial wars between 'English' and 'Irish' youth gangs erupted during a period of economic downturn in 1873. Sectarian convictions intensified in the wake of chronic youth unemployment, and the level of violence in the city's 'slums' was inflamed by aggressive police campaigns against street gambling and breaches of the licensing laws (ibid. 410–14). Weinberger claimed that the municipal authorities were largely indifferent to outbreaks of communal violence that were effectively restricted to the 'slums' (ibid. 416–17). Echoing Humphries, Weinberger concluded that youths formed gangs within a context of chronic economic disadvantage and political powerlessness: 'it was precisely their sense of exclusion from the larger society which gave rise to . . . street gangs in the first place. However misconceived, gang warfare at least gave the participants a chance to acquire some local power and prestige which was denied them at any other level of public life' (ibid. 417).[5]

'Scuttling' in Manchester and Salford

In late Victorian Manchester and Salford, gang members called themselves 'scuttlers'. In local slang, the noun 'scuttle' had long been used to refer to a fight between groups of boys from different streets (Rowley, 1875: 48). In the years 1870–1 the term was adopted by police officers and journalists to describe a spate of gang fighting in the 'low' districts of Angel Meadow and Ancoats situated on the north-eastern edge of Manchester city centre. According to the police, sectarian antagonisms between the 'English' and 'Irish' schoolboys of Angel Meadow had been stirred by newspaper reports of the Franco-Prussian War. Rival armies had been formed in 'the Meadow' with 'English' (Protestant) boys flocking to the 'Prussian' cause and young Catholics – many of them Manchester-born, but most of Irish descent – marching behind a banner on which had been painted the single word 'French' (Davies, 2008: 38–44).

According to the police, 'scuttling' intensified significantly during the 12 months to October 1871. Territorial skirmishes were fought on a nightly basis. Youths aged from their mid- to late teens had been drawn into the conflicts and began to arm themselves with knives and, in some instances, iron swords and firearms. Police made more than 500 arrests in the 12-month period, but failed to quell the violence. Quite the reverse: scuttling spread throughout the factory districts that ringed Manchester city-centre, although the sectarian basis of the conflicts was seemingly eclipsed by neighbourhood-based territorial loyalties, and by the mid-1870s, it was common for 'English' and 'Irish' youths to fight side-by-side in skirmishes between gangs from different districts.

Reports of scuttling – in the form of fights with weapons between territorially based teenage gangs – persisted for three decades before dwindling during the late 1890s. Whilst scuttling – like 'hooliganism' – was sometimes deployed by police officers and journalists as an umbrella term for a wide range of forms of youthful disorder, including rough 'horseplay' as well as fighting, those social commentators in closest contact with young people in Manchester's factory districts were adamant that many male youths actively identified as gang members. As Charles Russell put it, they: 'gloried in the name of "scuttler"' (Russell and Rigby, 1908: 12). Scuttlers distinguished themselves from other youths in working-class neighbourhoods by wearing a uniform of pointed, brass-tipped clogs, 'bells' (bell-bottomed trousers, cut 'like a sailor's' and measuring 14 inches round the knee and 21 inches round the foot) and 'flashy' neckerchiefs, often of silk. They had their hair cut short at the back and sides, but grew long 'scuttler's fringes' which were cut unevenly and left notably longer on the left than on the right. Peaked caps were worn tilted to the left and angled to display the fringe. This style of dress carried both status and risk, as any youth who adopted such identifiable dress codes became an immediate target for scuttlers from rival districts (Davies, 1998: 353).

Local social commentators identified large numbers of scuttling gangs – sometimes described as 'bands' – with regular meeting places that included beerhouses and street corners. They took their names from the districts where their members lived, or the main thoroughfares running through them. Reports of incidents involving well-known gangs such as the Bengal Tigers (from the streets and courts off Bengal Street in Ancoats – a district of Manchester) revealed evidence of continuity in membership as well as a clear sense of common purpose in defending territory and seeking out confrontations with youths from rival districts. Reports on trials of members of the Bengal Tigers at the Manchester City Police Court detailed their long-running feuds with rival gangs in Ancoats and Angel Meadow and highlighted the involvement of prominent individuals, some of whom had been jailed repeatedly for their part in the disturbances (Davies, 2008: 127–39, 159–69, 173–4).

Most of the surviving evidence of scuttling comes from the 'Police Court News' columns of the local press.[6] Newspaper reports on court hearings tended to be highly formulaic, providing the names, ages, addresses and sometimes the occupations of alleged 'offenders', followed by a brief description (usually given by a police officer) of the incidents leading to their arrest, and concluding with the verdicts and details of any sentences imposed by the magistrates. Stern pronouncements from the Bench made good copy, and magisterial rhetoric on the menace of scuttling was a staple feature of 'Police Court News' throughout the period from 1870–1 to the late 1890s. Newspapers published fuller accounts of more serious cases tried at the Quarter Sessions or Assizes.[7] These frequently incorporated statements by a series of witnesses and occasionally recorded prisoners' own responses under cross-examination.

Not surprisingly, witnesses' stories seldom converged and magistrates and judges railed repeatedly against what they took to be orchestrated perjury. Those accused of scuttling tended to depict themselves as the innocent victims of random violence: assaulted without provocation or warning by groups of youths they had never previously met. Police officers and prosecution witnesses told very different stories of premeditated brutality and these versions of events were generally accepted in court. For all their distortions – and silences – these sources frequently contain much useful incidental detail. They record the days, times and locations of encounters between groups of young people from different districts; the appearance of the same youth as victim, defendant and 'chance' passer-by in a series of trials spread over several years; and reveal glimpses of police operational strategies, including the routine patrolling in pairs or even threes of noted 'hotbeds' of scuttling.

The case-study of youth gangs in late Victorian Manchester and Salford presented here is based on a collection of more than 300 reported outbreaks of scuttling between 1870 and 1900. More than 800 young people were prosecuted in these cases; almost all of them were convicted. Where possible, newspaper reports have been cross-checked against surviving legal records. Depositions, or sworn witness statements, survive for a small number of cases tried at the Quarter Sessions or Assizes. More systematic information can be gleaned from the calendars of cases tried at the higher courts: these record previous convictions for indictable offences, which help to profile the criminal 'careers' of a number of prominent scuttlers. A sample of cases from the daily registers of the Salford Police Court for 1889–90 has been entered into a database: this reveals convictions against scuttlers for a wide range of petty offences and suggests that gang members were frequently apprehended for victimless crimes, as well as for crimes of violence (see below).

There are few surviving sources in which scuttlers were invited to speak for themselves, although an interview with a group of scuttlers – four youths from Ancoats – was published in the *Manchester Guardian* in 1898.[8] For accounts of their motives, we are heavily reliant on reports from middle-class commentators – notably two pioneers of the local lads' club movement, Alexander Devine and Charles Russell.[9] Both Devine and Russell (1905: 51–3) deplored scuttling, but they talked at length with gang members and Russell in particular showed considerable respect for their 'spirit'.

The social backgrounds of gang members

Historical evidence reveals clear patterns in gang membership in terms of age, class, occupation, gender and ethnicity. The first reports of scuttling in 1870–1 highlighted the involvement of schoolboys, but as the conflicts escalated the age profile of the participants quickly rose and by the mid-1870s those brought before the courts were overwhelmingly aged between 14 and 20. Seemingly without exception, they belonged to working-class families. They were the children of manual workers and they worked in manual occupations themselves – as labourers, factory operatives, dyers, colliers, carters or street traders.[10] It is rare, however, to find apprentices among those convicted of gang fighting. This is unsurprising given that apprentices had too much to lose. Having 'served their time', they stood to enter the elite ranks of skilled craftsmen, with the prospect of higher rates of pay and more secure employment. Few were willing to jeopardize their future prospects by scuttling.

The most notorious gangs were clustered in the 'slums' of Ancoats in Manchester and Greengate in Salford, or in the lodging-house districts of Angel Meadow and Deansgate – the reputed haunts of 'Criminal Manchester'. These were hotbeds of poverty and disease, renowned for drunkenness and 'vice' as well as for scuttling (Davies, 2008: 126–7 and 154). However, gang conflicts were not confined to the 'slums'. Scuttling also appeared in the heavy manufacturing districts to the north and east of Manchester's city-centre, such as Newton Heath, Gorton and Openshaw, and in the colliery districts of Bradford in Manchester and Pendleton in Salford. All of these districts were firmly identified as 'working-class', but they were generally considered to be 'superior' to Ancoats or Angel Meadow.

More than 90 per cent of those prosecuted following cases of 'scuttling' were male. Gang conflicts constituted arenas in which youths could demonstrate their masculinity (machismo) and 'prove' themselves as men, both individually and collectively. Public displays of aggression and acts of violence in clashes between opposing gangs allowed those on the brink of adulthood to derive considerable kudos and to imagine themselves as 'hard' men (Davies, 1998: 356–7). Young women were rarely prosecuted following outbreaks of scuttling and contemporary commentators frequently described girls as playing auxiliary roles within the gangs: as observers of masculine (macho) prowess; as 'handmaidens' (carrying the male gang members' weapons and/or nursing their wounds); and as witnesses, ever-ready to perjure themselves on behalf of their 'sweethearts' (Davies, 1999: 73). Some commentators feared that girls actively incited conflicts between rival gangs. To the *Manchester Guardian*, this was a 'natural' female role, since: 'Everyone likes to feel herself a Helen of Troy.'[11] In fact, close scrutiny of reports of outbreaks of scuttling reveal that young women sometimes took a more active part in fights between rival gangs as well as the intimidation of witnesses (Davies, 1999: 79–86). In Bradford, on the eastern fringe of Manchester, frequent disturbances during 1877 were attributed to two gangs of scuttlers: 'of both sexes, perhaps 200–300 in all', skirmishing with bricks, stones and sticks.[12] In Salford, the local press was much excited by the discovery of a 'gang of female scuttlers' in the Pendleton district in 1890.[13] On closer inspection, however, they turned out to be members of a long-established gang from Chaney Street (Davies, 2008: 250–2).

There were few traces of sectarianism in reports of scuttling after the early 1870s. The most notorious 'hotbeds' of scuttling such as Angel Meadow and Ancoats in Manchester and Greengate in Salford were all known to be districts of heavy Irish-Catholic settlement. However, none was a 'ghetto' and the population of the most 'Irish' district of all – Angel Meadow – is estimated to have been around 50 per cent Catholic by the late nineteenth century (Fielding, 1993: 27–9). Gangs from these districts reflected the communities from which they were drawn. Catholic youths, of Irish descent, were well represented in their ranks and among their leaders, but fought alongside their 'English', Protestant neighbours. Moreover, many of the fiercest rivalries were between gangs of scuttlers from different 'Irish' districts.

Territorialized patterns of conflict

Bitter feuds were frequently reported between gangs drawn from adjacent districts: Ancoats and Angel Meadow; Gorton and Openshaw in Manchester; Greengate and the Adelphi in Salford. Proximity appeared to breed resentment. In Salford, the Hope Street and Ordsall Lane gangs clashed on a weekly basis over a period of 18 months, culminating in the trial of 17 youths at the Salford Borough Quarter Sessions in June 1890 (Davies, 2008: 213–21). The two gangs drew their members from the districts either side of Regent Road – the main thoroughfare linking South Salford to Manchester city centre. Their regular meeting places were little more than five minutes' walk apart and members of the two gangs were well known to each other.

Gangs from districts throughout Manchester clashed at weekends in the city-centre music halls and the surrounding beerhouses. Reports of the ensuing court cases detail vicious confrontations between leading figures such as John-Joseph Hillier and Thomas Callaghan, who vied for the title of 'King of the Scuttlers' (Davies, 1998: 360–2). More surprisingly, gangs sometimes travelled three or four miles across the city to seek out opponents. Reports of incursions by gangs from Bradford and Openshaw, on the eastern outskirts of Manchester, into the central 'slum' districts of Deansgate and Salford, testify to a high degree of organization as well as a shared sense of common purpose.[14]

Districts such as Ancoats were effectively divided into distinct sub-territories, each of which 'belonged' to a particular gang such as the Bengal Tigers or Alum Street. To cross a major thoroughfare or canal bridge was deemed an act of provocation. Yet intense neighbourhood rivalries were periodically eclipsed by wider antagonisms between scuttlers from different parts of the conurbation. As the *Manchester Guardian* reported in 1898: 'All the scuttlers of Ancoats, for example, are the natural enemies of the scuttlers of Salford, and they might, under pressure, mingle their ranks against the common enemy.'[15]

Contrary to Humphries' (1981: 193) claim that weapons were carried 'largely as symbols of defiance and resistance', scuttlers routinely fought with knives and belts. They wore thick leather belts with heavy brass buckles; the straps were wrapped tightly round the wrist so that the buckles which, on impact could fracture a skull, might be used to strike at opponents (Devine, 1890: 2–3). Stabbings – or 'dosings' – by scuttlers were so frequent as to provoke the ire of hospital staff as well as police and magistrates. Dr Charles Robertson of Ancoats Hospital testified before the city magistrates following a Saturday night 'scuttle' in Jersey Street, Ancoats, in July 1884 in which three youths were stabbed. The doctor told the court:

> the three lads were brought to him about 8.40 p.m., all more or less injured and in a very exhausted condition from loss of blood. One was stabbed through the chest, one through the left shoulder blade, and other through the lower part of the chest, piercing the lung.

He continued:

> [T]his sort of thing was becoming an intolerable nuisance in the neighbourhood, scarcely a week going by without such cases being brought to the hospital.[16]

Similar complaints were voiced by staff at Manchester Royal Infirmary (Bent, 1891: 225).

Although scuttlers routinely fought with weapons, they seldom inflicted fatal injury. The local press attributed just five deaths to scuttling during the period from 1870 to 1900.[17] Doctors' courtroom testimonies pointed to a code of fighting whereby gang members generally sought to scar and maim their opponents: knife and belt wounds were generally to the face or upper body, and the rare cases of fatal stabbing appear to have been met with surprise – and some disapproval – within the scuttling fraternity.[18] Reputations were forged, and honour maintained, by 'dosing' rivals, or putting them to flight.

Policing the gangs

Scuttlers posed real difficulties for the police. Most beat constables patrolled on foot and, even when patrolling in pairs or in threes, intervened in fights between rival gangs at great risk to their own safety. Jerome Caminada, who served in the City of Manchester Police from 1868 to 1899, reflected on the dangers posed by gangs of scuttlers in a volume of memoirs published two years after his retirement:

> From time to time the people of Manchester are startled by some scuttling outrage, and the cry is raised 'Where are the police?' These are about the worst cases with which the police have to deal. Very little credit is given by the public to the man who interferes in such an affray, yet he is frequently injured in so doing, and is sometimes in peril of his life; for the ruffians who mix up in these battles will stand at nothing when their blood is up. Even in quarrels amongst themselves the knife is drawn on the smallest provocation. Many a good tussle have I had with other classes of criminals, but I would

rather face the worst of these than a scuttler; for though the former will use
their hands and feet freely enough, the knife is seldom thought of.

(Caminada, 1901: 404)

Caminada's sentiments were widely echoed among his fellow officers.[19]

Many clashes between rival gangs took place without police intervention. Faced
with dozens or even hundreds of young people, many of them armed, beat
constables frequently watched from the sidelines. Some did intervene, calculating
that the risk of arrest would cause all but the most hardened scuttlers to scatter. Yet
as Caminada (1901: 405) ruefully pointed out, rival gangs frequently joined
together to stone the 'bobby'. The Chief Constables of both Manchester and
Salford responded by stationing additional officers in those thoroughfares
identified as the meeting places of the most prominent gangs.[20] However, they
were powerless to prevent fresh outbreaks of violence. As Superintendent Charles
Godby of the City of Manchester police complained in 1871, scuttles were: 'no
sooner put down in one place than renewed in another'.[21] Twenty years later
Superintendent James Bent made a similar complaint, noting that the police found
it difficult to deal with the gangs effectively, 'not only because it is never known
at what spot in a wide district the scuttlers may suddenly assemble, but also on
account of the formidable opposition with which a body of fifty or so such reckless
men may meet them' (Bent, 1891: 225).

When arrests were made at the scene of a scuttling affray, it was rare for more
than two or three youths to be apprehended. Larger-scale police operations against
the gangs tended to be carried out by detectives, who might spend several weeks
rounding up suspected gang members in the wake of a high-profile case.
Detective-Constable Ernest Dillon of the Salford Borough Police took four weeks
to apprehend 10 of the Hope Street scuttlers following a clash with the Ordsall
Lane gang in April 1890 (Davies, 2008: 217).

The mutual antagonism between the Hope Street scuttlers and the police is
clearly documented in the registers of the Salford Police Court. The gang's
members faced criminal charges following outbreaks of street violence on around
20 occasions during 1889 and 1890.[22] Beat constables tried to break up the gang's
street corner gatherings, and made sporadic arrests for obstructing the footpath,
using profane language and 'disorderly conduct' – a charge applied to a wide range
of forms of behaviour from fighting to horseplay.[23] High-profile scuttling trials
coincided with clusters of cases in which the gang's members were arrested for
minor offences. These included victimless crimes, such as gambling at 'pitch and
toss' and bathing in the Bolton and Bury Canal.[24] Beat constables arrested only a
tiny proportion of those witnessed committing such offences and it appears that
the Hope Street scuttlers were consistently targeted. The scuttlers retaliated with
intermittent assaults upon the police.[25]

Scuttlers before the courts

Scuttlers were jailed in their hundreds. During the 12 months to October 1871, almost 500 boys were brought before the Manchester magistrates following outbreaks of scuttling. The magistrates imposed stringent fines – as high as 40 shillings – in the knowledge that the offenders and their families could not possibly pay them.[26] As a result the City Gaol at Belle Vue was flooded with juveniles: no fewer than 374 boys were admitted in 1871 alone and the following year local councillors expressed concern at the number of 12- and 13-year-olds languishing in prison on account of non-payment of fines.[27]

As scuttling spread across Manchester and the age profile of gang members grew older, the magistrates quickly resorted to mandatory prison sentences. In Salford, scuttlers aged in their mid- to late teens were frequently jailed for 14 days with hard labour by the mid-1870s.[28] The magistrates began to refer the most serious cases of scuttling to the Quarter Sessions. In August 1876, Walter 'Doll' Armstrong, a 16-year-old hawker from Salford, was charged with attempted murder following a fracas in which John Conway – a long-standing adversary – was stabbed. Armstrong was convicted of unlawful wounding and sentenced to five years' penal servitude (the maximum term permitted under English law).[29] The nature and severity of the sentence imposed on Armstrong was intended to serve as a powerful deterrent, and similar sentences were deployed with increasing frequency over the following decade.

During the 1880s, dozens of scuttlers were sent for trial at the higher courts. In December 1884, six Openshaw youths were tried at the Quarter Sessions following an incident in which a 19-year-old Gorton scuttler had been stabbed. Joseph Siderfin and John Gibbons, both aged 18, were found guilty of unlawful wounding and sentenced to five years' penal servitude. Three of their companions, found guilty of inflicting grievous bodily harm, were sentenced to 15 months' imprisonment with hard labour. Special punishment was reserved for the youngest of the six. At 15, Philip McDermott was legally classified as a juvenile: he was sentenced to 12 months' imprisonment, plus 30 strokes with the birch rod.[30] Court reporters noted that the sentences were greeted with considerable anguish in the public gallery, where the friends of the prisoners had gathered. The police posted notices throughout the surrounding districts, warning against the practice of scuttling and detailing the sentences at the Quarter Sessions. This concerted effort by the police and courts was to no avail: within a week, the Openshaw scuttlers raided Gorton once more, seeking retribution against a number of youths who had testified at the Quarter Sessions. Five more young men were jailed for 12 months as a consequence.[31]

From the middle of the decade, gang members began to appear with increasing regularity at the Assizes where they faced sentences of greater severity. In April 1885, two Angel Meadow scuttlers were convicted of the manslaughter of a Salford youth following a Saturday night fracas in Greengate. William Murphy, a 19-year-old blacksmith's striker, was sentenced to 20 years' penal servitude.

Patrick Grant, a labourer aged 20, got 15 years. The judge, Mr Justice Wills, declared that the sentences were a warning to the gangs of idle and disorderly 'ruffians' currently 'infesting' the streets of Manchester: 'the hand of justice would be too strong for them in the end'.[32] Any hope that the sentences imposed on Murphy and Grant would serve as a deterrent was soon dashed, however. Three months later, a group of six scuttlers appeared at the following Assize charged with riot.[33] In May 1887, Owen Callaghan from Angel Meadow received a sentence of 20 years' penal servitude for the manslaughter of Joe Brady of the Bengal Tigers.[34] On this occasion, Mr Justice Wills remarked:

> Scuttling was now pretty well known to all the judges, and they were convinced, as he was, that those who took part in it must, when convicted, be punished with the utmost rigour. Life in parts of Manchester was as unsafe and uncertain as amongst a race of savages.[35]

The judge's pronouncement divided readers of the liberal *Manchester Guardian* – the city's only newspaper of national standing. Letters to the editor appeared from outraged citizens demanding longer prison sentences and the re-introduction of flogging for crimes of violence, but also from social reformers, who blamed scuttling on the appalling living conditions in districts such as Ancoats.[36]

Police officers, magistrates and judges were much aggrieved when scuttlers emerged from lengthy terms of imprisonment only to re-offend within weeks of their release. In a widely publicized case in the spring of 1890, Peter Moffatt – leader of the Ordsall Lane scuttlers – led a raid on a beerhouse frequented by the Hope Street gang on the very day of his release following a nine-month sentence.[37] Moffatt's case was cited when Manchester and Salford's civic leaders appealed to the Home Secretary in December 1890 for magistrates to be granted fresh powers to have scuttlers flogged. The request was turned down by the Home Secretary, who pointed out that parliamentary opinion was 'very averse to punishment by flogging, especially in the case of big boys and men'.[38]

Calls for scuttlers to be flogged were renewed in 1892 following the fatal stabbing of 16-year-old Peter Kennedy in Ancoats. Billy Willan, also aged 16, was convicted of murder and sentenced to hang by Mr Justice Collins. Willan languished in the condemned cell at Strangeways prison for a week before his sentence was commuted to penal servitude for life on account of his youth.[39] Three days after Willan was reprieved, another stabbing took place during a fight between gangs from Ancoats and Angel Meadow. Three Ancoats scuttlers were sentenced to five years' penal servitude for unlawful wounding. Their leader, Alexander Pearson, was far from cowed. When the sentence was pronounced, he shouted: 'Five stretches for nothing. Wait till I come out!'[40]

Scuttling in the local press

Fights between gangs of scuttlers made sensational copy for local journalists. 'Police Court News' was a staple feature of all the local newspapers and youthful gang members made compelling rogues: Thomas Hyman, a painter from Queen Street in Greengate, Salford, for example, was described as 'a Professor of Riot and Disorder'.[41] Elizabeth McGregor, Matilda McStay and Alice McEwen, three 14-year-olds said to be 'connected with the Ordsall Lane gang of scuttlers', were labelled 'GIRL RIPPERS' after they allegedly threatened to 'rip up' one of the gang's former members if he testified at a forthcoming trial.[42]

Editorial commentaries on scuttling greatly exaggerated the dangers posed to the wider population. News reports on clashes between rival gangs confirmed that injuries were generally restricted to the opposing bands of scuttlers. By contrast, editorial columns tended to characterize scuttling in terms of wholly random assaults upon peaceable passers-by. In June 1890, the *Salford Chronicle* reflected on the menace of scuttling following the trial of 17 members of the Hope Street and Ordsall Lane gangs at the Salford Borough Quarter Sessions:

> Everybody in Salford is by now aware what scuttling is. Gangs of youths and young men assemble in the public streets and, for no earthly reason beyond that of wanton mischief, attack any peaceably inclined citizen who happens to be passing. Without even the semblance of compunction, they freely use knives, belts, and sticks to whoever may have the misfortune to pass their way. They create terror among the inhabitants, and frequently their violence is such that even the police, unless in formidable numbers, are afraid to tackle them.[43]

Of course, dwelling on the threat to 'peaceably inclined citizens' made scuttlers much more newsworthy.

Scuttlers enjoyed their notoriety. They revelled in press coverage of their exploits, and adapted both gang names and individual 'street' names to glory in newspaper headlines. A letter to the *Gorton Reporter* in August 1877 describing a huge *mêlée* involving 200–300 scuttlers in which a youth was 'kicked almost to death' was published under the remarkable heading: 'BULGARIAN ATROCITIES OUT AND DONE IN OPENSHAW AND BRADFORD'.[44] Taking their cue from the newspaper, the respective gangs promptly re-named themselves the 'Russians' and the 'Turks'.[45] Individual scuttlers were no less shy of adopting newspaper soubriquets. When John-Joseph Hillier (alias 'Red Elliott') was christened 'King of the Scuttlers' by the *Salford Reporter* in 1894 he revelled in the title. Hillier took to parading the streets of Salford and Deansgate wearing a jersey into which both his street name and the legend 'KING OF SCUTTLERS' had been sewn. Elderly Salfordians still recalled Hillier's fights – and his jersey – 70 years later (Davies, 1998: 362).

The decline of scuttling

Reports of gang conflicts in Manchester and Salford tailed off rapidly during the late 1890s. A cluster of high-profile scuttling cases in 1895 captured the attention of newspapers throughout Britain, yet by 1898–9 only a few isolated incidents made the pages of even the Manchester press and, as the century drew to a close, local commentators were in little doubt that scuttling was dying out. By November 1904, Charles Russell was confident that the scuttler: 'has now almost disappeared from our midst'.[46] Russell (1905: 48 and 51–3) admitted that 'kindred forms of ruffianism' had not disappeared from Manchester's streets altogether, but he was adamant that they were not nearly as prevalent as they had been a few years previously.

Following Pearson (1983: 82–3), historians have tended to assume that reports of increased violence and disorder among young people reflect changes in levels of reporting rather than real changes in patterns of behaviour (Schwarz, 1996: 106). This begs a number of questions relating to the apparent demise of scuttling during the late 1890s. Did the local press finally lose interest after three decades of reporting on scuttlers and their exploits? Did the police find new methods of dealing with the gangs, so that scuttling was finally suppressed? Alternatively, is it possible to identify broader changes in young people's behaviour that might explain why territorial gang conflicts diminished in Manchester and Salford at the very moment that 'hooliganism' was identified as a growing threat to public order in London?

Charles Russell (1905: 53) asserted that in Manchester, scuttling was: 'put down, not without trouble, by vigorous action on the part of the police'. It appears that police tactics changed following the appointment of Robert Peacock as Chief Constable of Manchester in 1898. Peacock was the first head of the Manchester force with experience as a beat constable. Under his leadership, the police launched a campaign to clear young people from the street corners of districts such as Ancoats. Even those gathered in twos or threes were ordered to 'move on' or face arrest for 'obstruction'.[47] By 1903, the *Manchester Guardian* grew concerned that the police were showing too much zeal in sweeping youths off the streets.[48] The *Guardian*'s concern was prompted by a letter from Charles Russell, who complained that beat constables were arresting youths who were merely standing talking to their friends. The boys and young men were brought before the magistrates, costing them a day's work and, in some cases, their jobs.

Local police lore was unequivocal: new recruits to the Manchester force in the 1920s were regaled with tales of how their predecessors had 'subdued' the scuttlers (Davies, 2008: 300). Yet the police – and courts – had adopted stringent measures to deal with the gangs from the early 1870s onwards, with little deterrent effect for three decades. Local commentators identified wider social changes around the turn of the century that help to explain the reported decline of scuttling. Foremost among these was the growth of the Working Lads' Club movement.

The first Manchester clubs were formed in response to the reported escalation of scuttling during the late 1880s. They were founded and initially run by middle-class philanthropists who combined a sense of civic duty with a Christian compassion for the youth of the 'slums'. The clubs held religious services and offered educational classes and craft instruction with the aim of converting 'rough' lads into good Christians and diligent workmen. However, the clubs' main purpose was to put down scuttling. As a long-serving teacher at the Adelphi Ragged School in Salford declared at a ceremony to mark the laying of the foundation stone of the new, purpose-built premises for the Adelphi Lads' Club in 1889: 'I look forward to the time when, as a result of the establishment of lads' clubs, the Gorton scuttler would lie down with the Salford lamb and the Manchester rough would make a pleasing trio of law-abiding citizens.'[49]

Lads' clubs were built in precisely those districts most associated with scuttling. Four separate clubs were established in Ancoats between 1888 and 1890 (Russell and Rigby, 1908: 402 and 406). Three clubs were built in Salford. The clubs provided extensive facilities for recreation, with reading rooms, concerts, lantern-slide shows and opportunities to play sport. In practice, it was the latter that ensured that the clubs quickly took root. Clubs across the Manchester conurbation established football, rugby and cricket teams, and promoted gymnastics, athletics and swimming. They found hundreds of willing takers (Davies, 2008: 293–4).

Lads' clubs did not convert the existing ranks of scuttlers. Indeed, one of the early meetings of the Adelphi Lads' Club in Salford was invaded by a hostile gang of 'roughs' (Hill, 1949: 5). However, the clubs were more successful in recruiting 12- and 13-year-olds. As the clubs grew during the early 1890s they appear to have depleted the numbers of recruits into scuttling gangs. Moreover, the clubs helped to promote the spectacular growth of football as both spectator and participant sport. The proliferation of street-based football teams offered a new outlet for neighbourhood rivalries (Russell, 1905: 61–4). Whilst football increased steadily in popularity during the 1890s and 1900s, a new form of entertainment – the cinema – swept through the 'slums' of Manchester and Salford with astonishing rapidity. Within a decade of its inception in 1896, the cinema had begun to eclipse the music hall in Manchester. By 1914, there were 111 cinemas in the city – most of them located in working-class residential districts. Salford had 17. As cinema-going grew in popularity, convictions for drunkenness and assault declined (Davies, 2008: 305–6). The reported demise of scuttling appears to have owed as much to the growth of the Lads' Club movement and wider changes in the leisure patterns of working-class youths as to the determined efforts of the police and courts.

Conclusion

The periodization that emerges from this case-study of Manchester and Salford, where concern with scuttling diminished during the late 1890s, is distinctly at odds with the emergence of hooliganism in London in 1898. Further research is required to trace the rise – and decline – of concern with youth gangs in late Victorian and Edwardian London, whilst a parallel study of Liverpool with its distinctive, port-based economy and history of sectarian antagonisms would yield a useful further point of comparison.[50] However, despite the gaps in our historical understanding, there are clear resonances between late Victorian and present-day concerns with youth gangs, territoriality and violence. These include: the localities affected – urban, working-class and ethnically diverse; the correlation between gang membership and restricted educational and employment opportunities; the ready resort to weapons in defence of honour or 'respect'; and widespread alienation from the police and criminal justice system among young people in Britain's major cities. Historical research suggests that although patterns of gang formation and violence are by no means constant, these phenomena are much more deeply rooted than current political and media debates acknowledge.

Notes

1 'Gangs are Getting Younger and More Violent, Met Chief Warns', *Guardian*, 20 December 2008.
2 For an example of Victorian reportage, see 'Reign of Terror in South London', *Lloyd's Weekly Newspaper*, 24 July 1898.
3 The most explicit attack on 'gangsta' rap was made by the the then Home Secretary David Blunkett in January 2003: 'Blunkett Condemns Violence in Gangsta Rap Lyrics', *Independent*, 7 January 2003.
4 For further discussion of 'hooligan' as 'one of the keywords of modernity,' see Schwarz, 1996: 106–21.
5 In Birmingham, anxieties surrounding gang formation and street violence peaked in 1875 and again in 1897–8. On both occasions, concern intensified following incidents in which police officers were fatally injured by young 'roughs' (Davies, 2006: 110–12).
6 The term 'Police Court' was widely used to refer to a Magistrates' Court. Reports of 'scuttling' cases have been collected from the *Manchester City News, Manchester Courier, Manchester Evening News, Manchester Guardian, Manchester Weekly Times, Salford Chronicle, Salford County Telephone, Salford Reporter, Salford Weekly News* and *Gorton Reporter*.
7 After 1848 most indictable offences were tried at the Quarter Sessions. Only those offences carrying maximum sentences of life imprisonment, or cases of burglary, were normally referred to the Assizes (Sindall, 1990: 17).
8 *Manchester Guardian*, 5 February 1898.
9 For portraits of Devine and Russell, see Davies, 2008: 14–19 and 292–300.
10 A feud between gangs from Bradford and Openshaw (a district of Manchester) during the spring of 1879 culminated in the appearance of ten scuttlers at the County Police Court at Strangeways. The prisoners were aged between 16 and 21. Three of them worked as colliers and two as foundrymen. The others gave their occupations as dyer, tailor, labourer, hawker and cotton factory operative: *Manchester City News*, 31 May 1879.
11 *Manchester Guardian*, 5 February 1898.
12 *Gorton Reporter*, 25 August 1877.
13 *Salford Chronicle*, 15 March 1890.
14 *Salford Weekly News*, 13 September 1879.
15 *Manchester Guardian,* 5 February 1898.
16 *Manchester Courier*, 8 July 1884.
17 The victims were John O'Toole (1873), William Jackson (1884), Christopher Sheffield (1885), Joe Brady (1887) and Peter Kennedy (1892). These cases are examined in Davies (2008).

18 See the case of Billy Willan, convicted of the murder of Peter Kennedy in 1892 (Davies, 2008: 225–9).
19 Individual officers who tackled gangs of scuttlers were rewarded for their bravery by the Watch Committees of both Manchester and Salford. For one example, see the *Manchester Weekly Times*, 13 July 1894.
20 *Manchester Courier*, 2 October 1876.
21 *Manchester City News*, 28 October 1871.
22 Information derived from the registers of prisoners' offences (hereafter P.O. Registers) at the Salford Police Court, 1889–90. The registers are currently held at Salford Magistrates' Court.
23 P.O. Register, 3 June 1889, no. 45 (Edward Lavin), 28 June 1889, no. 11 (Herbert Howard), 23 Sept. 1889, no. 39 (Robert Alfred Verney).
24 P.O. Register, 6 June 1889, no. 5 and 10 June, no. 41 (Samuel Thornhill).
25 *County Telephone*, 11 January 1890.
26 *Manchester City News*, 28 October 1871.
27 *Manchester Weekly Times*, 19 October 1872.
28 *Salford Weekly News*, 25 September 1875; 11 December 1875; 7 October 1876.
29 *Salford Weekly Chronicle*, 5–26 August 1876.
30 *Salford Weekly News*, 6 December 1884. On the legal provision for the whipping of juveniles, see Radzinowicz and Hood, 1986: 718.
31 *Manchester Evening News*, 12 December 1884; *Manchester City News*, 17 January 1885.
32 *Manchester City News*, 25 April 1885.
33 *Manchester City News*, 25 July 1885.
34 *Manchester Guardian*, 7 May 1887.
35 *Sunday Chronicle*, 8 May 1887.
36 *Manchester Guardian*, 10–25 May 1887.
37 *Salford Reporter*, 26 April 1890.
38 *Manchester Guardian*, 13 December 1890.
39 *Manchester Courier*, 21–24 May 1892; *Manchester Evening News*, 1 June 1892.
40 *Manchester Guardian*, 20 June 1892.
41 *Free Lance*, 27 April 1877.
42 *County Telephone*, 21 June 1890.
43 *Salford Chronicle*, 14 June 1890.
44 *Gorton Reporter*, 25 August 1877. The previous year, reports had reached the British press that Turkish troops were massacring Christians in Bulgaria, then part of the Ottoman (Turkish) Empire.
45 *Manchester Courier*, 11 September 1877.
46 *Manchester Guardian*, 16 November 1904.
47 The Borough Police Act of 1844 forbade the people of Manchester 'standing, loitering, or remaining together with other persons on any footway without reasonable cause'.
48 *Manchester Guardian*, 16 September 1903.
49 *County Telephone*, 16 November 1889.
50 Sindall's (1990: 68–9) fragmentary account of Liverpool's 'High Rip' gangs suggests that they were more concerned with street robbery that territorial supremacy. For a 'true crime' account of the city's gangs, see MacIlwee (2006).

References

Bent, J. (1891) *Criminal Life: Reminiscences of Forty-two Years as a Police Officer.* Manchester: John Heywood.

Caminada, J. (1901) *Twenty-five Years of Detective Life, Volume 2*. Manchester: Jerome Caminada.

Cohen, S. (1987) *Folk Devils and Moral Panics: The Creation of the Mods and Rockers*, 3rd edition. Oxford: Basil Blackwell.

Davies, A. (1998) 'Youth Gangs, Masculinity and Violence in Late Victorian Manchester and Salford', *Journal of Social History*, 32(2): 349–69.

—— (1999) '"These Viragoes are No Less Cruel than the Lads": Young Women, Gangs and Violence in Late Victorian Manchester and Salford', *British Journal of Criminology*, 39(1): 72–89.

—— (2006) 'Youth, Violence and Courtship in Late-Victorian Birmingham: The Case of James Harper and Emily Pimm', *The History of the Family*, 11: 107–20.

—— (2008) *The Gangs of Manchester*. Preston: Milo Books.

Devine, A. (1890) *Scuttlers and Scuttling: Their Prevention and Cure*. Manchester: Manchester Guardian.

Fielding, S. (1993) *Class and Ethnicity: Irish Catholics in England, 1880–1939*. Buckingham: Open University Press.

Hill, H. (1949) *The Story of Adelphi: Sixty Years' History of the Adelphi Lads' Club, 1888–1948*. Manchester: Adelphi Lads' Club.

Humphries, S. (1981) *Hooligans or Rebels?: An Oral History of Working-Class Childhood and Youth, 1889–1939*. Oxford: Basil Blackwell.

MacIlwee, M. (2006) *The Gangs of Liverpool*. Preston: Milo Books.

Pearson, G. (1983) *Hooligan: A History of Respectable Fears*. London: Macmillan.

Radzinowicz, L. and Hood, R. (1986) *A History of English Criminal Law and its Administration from 1750. Volume 5: The Emergence of Penal Policy*. London: Stevens & Son.

Rowley, C. (1875) 'Glossarial Notes on the Slang of Boyhood (1864)', in G. Milner (ed.) *Selections from 'Odds and Ends': A Manuscript Magazine. Volume 1: 1855–1869*. Manchester: St Paul's Literary and Educational Society.

Russell, C. (1905) *Manchester Boys: Sketches of Manchester Lads at Work and Play*. Manchester: Manchester University Press.

Russell, C. and Rigby, L. (1908) *Working Lads' Clubs*. London: Macmillan.

Schwarz, B. (1996) 'Night Battles: Hooligan and Citizen', in M. Nava and A. O'Shea (eds) *Modern Times: Reflections of a Century of English Modernity*. London: Routledge, pp. 101–28.

Sindall, R. (1990) *Street Violence in the Nineteenth Century: Media Panic or Real Danger?* Leicester: Leicester University Press.

Weinberger, B. (1991), 'L'Anatomie de l'Antagonisme Racial et de la Violence Urbaine: les bandes à Birmingham dans les années 1870', *Déviance et Société*, 15(4): 407–18.

Chapter 3

'It's just an area – everybody represents it'

Exploring young people's territorial behaviour in British cities

Keith Kintrea, Jon Bannister and Jon Pickering

'Gangs' and disadvantaged places

This chapter explores the territorial roots of problematic youth groups in British cities and the consequences of territoriality for young people. By territoriality, we mean a situation where a claim is made over an identified geographical space and there is a willingness to defend that space against others. The empirical research upon which the chapter rests primarily concerns youth groups in the 'lower reaches' of the 'gang' activity spectrum (Leap, 2007; Young et al., 2007). Such groups are generally loosely organised and carry out low-level offences. However, the evidence also implies that there is potential for territorial groups of this nature to transmute into more highly organised, criminally sophisticated and violent 'gangs'.

The starting point here is a mission within urban studies research to examine whether, and if so how, living in disadvantaged neighbourhoods can lead to further forms of disadvantage for residents (see Blasius et al., 2007; Ellen and Turner, 1997; Jencks and Mayer, 1990; Leventhal and Brooks-Gunn, 2000; Sampson, 2001; Sampson et al., 2002). Although the evidence, on the whole, supports the proposition that disadvantaged neighbourhoods have a negative influence on individuals' life chances (even if they are less important than family background), questions remain about how exactly social processes within neighbourhoods impact upon residents.

Central to the question of 'neighbourhood effects' is the nature and scope of social relations within disadvantaged areas. A key dimension of this is the extent to which everyday lives are spatially constrained (Atkinson and Kintrea, 2000; Johnston et al., 2000; Loader, 1996; MacDonald and Marsh, 2005). In a globalised era in which it is claimed that social relations are increasingly disembedded from face-to-face contact and locality (Giddens, 1991), place still seems to matter to many people in disadvantaged areas. This can be in part explained by peripheral locations and transport possibilities, and by the attitudes of outsiders towards residents (Bauder, 2001; Goldson, 2003; Hastings and Dean, 2003). However, there is also often a strong, inward-looking place attachment and a surfeit of bonding social capital.

Accounts of 'gangs' have routinely acknowledged the poverty of the neighbourhoods in which they originate and operate, reaching back to the Chicago School studies of the 1920s (Park et al., 1925) and remaining within the most recent British research (Aldridge et al., 2008). Van Gemert and Decker (2008: 25) comment:

> the neighbourhood context has been one of the enduring variables in the study of gangs across the last century and between continents . . . gangs are described as springing from ghettos, whether isolated for ethnic or economic reasons, where marginalisation and lack of social capital dominate spatial relations.

But the importance of neighbourhood context is not limited to the origins of 'gangs' within poor places; there is also the important question about how disadvantaged neighbourhoods might shape 'gangs'. In some of the US literature there is acknowledgement that place attachment is a significant factor in gang formations (Spergal, 1995; Sullivan, 1989) and Jankowski (1991) showed that 'gangs' could be functional in neighbourhood defence. In UK research, the importance of place (and class) for young people's lives has been emphasised (Furlong and Biggart, 1999; Goldson, 2003; MacDonald et al., 2005; Shildrick et al., 2009) within which the significance of place for 'gangs' has not escaped attention. Young et al. (2007), studying 'gangs' across England, identified territorially based allegiances amongst young people in five urban locations, although they also suggest that neighbourhood gang networks spread outwith core neighbourhoods, based on friendship and other links. Most recently, Ralphs et al. (2009) have shown how living in an identified 'gang area' can impact negatively on the lives of young people who are not themselves members of 'gangs'. This chapter aims to provide greater understanding of how 'gangs' originate and the social and economic factors that shape them.

Research methods and data

The results here are from an exploratory qualitative study based in six British cities and undertaken over two phases between 2006 and 2008 (Kintrea et al., 2008). Previous research focusing explicitly on territoriality is limited and in order to address this the research centred upon local projects that had been established specifically to counteract, or to manage, problematic territoriality among young people in Glasgow, Sunderland, Bradford, Bristol, Peterborough and the London Borough of Tower Hamlets. The case study areas – particularly Glasgow and Tower Hamlets – all have significant concentrations of deprivation. Ethnic diversity varies across the locations; Glasgow and Sunderland are relatively homogeneous – mainly white – areas whilst, by contrast, Tower Hamlets has only a relatively small majority white population.

In carrying out the fieldwork we aimed to bring to the surface authentic experiences and understandings, rather than impose any preconceptions. Working with managers or co-ordinators in each of the six projects we identified potential interviewees, including youth and community workers, local police, residents leaders, school head teachers and other adults who had direct contact with young people and active knowledge of their neighbourhoods and, of course, young people who were 'clients' of the 'anti-territorial' projects, and other young people who lived in the neighbourhoods but had no involvement with the projects. In the first phase of the study we undertook face-to-face interviews with up to six adults in each area who had close involvement with the projects. In the second phase we selected four of the six projects – omitting Bristol and Sunderland – and interviewed between two and six further adults, this time including some who had no direct involvement in the projects. We also ran between two and five focus groups with young people aged between 11 and their early 20s. Altogether over 40 interviews and 15 focus groups were completed, each shaped by semi-structured 'topic guides'. The principal aim was to open up a dialogue rather than to impose a predefined agenda, and the overall approach was to allow the interviewees to introduce issues pertaining to territoriality spontaneously rather than for the research team to ask about them specifically.

Some limitations arising from the asymmetry of the case studies emerged. The spatiality of territoriality does not always lend itself to comparison and there was some variation in the age profiles of young people across the different focus groups, even though young people in their mid-teens were interviewed in all cases. Furthermore, some of the young people and, indeed, some of the youth workers who we interviewed had been involved in criminal activity and/or were acquainted with active offenders and as such they were reticent on some topics.

Identifying territoriality

The means by which territoriality shaped the experiences of young people was readily identified in all the case study areas. Transcripts from a Bradford focus group, for example, illustrate how young people are keenly aware of subjective boundaries and how such boundaries serve to inhibit social interaction:

> 'Certain people keep to their own parts of the areas, like the top end . . .'

> 'That's right, at the top, keeps to their own side. We won't, we don't mix with them lot there; we keep to our own side. If you look out that window, that's us right up the top, there . . . up the top end, they won't mix with the bottom end of the estate.' (BDFG1: two white males, one 'mixed race' male, all 16)[1]

The scale and scope of the territories varied across the six principal locations but most were small. In Glasgow, Sunderland and Bradford, a recognisable territory could be as restricted as a 200-metre block or area. In Tower Hamlets, territories were hardly any larger, estimated at under half a mile across. Figure 3.1 shows an 18-year-old black male's depiction of his area in Peterborough. The streets marked with wavy lines are considered to be 'safe'; the cross hatched areas are located outside of his 'territory' and regarded as unsafe.[2]

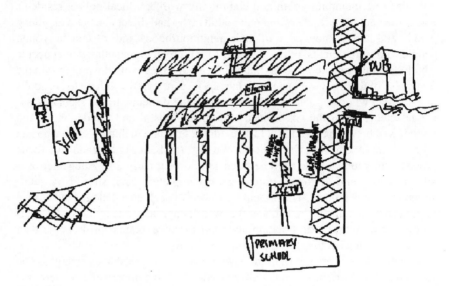

Figure 3.1 Tight boundaries in a Peterborough neighbourhood, black male, age 18 (PBFG3).

In some places tensions *between* areas were heavily overlaid by ethnic residential segregation, which was present to some degree in all the case study locations. But it was also clear that territorial division exists *within* areas of particular ethnic group concentration. For example, in Bristol, there was territorial conflict between two black groups who lived in two areas separated by a motorway, but there was also conflict between different ethnic groups who lived in adjoining parts of the locality. In Sunderland, with just one recognisable area of minority ethnic settlement and one principal minority ethnic group, the pervasive territoriality across the poor white areas of the city was said to be further accentuated. In Bradford, it was reported that white groups from rival estates would combine to oppose Asian groups, and then go back to fight each other, suggesting an ascendancy of ethnicity (racism) over territoriality.

Territorial rivalries were associated in all cases with violence, although its frequency and intensity varied greatly. Generally, violence operated at a 'low level', although conflicts sometimes involved a large number of young people, a range of weapons, and there were occasions when serious injuries and even deaths ensued:

> There's violence, physical contact. Twenty years ago it was a punch up, now it's blunt instruments, rocks, bricks, and knives. (SU4)

In Glasgow, where 'gang fighting' was comparatively widespread and frequent, there was a high awareness of the possible impacts:

You can get stabbed, or hit an artery or something. (white male, 14)

Smashed in the head with a brick, get brain damage. (white male, 15) (GLFG3)

Mostly, conflict occurred on the boundaries of territories – typically defined by roads, railway lines or other physical markers – or where there were incursions into another group's territory. Across all the areas it was clear that violence was primarily motivated by a territorial orientation in which group identity and the attitude towards other groups was shaped by strong neighbourhood sensibility. In each of the sites it was very striking that young people had a keen sense of who they were and where they came from. For example, in Peterborough:

> You live in a certain area, you get to a certain age, you go to a certain youth group, you hang out with certain people, and you are part of that crew. You are their people. (PB2)

Similarly, in Tower Hamlets, young people demonstrated solidarity with each other and a close affinity with their area:

> Researcher (asking about a group just mentioned): 'So [neighbourhood name] Massive? Are you a member?'
>
> 'It ain't a gang that you apply for and that, it's not a gang like that.'
>
> 'It's just an area; everybody represents it.'
>
> 'If you grow up around here, you're a [neighbourhood name] boy.' (THFG2, South Asian males, 16 and 17)

A key motivation for conflict with other groups was the desire to protect the home neighbourhood. An acute sense of place attachment and group solidarity that could quickly lead to revenge activity if one group thought that another had caused offence. Thus:

> It's a lot to do with who your friends are, who you grew up with, where you lived because as you can see it's a very tight-knit community around here, everyone knows everyone ... You know it is safe in that sense. But if someone treads on someone's toes, the whole family knows about it. (PB2)

There was sometimes considerable pride expressed in an area's tough reputation:

> [neighbourhood name] has always been the hardest estate. This is where we're from. I'm not being funny and all but we are hard, and they think, they try and fight, they always see if they can come up and fight us. (BDFG5 white male, 15)

Neighbourhood solidarity, allied with rising sexual awareness, extended protective activities to include local young women, for example:

> And this girl . . . she got with a boy from . . . quite a, like a known area . . . and then she said . . . that he hit her. We said she said that he hit her, and then . . . the whole of [neighbourhood name] . . . there was like 80 to 100 lads were there. All tooled up like they had koshers, nun-chucks, baseball bats with nails came in the centre. Yeah riot vans come down, helicopters everything. And it was all over a girl. (PBFG1: white male, 18)

In all the areas it was apparent that territoriality was deeply ingrained and cross-generationally embedded. Nowhere was it a recent or new phenomenon and it was especially longstanding in the predominantly white estates of Bradford, Sunderland, Glasgow and Peterborough:

> Those areas just don't mix. It's just the way it's been since the year dot. (PB3)

There was a sense that territoriality was inevitable and its impacts inescapable. Older generations expected that young people would behave territorially and have their lives affected by those experiences:

> I think it's historical, it's very historical . . . it's just history and . . . you know, I'm in me 30s now, you didn't expect that thing to still carry on but this new generation now, it's still, it's still there . . . (PB2)

Interviewees often offered the view that territoriality was 'learned' and, importantly, that the stories told by older generations, combined with adults' own limited spatial horizons, were significant in passing it on:

> A 5-year-old doesn't know where they come from, they are told by their parents. (GL1)

> Parental advice leads to hysteria, it causes territoriality . . . parents never leave their territories; it's a rarity. It generates myths. (SU3)

> I can't say where it started from . . . they stigmatise themselves by going into these groups and having their territories . . . it just grows with them, and it stems down from the parents to the youngsters, it's throughout their lives, and the only way they are going to get away from that is . . . they've got to step out of that area, but it's hard for a lot of them . . . (BD5)

The history of settlement patterns in the localities exerted an important influence on such traditions. A common thread involved the resentment of long-established and 'settled' groups towards more recent arrivals who were frequently conceptualised as an inferior and unwanted presence, especially where the 'newcomers' were perceived to 'stick together'. For example, the origins of conflict involving South Asian neighbourhoods in Tower Hamlets was thought to derive from their congregation for protection against attacks by sections of the white population in the 1970s (see also Dench et al., 2006). In Bradford, conflicts arose between different Asian groups on the basis of who was there first.

Territorial groups and 'gangs'

In each of the research sites identifiable groups of young people were engaged in territorial conflict, although the impacts of such conflict spread to other young people who were not actively involved in street groups. Across the piece three categories of group behaviour were identified:

- The first category comprised groups of young people who socialised on the streets or in public areas but without any particular territorial affiliation. These groups were found in all six field work sites.
- The second category – which was also universal – included groups of young people with a strong territorial affiliation. Some of these groups called themselves 'gangs' and were often referred to in interviews and focus groups as 'gangs'. However, they are probably better described as territorial groups.
- The third category comprised more recognisably organised 'gangs' more overtly associated with criminality and the control of neighbourhood-based drugs markets. This mode of organisation was less common and was not found in all the research areas.

A key point, then, is that territorialism and territory-based groups of young people are not necessarily synonymous with organised 'gangs'. In Peterborough, for example:

Young people may call themselves 'the [neighbourhood name] Massive', but it's a group of friends. It is very much, you hit my friend and I will hit your friend. (PB2)

Just hanging out on the street, drinking, talking. That's basically it. (PB6)

They grew up together, they do everything together. They might look like a gang but they are not. They might do certain things that are a bit naughty a bit illegal but they are not an organised gang. (PB7)

In Glasgow, interviewees observed that the distinction between Categories 1 and 2 (above) was that Category 2 'marked' their territory and engaged in other 'anti-social behaviours', with an aggressive, even violent, presence: 'young people will strut; gang members will strut with weapons' (GL1). Similarly, in Tower Hamlets, interviewees identified groups as being involved in minor antisocial behaviour and vandalism – including random fighting with each other – whereas 'gangs' were very much linked to the control of the supply of drugs whereby violence was more purposeful and organised. There was a reported relationship between 'territorial groups' and 'gangs', however: 'Groups always exist in areas where gangs exist' (TH1), which we discuss further below.

Some territorial groups (Category 2 above) were organised and adopted clear identities, but this did not apply everywhere. In Glasgow, Peterborough and Tower Hamlets all groups assumed names, mostly derived from places. In Bradford, postcodes formed the basis of group identity: 'what we have a lot of problems, round here, is postcode wars' (BDFG1: white male, 16). Similarly, in Bristol, postcodes were adopted as primary identifiers, whereas in Sunderland groups did not seem to assume specific names. In areas where names were adopted the spraying, drawing and visual identity of group names on walls, houses and such like was commonplace. In Glasgow and Tower Hamlets, the presence of territorial groups was signalled by 'tags'. In Bristol the first three digits of the postcode relevant to the 'gang's' origin were sprayed in another 'gang's' territory, designed to insult their counterparts and demonstrate boldness.

Adult interviewees reported that it was only a minority (estimated at between 5 per cent and 10 per cent in Glasgow and Bristol) of young people from a given area that took part in problematic territorial behaviour, even if the broader community perceived most young people from the area to be participants. It was suggested that a 'gang' would typically have 'hard-core' and 'peripheral' members. While the core usually could be easily identified, the membership of those on the peripheries was unclear, and the distinction between peripheral and non-members was blurred. Those who regarded themselves as 'non-members' might still participate in some activities. Consequently, it is hard to define the number of young people involved in any given group or 'gang'. In Bristol, one was said to consist of approximately 50 members. In Glasgow, Peterborough and Sunderland adult interviewees noted that groups normally comprise much smaller numbers but, in less common cases, could number as many as 70.

Most participants reported to be involved in territoriality were boys or young men; only in Sunderland was there a sense that as many girls could be associated with territorial groups as boys. Girls were 'invisible' in the areas dominated by South Asian groups. More generally, girls and young women assumed more minor roles; they were less often involved in conflict and they were less constrained by territoriality, and it was believed that the negative impact on their prospects and opportunities was much less marked than for boys. A typical comment about girls' role was:

> The girls play a background role to the gang. They are there, and they are there for their boys but they are not as territorial as the boys are. They are proud of their areas and they are proud of where they come from and they stick by their lads, but they are not as visible . . . for the girls it's part of hanging out with the lads. (PB6)

Elsewhere, however, girls played important roles in encouraging territorial activity. In Glasgow, for example:

> Girls can feed it through wanting to have a boyfriend who is the biggest, baddest guy in the scheme, through wanting to make boys in their area jealous by deliberately cultivating friendships with guys from other areas. There are some negative aspects to girl power and that is one of them. (GL2)

The age of territorially conscious young people varied from place to place and also according to the prevailing degree of criminality. Some younger children were involved, especially in Glasgow; typically those between the ages of 11 and 13 associated as 'wannabe' group members, displaying imitative behaviour and 'junior' group identities and adopting terms such as 'wee', 'baby' or 'young' as prefixes to established group names.

It was typically young people aged between 13 and 17 who were most territory-conscious, most active, most visible and most likely to carry weapons:

> 13 to 16 [-year-olds] perceive territoriality more than older teenagers, because [the older ones] are exposed to wider experiences, if it's only going down to the bloody dole office! (BD2)

Territoriality was also closely associated with transitions to adulthood. Some interviewees explicitly discussed it as a rite of passage or an inevitability of growing up in a given locale. By the age of 18 or 19, activity was reported to decline, as young adults progressed into jobs and/or long-term relationships. In Bradford, for example, group interviewees gave key reasons for 'moving on':

> Because they get a life. They get to go down the pub, and they get more money. (BDFG1: Asian male, 15)

> What's the point in coming in with a bloody face with your kids, man? They're going to think something's up, so they've stopped it, they've settled down. (BDFG1: 'mixed race' male, 16)

However, it appeared that the stronger the affiliation with the group the more difficult it was to desist. Interviewees in Glasgow reported that the only way to 'escape' was to move out of the area or join the army. It was very difficult for young people to turn their back on their entire friendship group. Similarly, in Peterborough, one focus group participant explained:

> You know you said earlier [name] is never gonna grow out of it 'cos he can't, man, think how many people he beat up when he was younger yeah. Now they all wanna get him back, how can he like stop hanging around with boys that are gonna have his back yeah? (PBFG1: white male, 18)

The impacts of territoriality

The strong identification with place and the violence between youth groups that is wrought by territoriality serves to intensify the disadvantages that young people face in their transitions to adulthood (Kintrea et al., 2008; forthcoming). Adult respondents at all of the sites concurred that territoriality places limits on young people's freedom to travel beyond their own neighbourhoods, especially during evenings and weekends. Because territoriality is associated with physical conflict young people are fearful of attack when they move beyond their own areas. The extent of fear varied according to young people's level of involvement with groups and/or 'gangs' and from area to area. However, for boys and young men in particular, living in the areas affected by territoriality – even if they did not associate themselves with a group or 'gang' – leads them to be fearful outside of their own immediate neighbourhoods. Young people from Tower Hamlets, for example, explained:

> Researcher: 'If you go into another area, what happens?'
>
> 'They will stop you and ask you who you are.'
>
> 'They will pick you up, take your phone, and after that take your money, innit?' (THFG2: South Asian males, 16 and 17)

Equally and reciprocally, it was also the case that young people from elsewhere would not go into the case study area:

> And some of the areas are very notorious; you know . . . you wouldn't expect to see youth ever coming into this area. Someone from another area? They would never, ever come. (THFG1: South Asian male, 16)

In areas of mixed ethnicity the impact of territoriality on movement appeared to be exacerbated. In Peterborough, for example, some areas were perceived as 'Asian' and some as 'white', which meant that young people were all the more visible in the 'wrong area'. In Bradford it was said that even driving through some areas could be unsafe:

> If you're in the middle of [name of neighbourhood], if you're a young white lad driving down that road, you're very lucky to get out the other side without a smashed window or getting beaten up. (BD2)

The consequence of this was that fear of moving between and across designated areas made it hard for young people to access services and facilities, even a short distance away, if it necessitated crossing territorial boundaries, thus making it feel like: 'being stuck in a sardine tin and not getting out' (THFG2: South Asian male, 19). There is a clear risk that access to employment and further education opportunities are restricted if fear inhibits travel beyond the immediate home neighbourhood, as an interviewee in Glasgow explained:

> If your horizons are limited to three streets, what is the point of you working really hard at school? What is the point of passing subjects that will allow you to go to college or university if you cannot travel beyond these streets? What's the point of dreaming about being an artist, a doctor, etc., if you cannot get on a bus to get out of the area in which you live? (GL2)

When asked about specific opportunities potentially foregone, young people were often vague; some had remarkably little exposure to areas beyond their immediate neighbourhood. In Tower Hamlets, for example, the 16- and 17-year-old South Asian male participants seemed completely oblivious to the possibilities of life in the wider London. A similar set of constraints operated in majority-white Sunderland:

> There's a lack of knowledge about what's beyond the estates. You're brought up . . . you don't leave, you blend in. It deters young people from spreading themselves around . . . it accentuates inward-looking behaviour. (SU4)

Territoriality and 'gangs'

Although the overall study revealed young people's routine involvement in group formations there was some evidence that territoriality might be an escalator to more organised and more violent forms of crime, principally involving illegal drugs. The tendencies for territorial groups to transmute to criminal 'gangs' over time varied a great deal, however, between the case studies. In Glasgow, with its ubiquitous territoriality and large numbers of group-engaged young people, connections to the world of organised adult criminal networks were considered to be weak or non-existent. Territorial groups based on place-identity had no direct connection to criminal 'firms'. In Bradford, similarly, none of the adult interviewees reported any awareness of territorial criminal 'gangs', rather drug-related 'crime firms' were not specifically area based.

Alternatively, in Peterborough, Tower Hamlets and Bristol 'upward' linkages between young people's territoriality to organised 'gangs' with criminal intent were reported. Perhaps Peterborough was the least serious case. Of the dozens of identifiable neighbourhood-based groups, most were reported to have little, if any, organised criminal networks. In Tower Hamlets, however, young people's involvement in territorial groups was perceived by adult interviewees to lead to an increased risk of involvement in criminal 'gangs'. Moreover, discussions with young people suggested that the area was saturated with drug dealing, so that young people and drug dealers were inescapably in contact on the streets. Young people in the focus groups complained that it was hard to avoid trouble, and drug dealing featured in the 'maps' that they drew of their home areas. In one case, a young South Asian male's 'map' omitted any other feature of his community (Figure 3.2).

Figure 3.2 Sketch of home neighbourhood in Tower Hamlets by South Asian male, age 17 (THFG2).

Adult interviewees in Tower Hamlets believed that, although 'traditional' territoriality was still prevalent, it increasingly included more 'material' forms involving drug dealing and 'scams':

> Illegal substances have a profound effect on how gangs operate and how they're structured. And today it's inextricably linked with territorialism and gang behaviour; they use and supply the drugs, OK? So with that I make the distinction between who we really say are gangs and gangsters, and young people who are out associating themselves with their friends, local youth and stuff like that. (TH1)

In Bristol, much more attention was given by interviewees to territorially based drug 'gangs' than in the other locations. Some of the interviewees were former gang members who had direct experience and contacts with current criminals. A black man in his thirties from the area suggested that divisions between identifiable neighbourhoods were longstanding and apparent in the early 1990s, perhaps rooted in settlement patterns, but it was the coming of drugs that made the difference:

> Those kind [referring to patterns of settlement] divided a lot of things before I was born, you know what I'm saying. Now crack, heroin, and drugs divided

it even more, you know what I mean. So young people's starting selling crack, young people's getting attacked, and young people start joining gangs. (BR3)

Equally, such phenomena invokes periodic violence:

> There is shooting but not really that much. We're getting more knives, more stabbing. There's been a lot of stabbing and some that's been revealed to TV, some that hasn't. Really I've had some experiences, relatives have had some experiences . . . well, that is how it is. (BR2)

In Tower Hamlets and Bristol, but also elsewhere, adults repeatedly emphasised that the life of a 'gangster' was often presented and conceptualised as glamorous and attractive to young people, who found it difficult to imagine ways in which they could make decent money through conventional employment. It was also said to be attractive to young people, from a variety of ethnicities, who were seeking a sense of identity. In Tower Hamlets, for example, it was suggested 'they all want to be gangsters now' (TH2) and, in particular, that youths look to black US rappers as role models.

Overall, the evidence drawn from the study suggests that there is no deterministic connection between youth territoriality, 'gang' formation and organised violent crime. What is clear, though, is that the regular presence of young people within territorially bounded spaces presents adult criminals with readily identifiable potential recruits for their enterprises, especially where such enterprises operate within coterminous spatialised 'markets'. In Tower Hamlets, for example, both adults and the young people themselves sensed a susceptibility to 'turning out bad' as the level of drugs-related activity appeared to be rising. In Bristol, the 'tipping point' had apparently already been reached and problematic territoriality was now said to be less about teenagers involved in conventional territorial turf conflicts and more about men in their 20s involved in the defence of lucrative and established neighbourhood-based drug markets.

Conclusion

The research reported here is exploratory and there is a manifest need for both further investigation in order to yield deeper understanding of the processes that have been outlined above, and more extensive inquiry across other cities and areas. As it stands, however, the research contributes to a developing appreciation that place matters – particularly in poor neighbourhoods – and that people's lives are shaped in important ways by their immediate social relations. Recent research in working-class areas in the UK undertaken by Gore et al. (2007) makes the case for greater recognition of the local sphere, whereas Green and White (2008) and MacDonald and Marsh (2005) reveal that the circumscribed conceptualisations of labour markets held by many young people from poorer neighbourhoods derive directly from inward-looking perspectives. The findings here are consistent with such work and, more generally, elide with the recognition that social class is a key determinant of young people's culture and identity (Goldson, 2003; McCulloch et al., 2006).

In the areas we have considered, an established tradition of territoriality is passed down, in part through immediate siblings and 'olders and youngers', but it is also remarkable how deeply embedded territoriality is. Successive generations have been, and are, involved in similar behaviour, and adults often condone territoriality as an inevitable part of growing up. Territoriality also transgresses simplified notions of inter-racial and ethnic divisions; it exists *within* and *between* groups from similar ethnic backgrounds even if it appears to be accentuated where neighbourhood boundaries coincide with ethnic divisions.

Territoriality might be conceptualised as 'hyper place attachment' wherein it builds upon young people's close identification with their immediate neighbourhoods. Their estates or inner urban areas are the places that they feel they belong to and, in turn, belong to them, and they are ultimately prepared to defend them. Territoriality is part of everyday life and is shaped by young people's routine use of the streets as a place of assembly and recreation. While such strong loyalties to localised place may appear irrational to 'globalised' outsiders – especially as these neighbourhoods might seem to be unattractive or mundane places – there is a sense that territorial identities and friendship networks become a parallel to, or maybe a substitute for, adverse social and familial conditions. But territoriality is also shaped by the (sometimes) oppressive world outside the neighbourhood. Young people themselves have few resources and, in contexts of de-industrialised urban spaces and socially segregated, stigmatised neighbourhoods, their expectations of the labour market are low (and perhaps not irrationally so), and their opportunities appear sparse. In these settings territoriality is, as an interviewee commented: 'having a sense of belonging, that no-one can take away from you' (Kintrea and Suzuki, 2008: 58). Territoriality also has a recursive effect, however, in that it is both shaped by disadvantage and it contributes to it by restricting young people within tight boundaries where opportunities are few.

The findings are also apparently consistent with other recent UK research (Bullock and Tilley, 2002; Pitts, 2007; Aldridge and Medina, 2008) that some of the most violent 'gangs' have neighbourhood origins, even if they do not remain fully territorial. Our study suggests that territoriality can be a ramp to involvement in more violent and criminal 'gangs' and that territorial behaviour in some neighbourhoods can become more virulent and violent over time.

This study has been conducted at a time when there is a high level of concern about youth 'gangs' across the UK and a range of policy measures are emerging, ranging from strengthening law enforcement and the powers of the courts (Home Office, 2008a), promoting partnership between enforcement and preventative agencies (Home Office, 2008b) through an array of social inclusion and development measures aimed at children and young people (Department for Children, Schools and Families, 2007; 2008). While enforcement measures might be expected where public safety is believed to be at risk and programmes to support more vulnerable young people can be welcomed, the embeddedness of territorial 'gang' conflict as expressions of longstanding 'cultural' neighbourhood social relations suggests that a different, more place-aware approach is required. A core aspect of policy in relation to 'sustainable communities' (Bailey et al., 2006) is to sponsor new forms of neighbourhood social dynamics in 'mixed income' communities through housing regeneration strategies. 'Social mix' policies in land use, planning, regeneration and housing have struggled, however, against long-term trends towards the consolidated segregation of disadvantage and the use of social housing as a repository for the poor (Hills, 2007; Kintrea, 2008; Lupton et al., 2009). It is difficult to be particularly optimistic about the task of sponsoring new roles and new sets of social relations in disadvantaged places, particularly at a time of recession and a deepening retrenchment in public expenditure.

Acknowledgements

We are grateful to the Joseph Rowntree Foundation for funding the study on which this chapter is based, and to Naofumi Suzuki and Maggie Reid who contributed to the fieldwork.

Notes

1   Quotations are identified by location: GL Glasgow; SU Sunderland; BD Bradford; PB Peterborough; BR Bristol; TH Tower Hamlets. FG indicates Focus Group.
2   The shading of the 'safe' and 'unsafe' areas in Figure 3.1 has been altered by the authors in order to make it legible in black and white production.

References

Aldridge, J. and Medina, J. (2008) 'Youth Gangs in an English City: Social Exclusion, Drugs and Violence', *Research Report ESRC RES-000 23–0615*. Manchester: University of Manchester.

Aldridge, J., Medina, J. and Ralphs, R. (2008) 'The Dangers of Doing Gang Research in the UK', in F. van Gemert, D. Peterson and I-L. Lien (eds) *Street Gangs, Migration and Ethnicity*. Cullompton: Willan.

Atkinson, R. and Kintrea, K. (2000) 'Owner-occupation, Social Mix and Neighbourhood Impacts', *Policy and Politics* 28(1): 93–108.

Bailey, N., Haworth, A., Manzi, T., Paranagamage, P. and Roberts, M. (2006). *Creating and Sustaining Mixed-Income Communities: A Good Practice Guide*. Coventry: Chartered Institute of Housing.

Bauder, H. (2001) 'Culture in the Labour Market: Segmentation Theory and Perspectives on Place', *Progress in Human Geography* 25(1): 37–52.

Blasius, J., Friedrichs, J. and Galster, G. (2007) 'Introduction: Frontiers of Quantifying Neighbourhood Effects', *Housing Studies* 22(5): 627–36.

Bullock, K. and Tilley, N. (2002) *Shooting, Gangs and Violent Incidents in Manchester: Developing a Crime Reduction Strategy*. London: Home Office.

Dench, G., Gavron, K. and Young, M. (2006) *The New East End*. London: Profile Books.

Department for Children, Schools and Families (2007) *The Children's Plan: Building a Brighter Future* (Cm 7280). London: DCSF.

—— (2008) *Youth Taskforce Action Plan*. London: DCSF.

Ellen, I. and Turner, M. (1997) 'Does Neighbourhood Matter? Assessing Recent Research Evidence', *Housing Policy Debate* 8(4): 833–66.

Furlong, A. and Biggart, A. (1999) 'Framing "Choices": A Longitudinal Study of Occupational Aspirations Among 13- to 16-Year-Olds', *Journal of Education and Work*, 12: 21–35.

van Gemert, F. and Decker, S. (2008) 'Migrant Groups and Gang Activity: A Contrast Between Europe and the USA', in F. van Gemert, D. Peterson and I-L. Lien (eds) *Street Gangs, Migration and Ethnicity*. Cullompton: Willan.

Giddens, A. (1991) *The Consequences of Modernity*. Cambridge: Polity Press.

Goldson, B. (2003) 'Youth Perspectives', in R. Munck (ed.) *Reinventing the City? Liverpool in Comparative Perspective*. Liverpool: Liverpool University Press.

Gore, T., Fothergill, S., Hollywood, E., Lindsay, C., Morgan, K., Powell, R. and Upton, S. (2007) *Coalfields and Neighbouring Cities: Economic Regeneration, Labour Markets and Governance*. York: Joseph Rowntree Foundation.

Green, A. and White, R. (2008) 'Shaped by Place: Young People's Decisions about Education, Training and Work', *Benefits* 16(3): 213–24.

Hastings, A. and Dean, J. (2003) 'Challenging Images: Tackling Stigma Through Estate Regeneration', *Policy and Politics* 31(2): 171–84.

Hills, J. (2007). *Ends and Means: The Future of Social Housing in England*, Centre for the Analysis of Social Exclusion (CASE) report 34. London: London School of Economics.

Home Office (2008a) *Tackling Gangs: A Practical Guide for Local Authorities, CDRPs and Other Local Partners*. London: Home Office.

—— (2008b) *Saving Lives, Reducing Harm: Protecting the Public: An Action Plan for Tackling Violence, 2008–2011*. London: Home Office.

Jankowski, M. (1991) *Islands in the Street: Gangs and American Urban Society*. Berkeley: University of California Press.

Jencks, C. and Mayer, S. (1990) 'The Social Consequences of Growing up in Poor Neighbourhood', in L. Lynn and M. McGeary (eds) *Inner City Poverty in the United States*. Washington DC: National Academic Press.

Johnston, L., MacDonald, R., Mason, P. Ridley, L. and Webster, C. (2000) *Snakes and Ladders: Young People, Transitions and Social Exclusion*. Bristol: Policy Press.

Kintrea, K. (2008) 'Social Housing and Spatial Segregation', in S. Fitzpatrick and M. Stephens (eds) *The Future of Social Housing*. London: Shelter.

Kintrea, K. and Suzuki, N. (2008) 'Too Much Cohesion? Young People's Territoriality in Glasgow and Edinburgh', in J. Flint and D. Robinson (eds.) *Community Cohesion in Crisis? New Dimensions of Diversity and Difference*. Bristol: Policy Press.

Kintrea, K., Bannister, J., Pickering, J., Reid, M. and Suzuki, N. (2008) *Young People and Territoriality in British Cities*. York: Joseph Rowntree Foundation.

Kintrea, K., Bannister, J. and Pickering, J. (2010) 'Territoriality and Disadvantage Among Young People: An Exploratory Study of Six British Neighbourhoods', *Journal of Housing and the Built Environment*.

Leap (2007) *Gangs Activity Spectrum*. London: Leap Confronting Conflict.

Leventhal, T. and Brooks-Gunn, J. (2000) 'The Neighborhoods They Live In: The Effects of Neighborhood Residence on Child and Adolescent Outcomes', *Psychological Bulletin* 126(2): 309–37.

Loader, I. (1996) *Youth, Policing and Democracy*. Basingstoke: Macmillan.

Lupton, R., Tunstall, R., Sigle-Rushton, W., Sabates, R., Meschi, E., Kneale, D. and Salter, E. (2009) *Growing Up in Social Housing: A Profile of Four Generations, 1946 to the Present Day*. London: Tenant Services Authority.

McCulloch, K., Stewart, A. and Lovegreen, N. (2006) '"We Just Hang Out Together": Youth Cultures and Social Class', *Journal of Youth Studies* 9(5): 539–56.

MacDonald, R. and Marsh, J. (2005) *Disconnected Youth? Growing Up in Britain's Poor Neighbourhoods*. Basingstoke: Palgrave Macmillan.

MacDonald, R., Shildrick, T., Webster, C. and Simpson, D. (2005) 'Growing Up in Poor Neighbourhoods: The Significance of Class and Place in the Extended Transitions of "Socially Excluded" Adults', *Sociology* 39(5): 873–91.

Park, R., Burgess, E. and Mackenzie, R. (1925) *The City: Suggestions for the Study of Human Nature in the Urban Environment*. Chicago: University of Chicago Press.

Pitts, J. (2007) *Reluctant Gangsters: Youth Gangs in Waltham Forest*. London: London Borough of Waltham Forest.

Ralphs, R., Medina, J. and Aldridge, J. (2009) 'Who Needs Enemies with Friends Like These? The Importance of Place for Young People Living in Known Gang Areas', *Journal of Youth Studies*, 12(5): 483–500.

Sampson, R. (2001) 'How Do Communities Undergird or Undermine Human Development? Relevant Contexts and Social Mechanisms', in A. Booth and A. Crouter (eds) *Does it Take a Village? Community Effects on Children, Adolescents and Families*. Mahwah, NJ: Lawrence Erlbaum.

Sampson, R., Morenoff, J. and Gannon-Rowley, T. (2002) 'Assessing "Neighborhood Effects": Social Processes and New Directions in Research', *American Review of Sociology* 28: 443–78.

Shildrick, T., Blackman, S. and MacDonald, R. (2009) 'Young People, Class and Place, *Journal of Youth Studies* 12(8): 457–65.

Spergal, L. (1995) *The Youth Gang Problem: A Community Approach*. Oxford: Oxford University Press.

Sullivan, M. (1989) *Getting Paid: Youth, Crime and Work in the Inner City*. Ithaca, NY: Cornell University Press.

Young, T., Fitzgerald, M., Hallsworth, S. and Joseph, I. (2007) *Groups, Gangs and Weapons*, London: Youth Justice Board.

Chapter 4

Collateral damage
Territory and policing in an English gang city

Judith Aldridge, Robert Ralphs and Juanjo Medina

Introduction

This chapter explores the relevance of 'territory' – variously understood – with regard to youth gangs, using data arising from an ethnographic study of youth gangs in an English city. Gangs are usually assumed or argued to be territorial entities in the popular imagination, by police authorities and even by academic researchers (e.g. Ley and Cybriwsky, 1974; Pitts, 2008). A consistent finding of research in the UK, and elsewhere, is that youth gangs appear to be grounded in territory (particularly place of gang members' residence) (e.g. Marshall et al., 2005). For some, territoriality is a defining characteristic of gangs. Klein (1997: 517), for example, distinguishes between highly territorial 'traditional' gangs and 'specialist' gangs that 'define territory by their criminal market'. The linkage between gangs and territories also has important policy implications. In the USA it has led, for instance, to targeted policing strategies based on mapping gangs and their 'turf' as a means of providing crime reduction (e.g. Kennedy et al., 1997). In the UK, following the American lead, the salience of territory is critical for understanding the application of gang injunctions used to limit the association of gang members in public spaces. Understanding how territory functions in youth gangs, therefore, is important in assessing both the appropriateness – and the theoretical groundedness – of such policy interventions.

We begin with the question of whether or not youth gangs in 'Research City'[1] map onto neighbourhood of residence. Gangs in the 'Inner West' part of the city developed directly from specific neighbourhood areas, and two of the gangs with the greatest notoriety and longevity (approximately 30 years) were named in connection with particular geographical localities. Notwithstanding this, over the ensuing decades what we term 'residential outsiders' have become more visible in these gangs. Residential outsiders arise for a range of reasons that we identify and discuss below, and they have important implications for how gangs are policed.

'Territory' has multiple and overlapping referents and its markers include: identifiable neighbourhoods marked by physical boundaries; particular streets or areas 'adopted' by a gang (see Tita et al., 2005); public or private venues such as gyms, youth centres, pubs; illegal (normally drugs) 'markets'; and the domiciliary positioning of people (especially family members and sexual partners, usually girls and women). In our research, gang members' accounts of their 'turf' were highly individualised, differing in the level of risk they perceived within particular areas and, thus, their spatialised patterns of movement. Young people in Inner West gangs, for example, sometimes reported 'hanging around' in public places, but only rarely did we directly observe this. Visible street presence was not the norm amongst the Inner West gangs of Research City – at least not to the extent that it appears to be amongst gangs in the USA – and we will consider possible reasons for this difference. We will also assess the implications of this finding for dominant conceptualisations of gangs that emphasise 'street orientation' as a defining criterion.

Moreover, as we have discussed elsewhere (Ralphs et al., 2009), 'space' and 'place' are significant for how non-gang-affiliated young people living in 'gang' neighbourhoods inhabit or avoid particular territory, both close to home and further afield. Here we investigate the means by which gang members and their families navigate space, and the risks they face both in 'home space' and in 'non-gang territory' – particularly the city centre. Although there are many similarities in the experiences of non-gang-affiliated young people and gang members in this regard – both experience restricted movements – paradoxically, gang members, and indeed their families (Aldridge et al., 2009), more often described actual victimisation, sometimes involving serious levels of violence and injury.

Police perceptions of young people's use of space and place are critical to the means by which they identify and police gang members. During the late 1980s and early 1990s in Research City, this was a fairly straightforward matter comprising observations of substantial numbers of gang-involved young people making sales within gang-dominated open drugs markets. However, the shift over the last two decades from open drugs markets (situated within clearly defined public places) to closed markets (where transactions are carried out in a range of often non-public locations) has created something of an 'intelligence vacuum' for the police in Research City. Furthermore, the fact that the police rely substantially on young people's use of space in relation to how they characterise, define and police gangs in the city – and determine their 'membership' – has serious implications, particularly in light of new legislation on 'gang injunctions'.

Research methods, sites and conceptual definitions

We conducted our study in a large English city where authorities had recognised the existence of a violent 'gang problem' and implemented explicit gang suppression and prevention measures. As stated – and explained in greater detail elsewhere (Aldridge et al., 2008) – we do not reveal the identity of the city in order to protect the identity of individuals we engaged with throughout the research, but also to avoid further stigmatisation of certain areas within the city. Other researchers have adopted a similar approach (e.g. May et al., 2005) and, apart from ethical and political considerations, it also served to facilitate access, win confidence and secure trust, even if it places certain limitations on the contextualisation of results.

Data were collected over 26 months between 2005 and 2008 by way of direct observation, individual interviews and focus groups (Aldridge et al., 2010). Additionally, administrative data was collected and collated in order to assist the contextualisation of our primary findings. The project employed five different field researchers, assisted at times by 'native' interviewers. Throughout, we worked closely with members of the community and individuals associated with gangs in Research City, and we studied and incorporated their critical feedback into our own interpretations. Observations involved: engagement in community activities and events; volunteering in youth centres and community groups concerned with gang violence; participation in police–community consultative groups; and meeting informally with gang members and associates, ex-gang members and others in the community (including friends and relatives of gang members). Field notes were kept deriving from such observation and engagement. We also conducted 130 formal interviews: 41 with 'gang members'[2] (ranging from individuals in their teens to others in their thirties); 62 with people who had a close connection to gang members (such as family members, friends and partners) and 27 with 'key informants'. Finally, these data were complemented by nine focus groups: three with non-gang youth; three with parents and three with agency and community representatives. We worked in six discrete areas of Research City and established access to six gangs that differed in terms of their longevity, ethnic composition, public profile and (to some degree) nature of criminal activity.

Each of the six areas comprised disadvantaged communities afflicted by structural youth unemployment and related indices of social disadvantage. As Hobbs (2001) has indicated, informal and distinctly localised social systems underpinned by criminality have been an entrenched feature of urban Britain for many decades. The areas we studied were no exception and each evidenced actors actively operating within the criminal economy. The six areas were essentially enveloped within two broader urban zones, which, for simplification, we refer to as *Inner West* (a corridor of historically marginalised neighbourhoods with a substantial black and minority ethnic population and an officially recognised gang and gun problem), and *Far West* (a large, predominantly white, council estate with a self-identified gang problem that was *not* officially recognised by local state authorities). The data underpinning this chapter are drawn from Inner West alone, for it is in relation to Inner West that issues around territory and territorialism are particularly pertinent, given the notorious status of the gangs there: highly criminal, gun-carrying, territorial and warring. Data arise primarily from two gangs in the *Belmont* neighbourhood: *Upperside* and *Lowerside* named after two residential streets in Belmont and, to a lesser extent, two other Inner West neighbourhoods: *Shanklytown* and *Windham*.[3]

There is considerable academic debate and disagreement regarding the definition(s) of gangs. Such definitional disputes have exercised researchers from the seminal work of Thrasher (1927) and they explain, at least to some degree, contrasting research findings. We used the 'Eurogang' definition in order to construct our sample. According to this international group of researchers, a gang is a durable street-oriented youth group whose identity includes involvement in illegal activity (Klein et al., 2006; Weerman et al., 2009). Hallsworth and Young (2008) have used a partially modified version of this definition in the UK in order to differentiate 'gangs' from less criminally involved peer 'street groups'. We believe that the 'Eurogang' definition provides a sensible starting point given both its international salience and its conceptual latitude, allowing us to engage with the diversity of groups that we found in Research City. However, as we argue later, we take issue with the 'street oriented' requisite of the 'Eurogang' definition.

Complexity and contestation: territory, 'turf' and policing

Although gang members (and gang discourses) often emphasise the significance of *territory* and '*turf*', we learned through our research that their conceptual-isations were much more complex than popular 'boys in the hood' representations imply. This raises core questions pertaining to the legitimacy of conventional modes of policing gangs.

Gang affiliation and neighbourhood: the evolution of 'residential outsiders'

Gangs in Research City evolved from neighbourhood areas. The two main Inner West gangs ('Upperside' and 'Lowerside') are named after areas within the neighbourhood of Belmont, divided by the bisecting Kendall Park Road. There was a common perception, amongst both gang members and the police, that it was the police themselves who first coined the gang names, although they were subsequently adopted to embody strong area-based identities. In other words, the 'labels'[4] were initially applied by the police, and then adopted by the gangs themselves before being recognised more widely within the communities and, ultimately, local and national media.

Over time, however, Inner West gangs evolved in such a way that terri-torial boundaries became more fluid and it was no longer necessary for gang members to be resident in neighbourhoods corresponding to their names. Husky, a 25-year-old Inner West gang member from Windham explains:

> Back in the day it used to be if you were Upperside you had to live on Upperside, if you were Lowerside you had to live on Lowerside, no ins or outs about it. It's not like that no more, they're just shipping in people from anywhere and everywhere. So you've got a guy from Shanklytown, chilling in Belmont, chilling with Lowerside. And then his mates might think, 'Well, they're chilling now with the Lowerside, and one of them Lowerside boys

> beat my sister's boyfriend up years ago, and give me a slap at the same time so fuck you, I'm gonna chill with Upperside.'

In the US context, it has long been recognised that gang members' territory and neighbourhood of residence are not necessarily directly coterminous (Moore et al., 1983). Similar divergence was evident in Research City, as explained by an Upperside gang member:

> Most gangs are people that live directly near each other, say five/ten guys are definitely from that estate. But as you get more established now you get people from all over that want to be with their cousin, friends, whatever, you know: meeting in jail, however you meet. Hanging around, going out for a few beers, you get part of the gang. I know people from Belmont gangs, probably ten/fifteen people that's not from Belmont, they haven't got addresses from Belmont.

So, whilst close neighbourhood affiliations may underpin the original names of gangs, over time membership often evolves to include what we term 'residential outsiders'. Members of Inner West gangs commonly had addresses outside of the immediate gang neighbourhood. Indeed, some had addresses in areas deemed to be 'rival' gang neighbourhoods. Residential outsiders arose as a result of three primary processes: first, re-housing; second, residing outside of the gang neighbourhood but having family members (usually fathers) residing within it and, third, transition between schools.[5]

Residential outsiders can result from gang members being voluntarily or involuntarily re-housed. Indeed, re-housing is a recommended gang 'exit strategy' advocated by the Home Office (2008) and it featured explicitly as part of the multi-agency gang strategy in Research City. In some cases we found that re-housing could produce positive outcomes in terms of gang exit. However, in many other cases, re-housing gang-involved young people and their families had little impact. We noted numerous examples of Inner West gang members being re-housed into neighbouring communities – sometimes a few miles away, sometimes further afield – but retaining their gang activity as residential outsiders. Alongside this, numerous gang members that we encountered in Inner West voluntarily moved from Belmont – where they considered attention from the police to be too great a hassle – to neighbouring areas. Crash, a 37-year-old Upperside gang member, refers to some in his gang moving out of Belmont to neighbouring areas: 'I think they moved, because obviously, the area's hot.' 'Heat' could refer to unwanted attention as a result of conflict with others in or outside of the gang, or arise from intensive surveillance from the police. The formation of a dedicated firearm/gang unit with a remit for high-profile policing – including regularly stopping suspected gang members and gathering intelligence on their movements – reinforced the view amongst some gang members that identifiable streets, parks and/or other venues associated with these Inner West gangs, are 'too hot' to spend time in.

The most common explanation for the existence of residential outsiders derived from the influence of family connections within the gang neighbourhood. This typically resulted where gang members were raised outside of Belmont by single-parent mothers, whilst their fathers resided in Belmont. Spending time with fathers – some of whom were gang-involved themselves – facilitated gang involvement. Deb (a 33-year-old former member of a girl gang), and her three brothers (all Upperside gang members), moved from Belmont to neighbouring Cortland when she and her siblings were still in primary school:

> We moved to Cortland. But my dad's been in Belmont from the start, and everyone around that area knows us, because we had a good relationship with everyone . . . So the connections that we had through [primary] school, we still kept, the boys included, in Belmont.

The third process giving rise to residential outsiders involved moving from one school to another. This was particularly common in the transition at the age of 11 from smaller local primary schools to larger secondary schools sometimes located outside of the neighbourhood of residence. Jon, Toby and Billy, three brothers ranging in age from 24 to 32 years, resided during their childhood in Cortland, a few miles out of Belmont, but after leaving their Cortland primary school, they travelled to the nearby Belmont secondary school (known for having a high proportion of gang members on its roll) and, as a consequence, became involved in the Upperside gang. In Research City, the likelihood that educational transition at the age of 11 would involve children and young people travelling to schools outside of their immediate neighbourhood was accentuated by the trend towards the provision of larger schools (in common with other cities and towns in the UK).

Gang 'turf', movement and street presence

The popular association of drug dealing with gangs often underpins the belief that gangs have clearly defined 'turf' on which they conduct and control their drug trade. Similarly, inner city violent crime – especially gun crime – is frequently associated with turf wars thought to erupt between gangs as they vie for control of area-based drugs markets. Such images were no doubt bolstered in the popular imagination when Conservative Shadow Home Secretary, Chris Grayling, commented in an August 2009 speech (Watt and Oliver, 2009), that some of Britain's inner cities were beginning to resemble Baltimore, USA. Baltimore had, of course, been portrayed in a popular television series – *The Wire* – in such a way as to suggest that open drugs markets routinely operate on street corners where violence is rife. Whether this specific representation of Baltimore is accurate or not, there is evidence to suggest that such drugs trading does feature within US cities (see for example Taniguchi et al., in press); within what has been termed gang 'set space' (Tita et al., 2005: 280): 'the actual area within the neighbourhood where gang members come together as a gang'. But is this being replicated in

Research City and other areas of the UK? Do Inner West gangs have 'set space'? Is such space recognised as gang space by others? Is it conceptualised as 'turf' over which gangs vie for control?

There was general awareness – amongst the police, gang members, non-gang young people, and adult residents of Inner West – that the residential areas on each side of Kendall Park Road were associated with the Upperside and Lowerside gangs respectively. Beyond this, locations such as particular streets, parks, youth and community centres, shops and especially fast food takeaways, were *sometimes* identified as 'belonging' to one gang or another. There was, however, dissensus as to what specific territorial areas 'belonged' to any one gang.

Indeed, gang members' accounts of territorial spaces were highly individualised; some felt their movements were curtailed and restricted in particular places whilst others did not. Furthermore, territory could be perceived as shifting and changing, depending upon who inhabits it at any one time. This is exemplified for some gang members in their attempts to venture into the city centre – the non-gang-affiliated 'down town' shopping and nightlife centre of Research City. Carl, a 23-year-old Inner West gang member, describes how:

> Some people can't go to town now to a club on their own with a girlfriend because the gang activity they're getting into so much, as I say, they can't afford to get seen on their own, doing their own thing.

Similarly, Darryl, a 25-year-old member of Lowerside explains that the presence of an adversary at certain pubs, clubs or city centre venues may restrict the movement of individuals, but not always of groups:

> Depends though who you go in there with. Why can't you go there? It depends on who's going. Maybe [someone just] can't go there on his own. [. . .] Where we used to go [. . .] we used to roll down there 30-handed and that. [. . .] You'd have to sometimes.

He continues to explain that venturing into non-affiliated territory like this could be extremely dangerous:

> We came out of the club and all that, and I had like pure mantrap. [. . .] I come out and like 20 of them lined up. And I was with five people. [. . .] I had me feet on [laughs] – you know, on the side of the pavement and all that, lipped up to fuck, trying to get me in the boot [of a car].

We also found members of the same family residing in the same home but belonging to different gangs, and others who professed allegiance to more than one gang, demonstrating that turf cannot be exclusively determinant of the movements gang members make within, or across, territory. The extent to which individuals were fearful of 'straying' or 'transgressing' was often linked more to previous conflict with particular individuals (sometimes even members of their own gang), than to rival gang status *per se*. In such cases, they were fearful in home territory, 'rival' territory and further afield (such as the city centre). Such observations contradict simple and straightforward coterminous mapping of territory – of delineated geographical space – to gangs.

As Tita and colleagues (2005: 273) have argued, 'gang set spaces' are places where gang members collect to 'hang out'. Younger gang members in Inner West sometimes referred to hanging out in parks, local youth centres and on streets (especially outside their houses). Older gang members sometimes referred to a particular bar or gym as being associated with their gang. However, manifest street presence was not the norm amongst the Inner West gangs of Research City and it was certainly not as prevalent as it appears to be amongst gangs in the USA. More often, gang members spent their time inside one another's houses and flats.

It is important to distinguish between 'hanging out' in public places and exerting control over such places. Our research indicates that Inner West gangs did not generally have, or attempt to impose, control over public places and social institutions in ways articulated by gang researchers in cities such as Chicago (Venkatesh, 2008) or Rio de Janeiro (Arias, 2006; Venkatesh, 2008). We found no evidence to imply that spatial boundaries were deliberately enforced to mark turf and, throughout the 26-month period of fieldwork, there was nothing to suggest that any fatal shooting incident occurring in Inner West was related to territorial disputes. Indeed, a key finding in our research was that violent conflict rarely derived from disputes over territorial drugs markets and/or protection rackets.

There is some evidence that turf wars may have been a characteristic of Inner West gangs in the Belmont area 20 years ago, when such formations comprised 'quasi-specialist' drug-dealing gangs (see Medina et al., 2010). Even then, however, those who operated successfully in such markets questioned this, as illustrated by 36-year-old ex-Upperside member Vader:

> That's never been the case. You know, when they say gangs fighting over drug territory and all that. How [one] gang made their money doesn't really – never really – had an effect on how [another] gang made their money. I've not seen that in my time.

Similarly, the following exchange with Levi about his experience in the Belmont open drugs markets of the late 1980s and early 1990s illustrates the blurred and fluid nature of territoriality and territorial conventions:

> We had like our own area, and they had their little area, and it was like a silent agreement, and once you go over there, you know . . . [Interviewer: But you knew clearly what your area was?] Yeh, yeh, you just know what boundaries not to step over and if you do, you know you might get in a bit of trouble. [Interviewer: Is that just to do with dealing drugs? Or is that to do with actually walking into an area [. . .], so basically, you can't just even go into

> an area?] You can go there but you would have to be more aware of what's going on when you go there. You have to be more on your toes when you do go in certain places. You know, it's like you can go and sell drugs anywhere you want really. But [you take a certain amount of risk] standing up and selling drugs in certain places.

In the USA, Block and Block (1993) have shown that the majority of gang-related incidents recorded by the police[6] were 'turf' related; that is, conflict over geographical space identified as belonging to one gang or another. In Research City, the evidence we have gathered suggests that the majority of conflict experienced between Inner West gangs was not over turf. Although inter-gang violence could result in tit-for-tat retaliatory action we found intra-gang conflict to be as, or more, important on a day-to-day basis. Jealousies and rivalries over illegal acquisitive opportunities tended to occur *within* rather than *between* gangs as one member explains:

> All of a sudden you start to sell drugs, obviously, and it starts to be like jealousy. We were clashing with each other so before you knew it everybody had like beef with each other. They started to rob people.

We regularly encountered girls and women being treated as the 'property' of gangs. As Hannah points out:

> If you are actually seeing a gang member, you're their girl. [. . .] If, for instance, I cheated on that guy then, you know, I don't know what would happen. Do you know what I mean? But obviously that didn't happen. I was well trusted in that sense.

Similarly, the identities of family members – especially sisters – were often defined in accordance with secondary gang 'affiliation'. In this way, Angie, the sister of one Lowerside member and the girlfriend of another, explained that she needed to be very careful which 'blues' [also known as 'shebeens': illegal African-Caribbean drinking/dance clubs] she attended as a result of having a brother in Lowerside gang:

> But I did go to a blues, I think it was on [X] Street. There was an Upperside guy in there [a prominent/leading member], and he asked me for a cigarette, and I didn't have one, so he head-butted me.

Angie also recounted how she became embroiled in a situation related to her brother's conflict one night when she tried to persuade him not to go out when there was trouble brewing:

> I said that I'm going with you then if you are going out. So we were arguing [laughs] and he's telling me to go home and then we saw two guys on bikes

riding towards us and they had pulled-down balaclavas. So he was just like 'run', you know when they were going in the coats [reaching for a weapon?], so we both ran in different directions and I ran and hid down this alley. It was open at both ends and I was scared because I just expected them to be at one end, whichever way I went. So I stayed in the alley for what felt like ages, but it was probably only about five minutes. I saw one of the kids on the estate on a bike and I said 'Have you seen any guys on bikes with balaclavas?' and she went 'They went that way, if you run quick now you can get home' and she was only like seven [years old], but she knew, like, what was going on. And then I got in and my mum was holding him in the house because he was trying to come out and look for me because he'd ran round and gone in the back, so it was like then you're living in fear as well because you're associated with that person and they would do something to you to get to them.

One signifier of gang-based territoriality that the local authority, related local state agencies and the police (especially the dedicated firearm/gang units), pay particular attention to is gang-connected graffiti in public places, known as 'tagging'. Spray-painted gang names or symbols are taken as marking out boundaries and, in particular, the police tend to treat new graffiti as evidence of gang activity. An interview with a senior police officer in the city's specialist 'gang unit', for example, revealed that graffiti was photographed and removed immediately. Our observations confirmed that graffiti rarely remained in place for more than 24 hours. In contrast to the perceptions and actions of the police, however, the young people involved in Inner West gangs attributed little importance to graffiti. Gang members were aware of children and young people tagging one gang name in another's territory but such activity was dismissed as having little real importance or significance. We found no evidence that graffiti was symbolic of gang identity in any meaningful sense for young people in Inner West gangs.

Overall, therefore, gang members understood, experienced and interpreted territory in complicated ways and held much less clearly defined spatial boundaries than accounts provided by city officials suggested. There was considerable dissensus amongst gang members about what constituted 'gang set space'. Gang members tended not to protect or guard territory, and rarely fought over control of territories defined as markets for illicit earning opportunities, such as the drugs trade, even though many participated in drug sales (especially cannabis). However, and in spite of the fact that we found conceptions of territory and turf to be contested, gang members and members of their families could sometimes feel and be restricted in their use of space.

Policing gangs, policing space

Young people's use of space and place is critical for police in identifying and policing gang members. We can see this in how police talked about the (ostensibly) gang-dominated open drugs markets in the Belmont of 20 years ago, as well as in how youth gangs in Inner West are policed today.

As stated, 20 years ago gangs in the Belmont area of Research City could best be described as 'quasi-specialist' drug-dealing gangs. Members were routinely involved in street-level dealing in open drugs markets (primarily heroin and crack cocaine), with a smaller number working as middle-level dealers involved in multi-kilo purchases and sales. We interviewed people employed by the police, both as officers and in civilian positions. Jake Jennings, who was specially tasked with policing the Inner West drugs market for over 25 years, described the process of closing down the gang-dominated open drugs markets in Belmont:

> We used what you call 'punter pulling' whereby you would take observations on the market. You just pull punters coming away to see what commodities . . . It was trying to associate [those drugs, that buyer] to a dealer . . . Then moved onto things like 'test purchase', using 'coverts'. It meant that you could tackle the market as a market and not the individuals within it. And there were several major operations that I was party to whereby we would take out between 15 and 20 dealers at the time . . . and in effect take out a large chunk of that gang.

Thus, the open drugs markets provided a specific locus for the policing of gangs and, in turn, gang affiliation could be determined by observing dealers working together in such markets (one part of Belmont being dominated by the Lowerside gang whilst another was recognisably Upperside territory). However, Jake was far less certain about the extent to which gang members were involved in the drugs trade in Inner West today. The move from open to closed – and thus less visible – drugs markets effectively created an intelligence vacuum with regard to gangs and drug sales. Like Jake Jennings, Detective Inspector Terry Cummings, an officer coming to the end of a 30-year career – mostly centred around policing illicit drugs markets – was unable to shed light on contemporary gang involvement in drug dealing in Research City:

> What's [been] lost is that intimate knowledge of the way gang members are involved in the drugs market. Everybody can say . . . 'it used to be like this and it used to be like that', as I've done that here. And I think every police officer in Research City could probably talk like that . . . Unless you're working specifically looking at [gangs] in relation to drugs, you can be out of date.

There are, no doubt, a range of reasons for this intelligence vacuum but it is clear that the absence of clearly identifiable territory in which open – and observable – drug dealing takes place, is key.

During the life of our fieldwork, the police continued to rely substantially on young people's use of space for the purposes of policing gangs, even though the open drugs markets had disappeared. The policing of Research City – in common with other 'gang' cities in the UK – is characterised by community or 'neighbourhood' style policing (Newburn and Reiner, 2007) that focuses attention on high-crime residential areas. This heavy concentration of policing in particular places and spaces is often combined with intervention and surveillance techniques developed in the US (Bullock and Tilley, 2008 describe one implemented in Manchester). The same approaches draw upon US-style 'gang databases' (Barrows and Huff, 2009) in which intelligence used to identify potential gang members is often based on people's associations with 'known' gang members. The overall result is the construction of 'suspect populations' (e.g. Quinton et al., 2000) in particular neighbourhoods, attracting high levels of police attention. In Research City the police reported that they explicitly employed intensive and focused techniques – akin to 'harassment policing' – in which young people were routinely stop-checked when they ventured into areas that the police associated with gang 'territory' (in practice, areas where known gang members resided, or in public places, such as parks, around them):

> If we suddenly see Crestside Crew emerging on Long Lane, bang, get over there, get our uniform lads to absolutely hammer them, harass them, do them for anything they can. So they basically think, 'We've had enough of this' and we can dampen things down [. . .] but [hanging around on the streets] from our point of view makes them a target. Lowerside lads can drive by, so if we're dispersing them and displacing them, it's diminishing the problem again.

This kind of policing was confirmed by young people living in 'gang neighbourhoods' like Belmont, whether they were gang-involved or not (see Ralphs et al., 2009). Moreover, patterns of association were ultimately taken to comprise 'proof', as this police officer indicates:

> OK, if somebody says to me, 'Is Joe Bloggs a gang member?' And I will obviously look at what we know about him and say, well, if he's been stop-checked once or twice with a known gang member, he's on the periphery. But he's getting stop-checked regular, then you've got to say, 'Well look, by the company that he keeps, we believe that he's a gang member.'

Policing gangs is based on the fundamental assumption that they comprise territorial, street-based entities. Territories of place and space are essential referents for the police in defining gangs and gang members, informing how they are assumed to function and, ultimately, determining how they are policed. In turn, these assumptions – and the policing activity that follows from them – serve to reify police understandings of gangs as territorial and street-based entities in forms that appear to substantially exceed the realities discussed above.

Rethinking gangs and gang control

We began this chapter by noting the typical constructions of youth gangs – as street-based entities operating within clearly defined territories – that commonly underpin explanatory accounts of urban conflicts. Such hegemonic conceptualisations dominate public and policy discourse and are embedded within criminal justice responses to youth gangs. The data presented here challenges this characterisation and, in doing so, it questions the legitimacy of policy responses to gangs based upon notions of clearly defined territorial boundaries. In drawing attention to the anomalies between gang members' use and negotiation of space on the one hand, and the methods of policing them on the other, we argue that territory-focused responses are based on outdated and/or stereotypical assumptions of gang membership.

The two gangs on which the analysis here focused – Upperside and Lowerside – had widespread notoriety across Research City and further afield and were routinely characterised as: highly criminal; highly likely to use firearms; highly territorial and permanently warring. Against this imaginary, our research has revealed substantial dissensus amongst gang members themselves, and between gang members and the police, with regard to what constitutes gang 'set space' and the levels of risk that they attribute to movement around the city.

Rather than gang members residing and spending most of their time in fixed 'gang' neighbourhoods, we found much greater mobility and fluidity with gangs in the Inner West area of Research City, comprising members who reside in areas across the city and, indeed, beyond the city's boundaries. A further blurring of spatial territorial boundaries was evident in that some gang members resided in areas widely viewed as rival gang territory and some even had members of rival gangs in their immediate families. This finding in particular – in addition to undermining a strongly territorial characterisation of these two Inner West gangs – further challenges simplistic understandings of gang members 'belonging' to the gang alone. Loyalties and ties are far more complex.

Furthermore, gangs in Inner West have evolved considerably over the past thirty years. Despite no longer organising around the sales of drugs in open markets, substantial resources are centred on policing them in ways that seemingly fail to take account of these changes. Certainly the police are aware of 'residential outsiders' but policing methods that heavily focus on neighbourhood and employ 'harassment techniques' are problematic. They serve to reify enduring (but outmoded) conceptualisations of gangs as highly territorial by focusing their attention only on young people residing in 'gang neighbourhoods'. Where this involves males – especially young black men – deemed to be 'at risk' of gang involvement (that is, being related to, or seen in the company of, 'known' members), net-widening and labelling ensues. In turn, this invokes 'disrespect' for the police amongst those non-gang-involved young people inadvertently captured via this territorial gaze (see Ralphs et al., 2009) whilst, paradoxically, gang-involved youth are residing or 'chillin'' elsewhere. Indeed, youth gangs were often conspicuous by their absence on 'gang neighbourhood' streets. Pervasive or 'ambient' policing (Loader, 2006), such as that found in Research City, may ultimately undermine citizen security – particularly for identifiable groups – rather than enhance it.

Although, Upperside and Lowerside gangs were noted for their relative absence of street presence, this did not necessarily detract from their engagement with violence and/or criminal activities (including drug dealing). All this raises profound questions of dominant conceptualisations pertaining to gangs. Indeed, as stated, having a street orientation is part of a set of defining criteria used to differentiate youth gangs from other youth formations in the internationally recognised 'Eurogang' definition (Klein et al., 2006). Our findings, therefore, imply that this definition might need to be modified to accommodate non-street-based groups and/or gangs. Heavy policing of public places, legislation prohibiting gang members from gathering in public places, court-mandated curfews and a global trend for young people to spend more time indoors – and especially online – may all be factors contributing towards a less conspicuous street orientation for gang members than was the case in previous decades.

We turn finally to the controversial question of gang injunctions. Legislation that limits the association of gang members in public spaces has existed in the USA since the 1980s (Rosen and Venkatesh 2007). Recent UK legislation in the form of the Policing and Crime Bill 2009 (part four, section 34, 'gang related violence injunction') contains provisions to prohibit individuals deemed to be in a gang from: being in a particular place; being with particular persons in a particular place; wearing specific types of clothing in a particular place; or being in charge of a specified species of animal in a particular place. 'Place', therefore, is key. The civil liberties implications that such legislation brings are obvious, insofar as injunctions can be used to prevent the ordinary activities and everyday movements of individuals who have committed no crime, but who are thought to be gang connected.

In the USA, where these injunctions are increasingly popular, the benefits for reducing crime and fear of crime have been shown to be variable (Maxson et al., 2005). More significantly, ethnic minority areas are disproportionately targeted and, perhaps inevitably, the excessive discretion that gang injunctions afford the police has been shown to lead to discrimination and stigmatisation:

> Some of these youth might be labelled 'associates' of gangs simply because they belong to racial minorities and share living quarters or public spaces with street gang members. Others might actively affiliate with street gang members but lack the specific intent to further a gang's criminal activities. Either way, anti-gang civil injunctions promise to perpetuate racial stigma and oppression.
>
> (Stewart, 1998: 250–1)

Given that just over a decade has passed since London's Metropolitan Police force was found to be 'institutionally racist' (Macpherson of Cluny, 1999), we might have similar concerns about the use of gang injunctions in the UK.

Rosen and Venkatesh (2007) argue that such policies and interventions rest upon a conceptualisation of the city as consisting of distinct and separate communities with clear boundaries. Our findings suggest that over time such boundaries begin to blur. Furthermore, gang injunctions appear to work on the premise that 'gangs need to operate in public to survive; take away their freedom of association and one dramatically reduces the likelihood that gangs will be able to function' (Rosen and Venkatesh, 2007: 624). But the research presented here demonstrates that: young people in gangs do not always have a street presence; many do not reside in gang neighbourhoods; and, most importantly, the policing of public spaces that is required when injunctions are applied often imposes damaging, net-widening and labelling effects (Aldridge et al., 2009; Ralphs et al., 2009; Medina et al., forthcoming).

Meanwhile, whilst new gang injunction legislation may well lead to young (particularly black) males – especially younger gang members with the greatest street presence and the most limited access to alternative locations to socialise – being disproportionately targeted, older and potentially more active and criminally involved gang members (who reside or hang out elsewhere) may well manage to evade them.

Acknowledgements

We would like to thank Jennie Lee, Phil Edwards, Julie Boyle and Yvonne Thorne for their capable research assistance. The research underpinning this chapter was supported by the Economic and Social Research Council (RES-000-23-0615).

Notes

1   The city in which we carried out the research remains anonymous in our public references to it (see later).
2   Only individuals for whom there was clear evidence of gang involvement were classified as 'members'. The 'gang' sample included many people considered to be 'original gangsters' from the late 1980s and early 1990s, together with current 'lead' figures in Research City gangs.
3   Pseudonyms for areas, neighbourhoods and gangs were derived in one of two ways: either by using generic names (for example, 'Inner West', 'Far West', 'Upperside' and 'Lowerside'), or by using the names of towns picked (randomly) from the state of Ohio in the United States. The 'real' towns in Ohio bear no intended resemblance to their corresponding neighbourhoods in Research City. Any similarity in size, population, demographics, socio-economic status (or indeed any other characteristic) is entirely coincidental. The names of all individuals referred to here and in all publications that emanate from the wider research are pseudonyms.
4   The effect of these gang labels in reinforcing and freshly generating deviance is a key issue in relation to youth gangs. We do not address this here, but have in Ralphs et al., 2009.
5   There are other possible processes that are not explored here, including associations made whilst in prison and the development of 'splinter groups' of a gang in its neighbouring areas.

6   It is important to note that the Chicago police department who generated the data on which this research is based defines street gangs as having a geographic territory. Findings that highlight the importance of territoriality and 'turf', therefore, may result in part through data collection specifically around territorial groups.

References

Aldridge, J., Medina, J. and Ralphs, R. (2008) 'Dangers and Problems of Doing "Gang" Research in the UK', in F. van Gemert, D. Peterson and I-L. Lien (eds) *Street Gangs, Migration and Ethnicity*. Cullompton: Willan, pp. 31–46.

—— (2010) 'The Problem of Proliferation: Guidelines for Improving the Security of Qualitative Data in a Digital Age', *Research Ethics Review*, 6(1): 3–9.

Aldridge, J., Shute, J., Ralphs, R. and Medina, J. (2009) 'Blame the Parents? Challenges for Parent-Focussed Programmes for Families of Gang-involved Young People' *Children and Society* (DOI: 10.1111/j.1099–0860.2009.00282.x).

Arias, E.D. (2006) *Drugs and Democracy in Rio de Janeiro*. Chapel Hill: University of North Carolina Press.

Barrows, J. and Huff, C.R. (2009) 'Gangs and Public Policy: Constructing and Deconstructing Gang Databases', *Criminology & Public Policy*, 8(4): 675–703.

Block, C.R. and Block, R. (1993) 'Street Gang Crime in Chicago', *National Institute of Justice: Research in Brief*. Washington, US Department of Justice, Office of Justice Programs.

Bullock, K. and Tilley, N. (2008) 'Understanding and Tackling Gang Violence', *Crime Prevention and Community Safety*, 10: 36–47.

Hallsworth, S. and Young, T. (2008) 'Gang Talk and Gang Talkers: A Critique', *Crime, Media, Culture*, 4(2): 175–95.

Hobbs, D. (2001) 'The Firm: Organizational Logic and Criminal Culture on a Shifting Terrain', *British Journal of Criminology*, 41(4): 549–60.

Home Office (2008), *Tackling Gangs: A Practical Guide for Local Authorities, CDRPs and Other Local Partners*. London: Home Office.

Kennedy, D.M., Braga, A.A. and Piehl, A.M. (1997) 'The (Un)known Universe: Mapping Gangs and Gang Violence in Boston', in D. Weisburd and T. McEwen (eds), *Crime Mapping and Crime Prevention*. New York: Criminal Justice Press, pp. 219–62.

Klein, M.W. (1997) 'What Are Street Gangs When They Get to Court?', *Valparaiso University Law Review*, 31(2): 515–21.

Klein, M.W., Weerman, F. and Thornberry, T.P. (2006) 'Street Gang Violence in Europe', *European Journal of Criminology*, 3(4): 413–37.

Ley, D. and Cybriwsky, R. (1974) 'Urban Graffiti as Territorial Markers', *Annals of the Association of American Geographers*, 64(4): 491–505.

Loader, I. (2006) 'Policing, Recognition, and Belonging', *The Annals of the American Academy of Political and Social Science*, 605(1): 201.

Macpherson of Cluny, Sir William (1999) *The Stephen Lawrence Inquiry: Report of an Inquiry by Sir William Macpherson of Cluny*. Cmnd 4262-1. London: Stationery Office.

Marshall, B., Webb, B. and Tilley, N. (2005) *Rationalisation of Current Research on Guns, Gangs and Other Weapons: Phase 1*. London: UCL Jill Dando Institute of Crime Science.

Maxson, C.L., Hennigan, K.M. and Sloane, D.C. (2005) '"It's Getting Crazy Out There": Can a Civil Gang Injunction Change a Community?', *Criminology and Public Policy*, 4: 577–606.

May, T., Duffy, M., Few, B. and Hough, M. (2005) *Understanding Drug Selling in Local Communities*. York: Joseph Rowntree Foundation.

Medina, J., Aldridge, J. and Ralphs, R. (2010) 'Gang Transformation, Changes or Demise: Evidence from an English City', in J.M. Hazen and D. Rodgers (eds) *Global Gangs: Comparative Perspectives*. Minneapolis: University of Minnesota Press.

Medina, J., Ralphs, R. and Aldridge, J. (forthcoming) 'Mentoring Siblings of Gang Members: A Template for Reaching Families of Gang Members?', *Children and Society*.

Moore, J., Vigil, D. and Garcia, R. (1983) 'Residence and Territoriality in Chicano Gangs', *Social Problems*, 31(2): 182–94.

Newburn, T. and Reiner, R. (2007) 'Policing and the Police', in M. Maguire, R. Morgan and R. Reiner (eds) *The Oxford Handbook of Criminology*. Oxford: Oxford University Press, pp. 910–52.

Pitts, J. (2008) *Reluctant Gangsters: The Changing Face of Youth Crime*. Cullompton: Willan.

Quinton, P., Bland, N. and Miller, J. (2000) *Police Stops, Decision-making and Practice*. London: Home Office, Police Research Series Paper No. 130.

Ralphs, R., Medina, J. and Aldridge, J. (2009) 'Who Needs Enemies with Friends Like These? The Importance of Place for Young People Living in Known Gang Areas', *Journal of Youth Studies*, 12(5): 483–500.

Rosen, E. and Venkatesh, S. (2007) 'Legal Innovation and the Control of Gang Behavior', *Annual Review of Law and Social Science*, 3: 255–70.

Stewart, G. (1998) 'Black Codes and Broken Windows: The Legacy of Racial Hegemony in Anti-Gang Civil Injunctions', *Yale Law Journal*, 107(7): 2249–79.

Taniguchi, T.A., Ratcliffe, J.H. and Taylor, R.B. (in press) 'Gang Set Space, Drug Markets, and Crime: Violent and Property Crimes Around Drug Corners in Camden', *Journal of Research in Crime and Delinquency*.

Thrasher, F. (1927) *The Gang*. Chicago: University of Chicago Press.

Tita, G.E., Cohen, J. and Engberg, J. (2005) 'An Ecological Study of the Location of Gang "Set Space"', *Social Problems*, 52(2): 272–99.

Venkatesh, S. (2008) *Gang Leader for a Day*. London: Penguin.

Watt, N. and Oliver, M. (2009) '"Broken Britain" is Like The Wire, say Tories', *Guardian*, Tuesday 25 August. Retrieved 25 August 2009 (http://www.guardian.co.uk/politics/2009/aug/25/tories-compare-britain-wire-tv).

Weerman, F., Maxson, C.L., Esbensen, F-A., Aldridge, J., Medina, J. and Van Gemert, F. (2009) *Eurogang Program Manual: Background, Development, and Use of the Eurogang Instruments in Multi-Site, Multi-Method Comparative Research*. Retrieved http://www.umsl.edu/~ccj/eurogang/Eurogang_20Manual.pdf.

Chapter 5

Place, territory and young people's identity in the 'new' Northern Ireland

*Siobhán McAlister, Phil Scraton
and Deena Haydon*

Introduction: the 'Chicago School' and beyond

The ubiquity and inconsistency of the term 'gang' in popular discourse and in diverse academic analyses raise doubts about its usefulness in understanding associations, affiliations and interactions between young people. Taken together, the relationship between 'organisation' and 'disorganisation', the significance of 'place' and 'territory', the dynamics of inclusion and exclusion, perceptions of group identity and internal hierarchy, and representations of reputation, constitute defining themes within discourses on gangs. These themes are particularly relevant in developing a critical analysis of the lives of children and young people in Northern Ireland. Before considering the broader context of our primary research, it is important to briefly review some of the key theoretical perspectives on young people – that almost exclusively focus on males – and gangs.

Writing in 1926, Park prefaced Thrasher's (1927/1963) classic, ground-breaking text on Chicago's gangs, noting they 'are not confined to cities, nor to the slums of cities'. Each 'village has at least its boy gang . . . composed of those same foot-loose, prowling and predacious adolescents who herd and hang together, after the manner of the undomesticated male everywhere' (Park, 1963: vii). The domain of 'predatory bands that infest the fringes of civilization' constituted a self-defining 'frontier'. They were simultaneously 'elementary' in organisation and 'spontaneous' in origin, 'grow[ing] like weeds, without consciousness of their aims, and without administrative machinery to achieve them' (ibid. vii–viii). Gangs required understanding in the context of 'their peculiar [unique] habitat' (ibid.). Thrasher (1927/1963: 3) noted that urban space was ever-changing, specifically the 'shadows of the [working-class] slum', and identifiable areas of transition or 'racial ghettoes'. Here gangs created 'a world distinctly their own . . . rough and untamed, yet rich in elemental social processes' (ibid.). Their 'delinquencies' were minor yet serious, spontaneous yet institutionalised.

Youth gangs, according to Thrasher (1927/1963: 6), were embroiled in persistent 'feudal warfare . . . disorder and violence escaping the ordinary controls of the police and other social agencies', occupying a world alongside 'wholesome' community organisations. Gang territories were 'regions of conflict . . . like a frontier . . . a "no-man's land", lawless, godless, wild'. The 'great domains' of Chicago's gang 'empire' further projected their existence at the margins of 'respectable' society: 'North Side Jungles'; 'West Side Wilderness'; 'South Side Badlands'. They formed 'interstices' between the central business district and the 'better residential areas' of the suburbs. National identity and ethnic origin mapped gang territory: 'Little Italy'; 'Little Sicily'; 'Polish colony'; 'negro colony'; 'Little Greece'; 'gypsies'; 'Mexicans'; 'Jewish gangs'; 'Lithuanian colony'; 'Mickies' (Irish). Each possessed demarcated districts within which gangs adopted neighbourhood names and tags, their emergence a 'manifestation of the economic, moral, and cultural frontier which marks the interstice' (ibid. 21).

Boys and young men sought to create social order 'for themselves where none adequate to their needs exist' (ibid. 32). Their collective 'association' provided the 'thrill and zest of participation . . . in hunting, capture, conflict, flight, and escape', with inter-gang conflict a key element in that fulfilment. It reflected the:

> failure of the normally directing and controlling customs and institutions to function efficiently in the boys' experience . . . indicated by the disintegration of family life, inefficiency of schools, formalism and externality of religion, corruption and indifference in local politics, low wages and monotony in occupational activities, unemployment, and lack of opportunity for wholesome recreation.
>
> (Thrasher, 1927/1963: 33)

Gangs – while contextualised as a 'symptom of disorganization in the larger social framework' – offered members camaraderie, tradition and structure in local neighbourhoods. Collective belonging, exclusivity, hostility towards rivals and the police, solidified gang tradition. Conflict created more profound 'integration' within gangs.

For Thrasher (1927/1963: 46) gangs were 'characterized' by: 'meeting face-to-face, milling, movement through space as a unit, conflict, and planning', thus generating 'the development of tradition, unreflective internal structure, *esprit de corps*, solidarity, morale, group awareness, and attachment to local territory' (ibid. 46). While some gangs remained loosely defined and temporary, others 'solidified' through 'extended conflict', became incorporated into mainstream communities or took on the mystery of 'secret societies'. Arising from the immediate 'environment and the patterns it discovers' locally, gang members possessed a 'fund of energy that is undirected, undisciplined, and uncontrolled by any socially desirable pattern' and given the 'opportunity for expression in the freest, the most spontaneous and elemental manner possible' (ibid. 83).

This brief excursion into Thrasher's research indicates how the 'Chicago School' focused on the 'context of the physical processes and the changing shape of the modern city' in early twentieth-century USA (Hagedorn, 2007: 14). In this analysis the roots of crime, conflict and violence were no longer conceptualised as essentialist biological and/or cultural pathologies, rather as consequences of social disorganisation, community upheaval and social transition. The emphasis on social and cultural context, however nuanced and contested, became central to academic research in the USA and the UK. It laid the ground for a critical approach that placed structural inequalities and societal relations of power at the centre of analysis.

In his groundbreaking research, Patrick (1973: 170) emphasised the 'interlocking network of inequalities' underpinning the inter-generational 'subculture of gangs in Glasgow . . . poverty, inferior education, a lack of even minimum opportunities, and a steadily deteriorating economic situation' resulting in 'feelings of frustration, rage and powerlessness'. In 'choosing violence as their form of adaptation', in becoming 'street fighters rather than drug addicts or political activists' and in not 'retreat[ing] into social despair or fatalistic acceptance of the *status quo*' he noted two responses. First was 'a strong subcultural emphasis on self-assertion and on a rebellious independence against authority as the means of attaining masculinity'. Second was the long history of 'economic hardship, suffered by generations of Glaswegians' that had 'narrowed down the possibilities of action' (ibid.).

By emphasising social, cultural and material contexts, Patrick focused directly on issues of power, authority, legitimacy and the structural inequalities of class. As Hagedorn (2007: 15) notes more recently, the 'human ecology framework . . . minimized the *active* role of institutions, particularly the political machine, real estate companies, and the rackets . . . the *role of the powerful*, as well as the powerless, needs to be more fully explored' (emphases added). Wacquant (2007: 35) – reflecting on the 'recent debate on racial division and urban poverty in the United States' – notes three dominant premises constituting an 'academic orthodoxy' derived in 'long-standing American conceptions of the poor – and particularly the black poor – as morally defective, and of the city as a nefarious place that disrupts and corrupts social life'. First is 'simply to designate an urban area of widespread and intensive poverty' as a 'ghetto' without historical understanding or sociological analysis of the 'racial basis and character of this poverty' (ibid.). Second is the unquestioning acceptance of the established 'tenet' that 'the ghetto is a "disorganised" social formation' conceptualised and framed 'wholly in terms of *lack and deficiencies* (individual or collective) rather than by positively identifying the principles that underlie its internal order and govern its specific mode of functioning' (ibid. 34–35). Finally, the ghetto is represented as exotic, 'highlight[ing] the most extreme and unusual aspects of ghetto life as seen from the outside and above . . . the standpoint of the dominant' (ibid. 35).

Addressing the 'contested' and complex realities of 'racial conflict and urban marginality in contemporary America', Wacquant (2007: 36) challenges the portrayal of the ghetto as a 'topographic entity or aggregation of poor families'. Rooted in its particular history, the ghetto is institutionalised. 'Space' and state interventions are objectified by defining processes of 'categorisation, discrimination, segregation and exclusionary violence' (ibid. 37). Responses within communities to concrete manifestations of institutionalised marginalisation are not haphazard, irrational or disorganised. On the contrary, what operates is organised and reflective – evident in 'collective self-production'. Communities 'endow their world with form, meaning, and purpose', demonstrating 'how the *activities of dominant institutions* . . . contribute powerfully to organizing the social space of the ghetto', not least its 'destabilisation' (ibid. 41). For the parameters of public services, provision and regulation inhibit the '*situated agency* of ghetto residents' (emphasis in original).

Wacquant (2007) argues that the 'trope of disorganization also has reinforced the exoticizing of the ghetto' through which the 'most destitute, threatening and disreputable residents of the racialized urban core are made to stand for the whole of the ghetto' (ibid. 41). The socio-cultural pathologisation of the ghetto, where institutionalised racism meets structural, endemic poverty, is derived in middle-class assumptions that label the poor as 'abnormal, offensive, or unduly costly' (ibid.). As Wacquant (ibid. 42) argues, the categories employed to pathologise communities are influential '*instruments of indictment*', dismissing the '*local social rationality*' adopted and adapted within communities to inform and sustain strategies of survival. He concludes that, '[e]ven in the most extreme circumstances social life is patterned, regular . . . endowed with logic and meaning' (ibid. 44).

These critical developments, focusing on the social and cultural dynamics of communities, their ideological portrayal and opportunist political responses, within historical and material structural contexts provide the analytical framework for our recent primary research with children and young people in the 'new' Northern Ireland.

Northern Ireland: identities within a divided society

Between 1969 and 1999, a total of 3,636 people died in the Conflict in Northern Ireland; of these, 2,037 were civilians (McKittrick et al., 1999). Of all household respondents in a 2003 survey on poverty and social exclusion, half knew someone who had been killed in the Conflict. Approximately 88,000 households were affected by the loss of a close relative, 50,000 contained an injured resident, 28,000 people were forced to leave work and 54,000 households relocated through intimidation, threats or harassment (Hillyard et al., 2005: 6). Those areas that endured the most serious violence, injuries and bereavement during the Conflict were often the most economically deprived wards – illustrating the 'strong, but complex, relationship between poverty and conflict' (ibid. xx).

The Conflict severely undermined economic investment and development, exacerbated child poverty, and contributed to high levels of mental ill-health resulting in impaired employment opportunities. Poverty remains a significant issue: one in three children live in income poverty, one in ten live in severe poverty (Magadi and Middleton, 2007). Between 2001 and 2004, some 21 per cent of children in Northern Ireland were trapped in persistent poverty, compared with 9 per cent in Britain (Monteith et al., 2008). Given that poverty remains pervasive in areas most affected by the Conflict, children and young people living in these areas experience multiple deprivations. This affects their health and well-being, educational attainment, access to safe play and leisure facilities, opportunities, self-esteem and relationships (McAlister et al., 2009).

The Belfast/Good Friday Agreement, signed by the UK and Irish Governments, provided the constitutional foundation for devolution of powers to a demo-cratically elected Northern Ireland Assembly. Following its election in 1998, and the establishment of full delegated powers in December 1999, the Assembly went through a protracted and bitterly contested period focused mainly on arms decommissioning. Finally, in October 2002, the Executive was suspended for the fourth time and UK Government direct rule was (re)imposed. In October 2006 the St Andrews Agreement pre-empted the resumption of the Assembly and seven months later devolution returned.

In this context of transition our research investigated the dual impacts of poverty and the legacy of the Conflict on the lives of children and young people. It questioned the claims of progress made by official 'post-conflict' or 'peace' discourse, particularly for communities most affected by political violence. In-depth primary research was conducted with adult community representatives, children and young people in six urban and rural communities, one in each Northern Ireland County. Communities identified as Catholic/Nationalist/Republican or Protestant/Unionist/Loyalist. The research report (McAlister et al., 2009) focuses on: images of children and young people; personal life and relationships; education and employment; community and policing; place and identity; segregation and sectarianism; violence in the context of conflict and marginalisation; services and supports; the rights deficit.

Our research confirms the centrality of 'place' and 'space' in establishing personal and community identity. Whatever their limitations, communities provide 'an important source of social recognition for individuals, providing a tangible sense of connection and identity: knowing who you are and where you belong' (Henderson, 2007: 129). In Ireland – given the history of colonisation, partition and conflict – place, space and identity have particular significance. While politicians and academics often refer to Northern Ireland as an international example of conflict resolution and progress towards a sustainable peace, long-standing divisions and tensions remain. The Northern Ireland Office maintains 53 'peace lines or walls' (*BBC News*, 1 July 2009), three times the number prior to the ceasefires (*Guardian*, 28 July 2009). Although cessation of community-based punishment beatings and shootings was central to the withdrawal of paramilitary activity in communities, between 1999 and 2009 there were 1,958 casualties from 'paramilitary-style' shootings and assaults (PSNI, 2009). Between April 2009 and January 2010 there were a further 109 incidents recorded (PSNI, 2010). Threats and intimidation continue to be directed towards children and young people accused of 'anti-social behaviour', particularly in economically deprived urban areas associated with high levels of conflict-related violence.

Physical separation of the two main religious or ethno-national groups (Catholics and Protestants) prevails. Approximately 95 per cent of social housing remains segregated by religious affiliation and over half the population live in neighbourhoods which are over 90 per cent Catholic or Protestant (NIHE, 2006). In 2007–8, only 6 per cent of the school population was enrolled in integrated nursery, primary or post-primary schools (DENI, 2008: 2). Ninety-four per cent attended segregated education in Catholic or Protestant schools. Despite efforts to 're-image' communities, public space remains labelled and politicised – demarcated by flags, murals and symbols in displays of identity, territory and 'ownership' of space. Cross-community contact remains limited for many, with leisure facilities and other services not accessed by children and young people living outside specific local communities.

Exploring the impact of fear at the interfaces between communities, Shirlow (2003: 86) found that many people would not travel through an area housing the 'other community' during the day, rising to 88 per cent at night. In Roche's (2008) research with young people, three-quarters of those living in segregated communities were fearful of the 'other community' or of entering 'other neighbourhoods'. Intimidation (real or feared), abuse, verbal and physical violence reinforce the legacy of 'no-go areas', sustaining exclusivity and maintaining geographical boundaries. Roche (2008) reports young people as 'cocooned' within their community, with few opportunities to mix with those of the 'other community'. From a young age they inherit negative attitudes towards the 'other religion or community' (Connolly and Healy, 2004). In our research, community representatives noted that very young children often sang sectarian songs without understanding the meaning or significance of the words (McAlister et al., 2009).

Sectarian views are subtly transmitted through families, schools, communities and media. Illustrating the power and pervasiveness of sectarian messages, young people spoke of difficulties resisting parental and adult views:

> Like, sectarianism, ok it's bad. But it's like the parents are the worst culprits of it because if young people were allowed to do what they wanted, it wouldn't be as bad as it is. It's the older people that are makin' it so bad, like . . . what ye have passed down, like, it just stays with ye sorta thing. (Co. Tyrone, aged 14–25)[1]

Attempting to depart from ascribed community identity risks exclusion. Regardless of its strengths, 'the very intimacy of local community can itself be experienced as something oppressive and limiting' (Hall et al., 1999: 510). In Northern Ireland, the Conflict has contributed to the creation of strong and coherent communities but this process also maintains or perpetuates attitudes and activities derived from the Conflict. As Boal (2002: 693) states:

> Segregation of Catholics and Protestants in Belfast . . . has helped underpin community solidarity for each group, providing an environment for the

intergenerational transfer of cultural tradition, a localised degree of security from physical attack and a modicum of psychological security. On the obverse, segregation . . . reduces the possibilities for inter-ethnic exchange.

Since the ceasefires there has been a significant reduction in violent, sectarian incidents. Yet children and young people – particularly those living at 'interfaces' – are exposed to and involved in sporadic outbreaks of violence or 'disturbances'. These include verbal attacks and throwing stones, bottles or fireworks (Hansson, 2005). Leonard's (2004) research with children and young people in Loyalist and Nationalist interface areas illustrates the durability of sectarianism and the consolidation of physical boundaries marked by continuing hostility. Reflecting on day-to-day negotiation of social space and possible cross-community inter-action, 'peace . . . remained a distant vision' (ibid. 107). Our own research reveals the continued impact of separatism and segregation on the everyday lives of children and young people, and the frustrations of adult community representatives with the political rhetoric of 'peace' and 'post-Conflict' (McAlister et al., 2009). As Connolly and Neill (2001: 124) conclude, all children:

> developed and internalized . . . a very acute sense of identity grounded in their experiences of the local area . . . [which] plays a central role for many of the children in terms of being the key source of their experience and the reference point by which they make sense of their lives.

'Youth gangs' or 'youth groups'? Common assumptions, local responses

Many young people interviewed for our research spend much of their leisure-time on the streets of their neighbourhoods. Limited finances and fear of sectarian intimidation restrict social and leisure opportunities. Age-appropriate and acces-sible facilities are not generally available and the streets offer the least threatening social space. Yet there are risks. Meeting friends and passing time regularly involves alcohol, increasing the likelihood of involvement in violence. 'Trouble' results from negative interactions with the police, community members and paramilitaries, or from 'loss of control'. It is considered acceptable to respond violently to 'someone slaggin' ya'. Standing up for personal reputation, for family, friends and community is part of local culture. It also informs group dynamics and solidarity against 'outside' threats. Yet young people devise strategies for staying safe and avoiding violence.

While 'the street' has been a consistent feature of working-class youth culture, historically it has been less significant in Northern Ireland given the high level of conflict-related violence. Since the ceasefires, however, young people spend more time 'hanging out' in their local communities. In our research this was a major concern, linked to perceptions of a growth in 'antisocial behaviour'. Street groups are labelled 'gangs' and those wearing hoods are considered a threat:

R: 'Say there was a group of young people standin' on the street, what do you
         think adults might think about them?'
YP1: 'They're gangsters.'
YP2: 'Look at them wee hoodies.' (Co. Antrim, aged 10–13)

Many young people claim they are discriminated against and demonised because
of their lifestyle, appearance and age:

YP1: 'It's just the look of us.'
YP2: 'It's your appearance. It's the way you dress – wearin' hoods, whereabouts
         you hang about – street corners, the types of things you're into – like cars
         and all this here. You know, they just automatically assume.' (Co. Derry,
         aged 15–19)

Children and young people criticise the media for fuelling such negative assumptions. Most consider the negative reputation imposed on young people to be unfair
and uninformed. The constant pressure of rejection and exclusion, together with
direct threats of violence, undermine self-confidence and, simultaneously, provoke
angry reactions. While some become introspective, evident in regular comments
about suicide, others respond violently – perpetuating the image of the 'violent
gang'.

Our research demonstrates the over-simplified application of the 'gang' label.
At first glance, many young people appear to display 'youth gang' characteristics.
They occupy the 'streets' within clear geographical boundaries. Groups have a
semblance of organisation or structure, often with one individual as particularly
influential. They wear similar styles of dress and share cultural identity. Their
routine includes sporadic 'criminal' and violent behaviour that is territorial. While
violence is not integral to group identity, it is ever-present. They risk attack from
others and are prepared to fight when necessary. There is no evidence of long-term
durability of the groups but, consistent with 'street corner youth' studied elsewhere
(MacDonald and Shildrick, 2007), the expectation is that eventually they will be
replaced by the next generation.

Young people congregate in particular locations for safety, familiarity and
belonging. Street-based leisure is about lifestyle, which is 'one manifestation of
more fundamental social and economic processes' (Smith, 1986: 92). State
regulation of young people's lifestyle, including policies for regulation and
dispersal, results in alienation, marginalisation and criminalisation. Invariably it is
the poorest and under-resourced communities that are targeted. In Northern
Ireland, removing young people from the relative safety of neighbourhood streets
puts them at risk of sectarian attack (McGrellis, 2004; Leonard, 2007).

Heightened fears about 'youth gangs' and 'gangland violence' have brought
increased surveillance, control, management and criminalisation of poor and
'serially excluded' populations (Hallsworth, 2006). According to Ralphs et al.
(2009: 491), being labelled puts young people at risk as 'the police adopted a

proactive method of harassment of people they identified as "gang members"'. In targeted areas, non-gang affiliated young people also experience increased police surveillance, regulation and control because of the reputation of the place and their associations with others. Hallsworth (2006: 306) argues that, 'what had been created was a production line system for producing serially alienated and angry young men whose distrust of the police and formal authority structures had reached endemic levels'.

In our research, young people stated that the police are often called because they are out on the streets. This creates conflict with the police, whose arrival has become synonymous with rioting:

> They [the police] are the problem. It's them that leads to people petrol bombin' and all that and then they just destroy the place. (Co. Armagh, aged 12–21)

Young people give numerous examples of 'police harassment': being continuously stopped, questioned, moved on and threatened with antisocial behaviour orders. They claim that name-calling and ridicule by police officers exacerbates violent confrontations. While violent confrontations are sometimes a consequence of sectarianism, many young people argue that fighting the police is an expression of their resistance to age discrimination. The outcome is predictable: 'Well, if the police are always fuckin' annoyin' ya you're gonna be bad and you're gonna hate the law' (Co. Fermanagh, aged 13–15).

Some young people also experience uncompromising threats of severe punishments from, and exiling by, dissident paramilitaries:

> They [adults] blame us for stuff and we get a bad name for it . . . and there's cops comin' up round here and there's paramilitaries lookin' round all the time and they blame ye. (Co. Derry, aged 15–19)

Lack of trust in the police, experience of intimidation and adults' failure to understand young people's behaviour and use of public space, are recurrent themes. This extends to threats to safety, security and life – within communities through punishments by quasi-paramilitaries and outside communities through sectarian attack.

My place: local identity and territory

In Northern Ireland there has been considerable debate about the politicisation of space and divisions *between* places as a consequence of residential segregation, 'peace lines' and other symbolic markers of inclusion/exclusion. Minimal consideration has been given to local divisions *within* 'single-identity' communities and their impact on daily life. 'Territory' has become synonymous with the regulation, control and defence of communities with specific ethno-national identities (Republican/Nationalist or Loyalist/Unionist). Our research finds that, for children and young people, their community and identity corresponds to the spaces they occupy and the facilities they use. In focus groups they are specific about immediate locations: 'my community', 'my street' or 'my part of the estate'. Attachment to place is localised. Their knowledge and perception about places or spaces within the area impact on their sense of self, feelings of safety and movement.

Internal divisions are evident, often visible, in all the communities. Particular neighbourhoods or clusters of streets have developed distinct identities and reputations, with consequences for individual and collective identity. A community representative describes divisions within their community:

> The areas are all separate and the people living there have graded themselves in social rank. The road acts like a river, like a natural divide. People won't mix.

The claiming of different and separate identities within neighbourhoods affected provision and use of local services. Within some communities, play parks and local shops are only utilised by those from one part of an estate or neighbourhood, and children and young people are aware of divisions within their communities. In two of the communities, community representatives explain that internal divisions originate in the arrival of families who share the same cultural tradition but have been exiled from their previous homes as a consequence of intra-community feuds. Because they are not local, they are labelled 'outsiders'. Resentment simmers about so-called 'blow-ins'[2] who move into the area, occupy housing 'built for local people' and 'act as if they own the place'.

In another community, adult representatives suggest there are 'different moralities' and cultures within the estate. They refer to a Republican ethos which impacts on the organisation of, and attendance at, particular programmes or events in one part of the estate. Some service providers are acutely aware that their provision has an established reputation based on the local historical context: 'The centre is associated with the Provisionals [Provisional IRA] . . . we had to work hard to get the community to realise we are not linked to paramilitaries'. Illustrating the enduring nature of labels and identities linked to local spaces, young people state they would not attend this centre because of its association with 'the boys, the RA [IRA]'.

In Nationalist rural communities, divisions between small towns and strong identities linked to local place are represented as 'football territories'. Not visiting or using services in nearby communities demonstrates loyalty, connection and pride in 'their' community:

> There are territorial issues. People won't go to other areas. Young people are separated after school. This is about identity issues not based on religion . . . Young people from small rural areas will often never meet because of [Gaelic] football rivalries.

Local, complex and deep-rooted meanings and assumptions attached to space create difficulties for service providers. Because children and young people do not access youth services outside their community and are reticent to utilise those in particular neighbourhoods of their community, mobile services have been established, often duplicating programmes within a community. Occasionally local divisions are perpetuated by adults working directly with children and young people.

While divisions often have their origins in housing policies and population movement prevalent at the height of the Conflict, they remain significant. In children's and young peoples' accounts they are connected to 'reputation'. These include perceptions about the 'good' and 'bad' side of the estate, the 'rough' and the 'respectable', the 'quiet' and the 'trouble-orientated', the 'poor' and the 'more affluent':

> I'm not trying to say that [the other part of the area] is bad or anythin'. But [where I live] would be tidier than bits of [the other part] and, like, there's not as many bad people in [my part] than what there is in [the other part]. (Co. Antrim, aged 10–13)

There is, however, considerable disagreement about local divisions:

YP Area A: 'I don't like it [Area B].'
R: 'Any reason you don't like it?'
YP Area A: 'Yeah, it's got nothin' to do.'
YP Area B: 'Sure there's nothing to do in [Area A].'
YP Area A: 'Play rounders.'
YP Area B: 'Whooo, sure you can do that in [Area B].'
YP Area A: 'I come from [Area A] and I feel safe there because there's more places to go, it's bigger than [Area B].'
YP Area B: 'The Area A crew!' [giggles sarcastically]
(Co. Antrim, aged 10–13)

While this exchange reflects apparently petty differences, it exemplifies a shared defensiveness of 'their place'.

Internal community divisions impact on children and young people in various ways. Experiences are markedly different within the same locality. Where they live and play locally affects what they witness and experience at a personal level. Many comment that free time and play is restricted to the street or part of the community where they live as this provides safety and a sense of belonging. Consequently, particular groups 'hang out' in different parts of the estate or attend clubs in 'their part'. The physical location of facilities identifies them exclusively with a particular 'type', group or, according to young people, 'gang':

> it's like all the one gang that goes to it, which means there's other gangs in [the area] won't go to it . . . they would have all the kind of tough boys among

them which means a lot of the younger, the quieter ones . . . wouldn't go near it . . . if ye go into the community centres you would never see one of the people from [one centre] down at [other centre]. (Co. Derry, aged 22)

The location of services and who 'runs them' affects their use. Subtle and local nuances exclude some young people from local services. A form of territorialism is established, with facilities located in 'their end of the estate' organised by workers who they know, trust and perceive as 'safe'. Others, however, believe they 'wouldn't fit in' and would be made to 'feel like a weirdo'. Explaining why they will not use youth services in nearby villages, children and young people living in rural communities comment: 'We wouldn't be welcome down there because everyone stays in the one place' (Co. Armagh, aged 9–15). As facilities have become synonymous with particular groups, those 'not belonging' are excluded. Expressed as 'territory', exclusion is deeply rooted in the historical division and local meaning of space. The 'choices' and 'rules' made by children and young people regarding access and movement within their area are learned quickly, including 'differences' within their communities and estates. Such awareness represents identity formation at a very local level.

Our place: segregation, sectarianism and territoriality

Ascribing the label 'youth gang' to young people congregating in a specific location, thereby inferring the classic relationship between 'the gang' and its 'territory', has particular consequences in Northern Ireland. In a divided society transitioning from 30 years of armed conflict, youth identity, 'place' and violence cannot be conceptualised without taking into account the pervasive significance of segregation and sectarianism. From 'conflict' to 'peace', the management and negotiation of identity and place are crucial aspects of ideological aspirations, as well as consequences of a political shift. Despite government inducements to re-image communities (particularly the removal of sectarian murals), neighbourhoods and streets remain visibly demarcated through 'cultural symbols' such as flags, murals and memorials. While reflecting a community's cultural tradition, they also transmit messages of inclusion and exclusion. As Forrest and Kearns (2001: 2107) note, 'strong in-group loyalty' can project 'strong out-group antagonism'.

As discussed above, from an early age children identify and understand these markers. They are taken-for-granted in their socialisation, determining their associations and movements. One group, in a mixed but highly segregated community, comments:

Ye can tell from the old flags hangin' on the posts – wherever that's outside, that's that territory. (Co. Tyrone, aged 14–25)

Young people living in a Protestant community consider the flags, flying from lamp-posts leading into their estate, to be an outward expression of their cultural identity. To adults in the community they mark territory – a visual reminder, or threat: 'This is our street, no-one is coming down our street.'

Hall et al. (1999: 509) note that 'knowing where others are from makes it possible to *place* them'. Beyond community boundaries, being 'placed' as Loyalist or Republican creates risk of attack. Regardless of their acceptance or rejection of cultural identity, young people have a clear understanding of 'spaces of risk and threat' (Leonard, 2007: 76). In our research, those living in one small Protestant/Loyalist neighbourhood feel imprisoned in their community, identifying it as the *only* safe space. While it has no youth or recreation facilities, young people will not access those in the town because, 'you wouldn't be long in gettin' an auld crutch in the face if you used it . . . if you walk up yourself then you wouldn't be seen comin' back out' (Co. Fermanagh, aged 13–16).

Within relatively small towns, local neighbourhoods and estates are perceived to have established cultural traditions. Visual cues also connect to cultural identity. In a society where schools are predominantly segregated by religious affiliation, school uniforms signify division. This extends to football shirts, caps, scarves, jewellery and sports played. Even 'neutral spaces', such as town centres, carry the threat of sectarian abuse or attack with identity ascribed by appearance. Young men negotiate this risk by moving around in groups:

> When you're off the estate you're always lookin' where the trouble might come from. Always lookin' over your shoulder . . . you always have to be in numbers. No way would I walk off the estate on my own. (Co. Fermanagh, aged 16–21)

Outside their communities children and young people manage or disguise their identities, often altering their dress. Attacks bring retaliation by family, friends or community members leading to violent exchanges across the religious divide.

Given the unambiguous symbols of religious and cultural difference in Northern Ireland, there is a definitive understanding of cultural identity. Young men protect themselves by staying in groups, being vigilant and expecting attack. They adopt a 'hard man' persona, prepared to retaliate, presenting an open expression and assertion of identity rather than a disguise. In some areas, perceptions of the community and its young people reinforce attachment to place – strengthening identity, group solidarity and cohesiveness.

Further demonstrating the relationship between identity and territory, some young Loyalists emphasise their hostility towards people from other cultures moving into their community. Acceptance is granted to 'people who move in, good people who think like you, are loyal like you'. Those 'not part of your culture' (Co. Fermanagh, aged 16–21) are forced out. For some young Nationalists, those of 'the other religion' are not welcome:

YP1: 'I know boys that know Protestants loads, but if they were seen near the Protestant side they'd get hit.'
R: 'And what about the other way round?'
YP2: 'Aye, if ye seen one [a Protestant] walkin' about here you'd take a swipe at him.' (Co. Derry, aged 16–17)

Clear physical divisions and symbolic markers of ownership map territory defended against 'the other'. As Kuusisto (2001: 59) states: 'Local turf is controlled and formed as a safe haven for members of the community'. Cultural identity, therefore, remains 'clean' and 'uncontaminated', providing long-standing culturally reproduced reasons for the defence and retention of local space.

In divided societies, transition from conflict to peace is slow, not least because ceasefires and arms decommissioning are 'change' moments in time, while commitment to particular cultures and identities remains resilient. In our research, a decade into the 'peace process' and conducted with a 'new generation', limited exposure to those outside their communities and strong beliefs within them consolidate young people's negative attitudes towards 'the other'. Expressing loyalty to 'their own', many children and young people articulate mistrust and hostility towards 'outsiders'. There is also a sense that many communities have been left behind, unprepared and under-resourced for change or to deal with the legacy of the Conflict.

Beliefs about persistent inequalities inform sectarian, and sometimes violent, responses. In Catholic/Nationalist areas, the prevailing belief is that the police offer concessions to the Protestant community: 'the cops . . . take sides' (Co. Derry, aged 16–17) and 'Protestants get all the protection they want, and we get nothing' (Co. Derry, aged 15–19). Young people in Protestant communities, however, consider that Catholics are given preferential treatment. In one community, they had removed Loyalist flags but remain angry and resentful that the Catholic community have retained their Republican flags. This is considered 'favourin' and bias', resulting in 'hatred for the police'. It is 'another example' of how 'Catholics get everything' (Co. Fermanagh, aged 13–16). Their concerns are not restricted to mistrusting the police or defending symbolic expressions of culture. They feel that Catholics have benefited from the 'new' political situation in Northern Ireland to the detriment of Protestants:

> Catholics get everything. Everything that goes up is in a Catholic area and we don't get nothin'. It's not like they be good to be treated to it, all the sprayin', all the burnt-out cars there used to be. (Co. Fermanagh, 13–16)

In this climate of resentment, rioting and sectarian clashes assert identity while symbolising resistance towards perceived inequalities. While some young people find 'enjoyment' in rioting, it is not, as has been claimed, solely 'recreational'. According to Protestant and Catholic young people it is rooted politically in cultural tradition:

If you're out there riotin' and you're not Republican and all this here, you'd have to think, 'What's the point?' So in a way ye have to be kinda standin' up for it . . . we're fightin' for our identity. (Co. Derry, aged 15–19)

While sectarian attitudes and violence are closely allied to cultural identity, there is minimal, informed understanding about 'the other culture'. All Protestants are portrayed as identifying with Britain/Unionism/Loyalism. All Catholics are portrayed as identifying with Ireland/Nationalism/Republicanism. Fighting to retain cultural identity is about fighting to defeat 'the other':

We're not having a united Ireland. I'd be the first away. But that's the way it's goin' and we have to fight for our culture. If the Catholics took over what would you have? Would you want to live in Ireland? We'd lose everything. Everything we've fought for. (Co. Fermanagh, 16–21)

YM1: 'We're fightin' for our identity. It's like they want Londonderry and we want Derry.'
YM2: 'It's Derry not Londonderry. London's got its own place and Derry's got its own place . . . There's no London in Derry.'
YM3: 'If there's any people in Derry want to support the Queen an' all, they can fuck off back to England.' (Co. Derry, aged 15–19)

These mutually exclusive positions reflect a view held by some young people that their communities had 'fought for nothing'. Progress towards equal representation, power-sharing and the de-politicisation of shared space through the removal of sectarian symbols are depicted as 'concessions' to one community and 'punishments' to the other. Young Protestants explain marches, flags and bonfires as meaningful expressions of their cultural tradition. Their curtailment is considered a concerted attempt to 'to rip away our culture'. Elected politicians, who previously refused public association with Republican politicians or with the Irish Government, are now negotiating. 'Irish culture' is represented as flourishing, leading to suspicion and fear that 'reverse discrimination' challenges Protestant cultural identity. This compounds a sense of insecurity alongside increased defence of territory and resentment towards 'the other side'.

The driving force behind group sectarianism is a commitment to preserving a shared identity during a period of transition. Historically, intimidation and violence have been a means of asserting and maintaining identity, alongside rioting as an expression of resistance. The application of ill-informed labels, without recognising the particular circumstances of Northern Ireland and shared discontent, will further alienate the most marginalised young people. As a community representative states: 'If we are going to say that young people today are very sectarian we need to think about why that is and where they have gotten those messages from. We give it to them, then blame them'.

The perceived 'natural order' of divided space includes hostility towards recently arrived foreign nationals – illustrating the deep roots of exclusive identity regarding space and how segregation has been accepted as a response to dealing with 'difference' or fears about 'the other'. Thus, territoriality and 'ownership' of space extend beyond the religious divide. In the context of historical meaning attached to space and current fears about loss or dilution of identity and culture, a new 'outsider' has emerged as a common threat. The implicit and sometimes explicit racism expressed by children and young people in our research reflects a prevailing history of sectarian divisions, fear and mistrust of 'outsiders'.

Young men: masculinity and violence

Community representatives regularly comment on how the legacy of the Conflict affects young men – those traditionally brought up to fight for and defend their cultural identity. Since the ceasefires, however, the expectation of paramilitary recruitment has been reversed – the war is over, peace has been agreed. Yet reminders of the past persist through family and community inheritance, images in the form of murals and remembrance events:

> At the end of the day, we're goin' by what our grannies and granddads are tellin' us. And they're puttin' it on the news and they're makin' films about it. And what are we supposed to think when they make a film about Bloody Sunday or they make a film about the bombings and what-not? . . . So of course young ones are goin' to fight back – 'Oh, you did this to my one' – you know, war stories you could say it is. (Co. Derry, aged 21)

While young people are constantly reminded that sectarian violence is no longer acceptable, they hear former combatants and politicians 'glorifying the war' and 'romanticising the idea of struggle'. Concerns are expressed across communities about influential adults perpetuating and actively encouraging the continuation of violence. Inevitably, some young people are influenced by the sectarian attitudes of significant adults. Messages, therefore, are mixed:

> All those ones that were at the Bloody Sunday [commemorative march] an' all, if you were out riotin' they're all like, 'Wise up, the war's over' . . . They went through all the wars like, they should know how it feels. But yet they still get into us for doin' it. (Co. Derry, aged 15–19)

Working-class young men with strong cultural and community identities experience a shared sense of loss – there are no locally available jobs, they place minimal value on education and there are few alternative possibilities. With paramilitary recruitment waning, young men's identity and place within their communities are uncertain. They are 'disillusioned and alienated from community life'; some responding to this dramatic change by violently asserting masculinity and sectarianism. Those involved in rioting and violence share stories with their peers and in interviews with great bravado and, no doubt, some exaggeration. This brings status among peers, reflecting the relationship between violent sectarianism and masculine identity (see Harland et al., 2005). But it contrasts with their vulnerability in revealing fears about leaving their community and being attacked by 'the other community'.

Previous research with young men in Northern Ireland noted their explanation of aggression as protection of themselves and their communities, while recognising it was occasionally 'unnecessarily violent' (YouthNet, 1999: 3). It was justified when someone from 'outside' entered the community or attacked friends. While some young women were involved in 'fighting', 'rioting' and aggressive behaviour, violence was most often linked to masculine identity. The relationship between masculinity and violence is particularly significant in Northern Ireland where violence, particularly paramilitary and sectarian violence, has been a defining reality and expectation for young working-class men. It is instrumental in maintaining difference; connecting masculine and 'political' identity.

At a time when the identity and position of working-class young men is uncertain, violence is a complex issue. Youth unemployment is rapidly increasing and young men 'left clinging to unattainable and unrealistic masculine aspirations are alienated from a world that has changed rapidly in the last 35 years' (Harland et al., 2005: 2). Alongside the perceived threat to community stability 'violence is often an expression of young men's hopelessness, frustration, isolation, boredom and energy' (YouthAction, 2001: 13). The violence of rioting or sectarian attacks also reflects a tradition of conflict embodying structural and perceived inequalities between opposing cultural groups. While superficially similar to US gangs, these Northern Ireland groups have not been highly structured or organised. Our research suggests that recent 'recruitment' of children and young people has been by a few adult men locally labelled 'armchair paramilitaries'.

Conclusion

Within academic literature and popular discourses about youth gangs, the orthodoxy was set by the early twentieth-century Chicago studies briefly discussed in the introduction to this chapter. Haphazard urban growth, 'zones of transition' and social disorganisation were represented as the backdrop to predatory, spontaneous and elemental gangs lacking in purpose and deficient in organisation. They occupied their territories, named their identities and created their meanings as alternatives to a mainstream world of family, school and work from which they were excluded. Further perspectives on subcultures oscillated between 'blocked goals', 'status frustration' and 'differential association' experienced by working-class youth as determinants of their 'delinquency' or 'deviance'. What emerged within some of the earlier research was a more structural connection between the frustration and powerlessness experienced by young people, particularly young men, in capitalist societies and their reactions and resistances to structural inequalities. These were purposeful responses, based on their negotiation of daily life and the lived reality of marginalisation and exclusion originating in experiences of poverty, racism and sexism.

Working-class communities were, and continue to be, portrayed as inhabited by a 'rabble' classified and categorised as inherently pathological, their families 'dysfunctional'. Yet they are neighbourhoods of collaboration, generosity and survival occupied by people of dignity whose space and place is determined and managed by external forces rooted in long-term economic disadvantage, institutionalised through under-investment and discriminatory practices of state agencies and demonised in popular discourse. This is not to argue that structural conditions over-determine personal volition and social capacity, but they are powerful external forces contextualising action and shaping opportunities.

Our research demonstrates that, for young people, space and identity are imbued with personal and collective meaning not reducible to simplistic portrayals of 'youth gangs'. It reflects a youth studies literature that reveals the complexity of historical meanings attributed to place and identity within communities with strong, socially reproduced cultural traditions. Children's and young people's understanding of place and the meanings attached to specific locations, while not always fully articulated, reinforce affinities. Their demarcation of local space and its negotiation is not concerned only with remaining safe or 'claiming' and 'defending' a space against others. It also involves 'fitting in', belonging and personal identity, derived in the historical and political meaning of local space inherited by children and young people.

While 'territorial' divisions within Northern Ireland's working-class communities are not dissimilar to those in UK working-class, white communities (Goldson, 2003; MacDonald and Marsh, 2005; McAlister, 2007; Kintrea et al., 2008 and this volume), our study emphasises the importance of understanding the particular circumstances in which young people ascribe meaning to place and identity. They define particular places as 'their areas', where they invest significant time and energy. They consistently defend their areas against outside, negative criticism. For young men in particular this often involves violence against 'other communities' and the police. Lifting expressions of identity and use of violence from their historical and contemporary contexts, and misrepresenting them as 'a problem of gangs', produces an analysis 'flawed on empirical, theoretical and methodological grounds' (Hallsworth and Young, 2008: 177).

The children, young people and community representatives in our study present unequivocal evidence that youth groups are coherent and consistent. They base their collective understanding of place, space and identity on a shared interpretation of their historical inheritance and contemporary circumstances. Their visible presence on the streets and their confrontations with paramilitaries, vigilantes or the police are part of their negotiation of space and identity in conditions of limited opportunities, particularly relating to schooling and work. In the context of the 'new' Northern Ireland, working-class children and young people are living through a complex process of transition. They experience the personal dynamics of communities shifting from conflict to peace and the consequent inter-generational tensions, including the long-term impact of trauma. Simultaneously, the promise of new opportunities and fulfilment is denied and frustrated by ongoing structural poverty and social exclusion. Our analysis affirms that the 'view from below' is central to understanding and interpreting how the lived realities of children and young people are specific to time and place. It is also relevant to the broader debate about contextual analysis of the formation of social groups. Rather than accepting dubious claims about 'gang culture' as a powerful social force binding together disaffected children and young people, it is important to place local tensions concerning the occupation and defence of space within the dynamics of structural inequalities, state regulation and societal transition.

Acknowledgements

Sincere thanks to all the children, young people and community representatives who gave their time generously to this project. We acknowledge the research partnership with Save the Children (NI), especially former Director Sheri Chamberlain, whose work has been inspirational, and The Prince's Trust (NI). We are grateful to our co-workers in the Childhood, Transition and Social Justice Initiative at Queen's University Belfast and to Rob MacDonald for their contributions to our analysis. Finally, thanks to Barry Goldson.

Notes

1   Focus group references give the age range of participants. Quotes reflect the group's agreement unless otherwise stated.
2   'Blow-in' is a term used to describe people who have moved into an area.

References

Boal, F.W. (2002) 'Belfast: Walls Within', *Political Geography*, 21: 687–94.
Connolly, P. and Neill, J. (2001) 'Constructions of Locality and Gender and Their Impact on Educational Aspirations of Working Class Children', *International Studies in Sociology of Education*, 11(2): 107–29.
Connolly, P. and Healy, J. (2004) *Children and the Conflict in Northern Ireland: The Experiences and Perspectives of 3–11 Year Olds*. Belfast: Office of the First Minister and Deputy First Minister.
DENI (Department of Education Northern Ireland) (2008) *Enrolments at Schools and in Funded Pre-school Education in Northern Ireland 2007–08*. Belfast: DENI, 26 February.
Forrest, R. and Kearns, A. (2001) 'Social Cohesion, Social Capital and the Neighbourhood', *Urban Studies*, 38(12): 2125–43.
Goldson, B. (2003) 'Youth Perspectives', in R. Munck (ed.) *Reinventing the City? Liverpool in Comparative Perspective*. Liverpool: Liverpool University Press.
Hagedorn, J.M. (2007) 'Gangs, Institutions, Race, and Space: The Chicago School Revisited', in J.M. Hagedorn (ed.) *Gangs in the Global City: Alternatives to Traditional Criminology*. Chicago: University of Illinois Press, pp.13–33.

Hall, T., Coffey, A. and Williamson, H. (1999) 'Self, Space and Identity: Youth Identities and Citizenship', *British Journal of Sociology of Education*, 20(4): 501–13.

Hallsworth, S. (2006) 'Racial Targeting and Social Control: Looking Behind the Police', *Critical Criminology*,14: 293–311.

Hallsworth, S. and Young, T. (2008) 'Gang Talk and Gang Talkers: A Critique', *Crime, Media, Culture*, 4(2): 175–95.

Hansson, U. (2005) *Troubled Youth? Young People, Violence and Disorder in Northern Ireland*. Belfast: Institute for Conflict Research.

Harland, K., Beattie, K. and McCready, S. (2005) *Young Men and the Squeeze of Masculinity: The Inaugural Paper for the Centre for Young Men's Studies*. Jordanstown: University of Ulster/ YouthAction Northern Ireland.

Henderson, S. (2007) 'Neighbourhood', in M. Robb (ed.) *Youth in Context: Framework, Setting and Encounters*. London: Sage/Open University Press, pp. 123–54.

Hillyard, P., Rolston, B. and Tomlinson, M. (2005) *Poverty and Conflict in Ireland: An International Perspective*. Dublin: Institute of Public Administration/Combat Poverty Agency.

Kintrea, K., Bannister, J., Pickering, J., Reid, M. and Suzuki, N. (2008) *Young People and Territoriality in British Cities*. York: JRF.

Kuusisto, A. (2001) 'Territory, Symbolism and the Challenge', *Peace Review*, 13(1): 59–66.

Leonard, M. (2004) *Children in Interface Areas: Reflections from North Belfast*. Belfast: Save the Children.

—— (2007) 'Trapped in Space? Children's Accounts of Risky Environments', *Children and Society*, 21(6): 431–45.

MacDonald, R. and Marsh, J. (2005) *Disconnected Youth? Growing Up in Britain's Poor Neighbourhoods*. Houndsmills: Palgrave.

MacDonald, R. and Shildrick, T. (2007) 'Street Corner Society: Leisure Careers, Youth (Sub)culture and Social Exclusion', *Leisure Studies*, 26(3): 339–55.

Magadi, M. and Middleton, S. (2007) *Measuring Severe Child Poverty in the UK*. London: Save the Children.

McAlister, S. (2007) 'An Ethnographic Investigation of "Underclass Youth": A Case Study of Blossom Hill, Teesside'. Unpublished PhD Thesis, University of Teesside.

McAlister, S., Scraton, P. and Haydon, D. (2009) *Childhood in Transition: Experiencing Marginalisation and Conflict in Northern Ireland*. Belfast: Queen's University/Save the Children/Prince's Trust.

McGrellis, S. (2004) *Pushing the Boundaries in Northern Ireland: Young People, Violence and Sectarianism*. London: London South Bank University.

McKittrick, D., Kelters, S., Feeney, B. and Thornton, C. (1999) *Lost Lives: The Stories of the Men, Women and Children Who Died as a Result of the Northern Ireland Troubles*. Edinburgh: Mainstream Publishing.

Monteith, M., Lloyd. K. and McKee, P. (2008) *Persistent Child Poverty in Northern Ireland: Key Findings*. Belfast: Save the Children.

NIHE (Northern Ireland Housing Executive) (2006) 'Mixed Housing Scheme is Launched'. Retrieved 30 October 2006 (www.nihe.gov.uk/index/about-us-home/media_centre/news-2.htm?newsid = 6630).

Park, R.E. (1963) 'Editor's Preface', in F.M. Thrasher, *The Gang*. Chicago: University of Chicago Press, pp. vii–x.

Patrick, J. (1973) *A Glasgow Gang Observed*. London: Eyre Methuen.

PSNI (2009) *Statistics Relating to the Security Situation 1st April 2008–31st March 2009*. Belfast: PSNI Central Statistics Branch.

—— (2010) *Statistics Relating to the Security Situation 1st April 2009–31st January 2010*. Belfast: PSNI Central Statistics Branch.

Ralphs, R., Medina, J. and Aldridge, J. (2009) 'Who Needs Enemies with Friends Like These? The Importance of Place for Young People Living in Known Gang Areas', *Journal of Youth Studies*, 12(5): 483–500.

Roche, R. (2008) *Sectarianism and Segregation in Urban Northern Ireland: Northern Irish Youth Post-Agreement. A Report on the Facts, Fears and Feelings Project*. Belfast: Queen's University.

Shirlow, P. (2003) 'Ethno-sectarianism and the Reproduction of Fear in Belfast', *Capital and Class*, 80: 77–93.

Smith, J. (1986) *Crime, Space and Society*. Cambridge: Cambridge University Press.

Thrasher, F.M. (1927/1963) *The Gang*. Chicago: University of Chicago Press.

Wacquant, L. (2007) 'Three Pernicious Premises in the Study of the American Ghetto', in J.M. Hagedorn (ed.) *Gangs in the Global City: Alternatives to Traditional Criminology*. Chicago: University of Illinois Press, pp. 34–53.

YouthAction (2001) *Work with Young Men in Northern Ireland: Everyday Life – Young Men and Violence Project*. Belfast: YouthAction.

YouthNet (1999) *Young Men and Violence Thematic Initiative: Summary*. Belfast: YouthNet.

Chapter 6

Beyond dichotomy

Towards an explanation of young women's involvement in violent street gangs

Susan A. Batchelor

Introduction

Both popular and academic accounts of gangs in the UK have tended to distinguish between two types of girls and young women who become gang-associated: first, those who regard themselves as 'one of the lads' and fight to defend themselves and, second, those who assume a more ancillary role as girlfriends of male gang members. In each account gang-associated girls are portrayed in highly gendered ways, whereby the focus centres on their deviation from traditional norms of femininity or, alternatively, their sexual exploitation by males within the gang (Batchelor, 2009). Yet in spite of these typologies, little is actually known about how British girls and young women view gang involvement, since most UK gang research has focused on boys and young men. What is more – being primarily located in end-of-award reports to research funders – the data on girls that do exist lack a clear theoretical foundation in relation to gender. Whilst this emerging empirical work is useful in generating much needed *descriptions* of female gang involvement, it is far less effective at *explaining* such involvement. Building on the insights of feminist work on gangs in the United States and drawing upon interview data from research with young women in Scotland, this chapter examines the ways in which gender inequality shapes female gang involvement and participation in violence. The findings suggest that whilst dichotomous 'tomboy'/'sex object' characterisations are present in young women's accounts, these categories are inadequate for capturing the complexities of their gender identities.

Feminist research on girls, guys and gangs in the US

The literature on gangs has long been dominated by a focus on male gangs and male gang members. Historically, the field of criminology has been a masculinist enterprise, primarily interested in understanding the more dramatic or 'exciting' offending of boys and young men (Millman, 1975). Traditional gang research trivialised or ignored female participation, discussing girls and young women 'solely in terms of their . . . relations to male gang members' (Campbell, 1984/

1991: 166). Classic US studies emphasised the auxiliary or peripheral nature of girls' gang involvement, resulting in an almost exclusive focus on their sexuality and sexual activity with male gang members. Frederic Thrasher's (1927) seminal survey of 1,313 gangs in Chicago, for example, included only a few pages about girls' gang involvement. The minimal attention that Thrasher did actually afford to girls included: (i) the maladjusted 'tomboy', who 'is ill at ease with those of her own sex' and, therefore, seeks the company and approval of boys and young men (ibid. 158); and (ii) the older adolescent 'sweetheart', who 'may be taken under [the gang's] protection or in other cases may actually become [a member] of the gang in their sexual capacity' (ibid. 155). Irving Spergel (1964) presented a similar picture, drawing on his research with male gang members in New York to depict women's utility as carriers of weapons and as decoys or spies for the purposes of infiltrating rival gangs. Girls and young women, Spergel's respondents claimed, were the manipulators and instigators of group fighting amongst boys and young men: they were 'the carrier of tales – the magnifier, the distorter, and fabricator of derogatory remarks which served to instigate conflict amongst the various clubs' (ibid. 88–9).

In the US, these sexist and stereotypical images were robustly challenged by second-wave feminist researchers who engaged directly with female gang members in order to provide a more nuanced ethnographic portrayal of the experiences of girls in gangs. The landmark study was Anne Campbell's (1984/1991) *The Girls in the Gang*, which explored the lives of African-American and Latina gang members in New York. In contrast to earlier depictions of female gang members as completely subservient to male gang members, Campbell's research revealed that female gang involvement was neither wholly dependent upon – nor focused solely around satisfying – males. One of Campbell's key claims was that gang membership could be liberating for girls and young women because it provided them with otherwise unavailable opportunities for solidarity and self-actualisation. Developing a reputation as a good fighter, for example, afforded young women protection (for themselves and their female friends) and gave them a sense of self-respect and status. Most of the young women grew up in families characterised by male domination – particularly physical domination – and as a result consciously rejected a subordinate view of female life. According to Campbell (1987/1999: 116), their association with the gang was 'a public proclamation' of their refusal to martyr themselves and tolerate male abuse: 'Even as they extolled the importance of being a good mother, the girls opposed a view of themselves as being at the mercy of men. They took pride in their autonomy and rejected any suggestion that they could be duped or conned by males' (ibid. 112).

The view that gang involvement could be 'liberating' for lower-class girls and young women was problematised by later feminist works, which pointed to the persistent and pervasive influence of patriarchy in such girls' lives. For example, Joan Moore's (1991) research with Mexican-American former gang members in Los Angeles discovered that, despite protestations to the contrary from female gang members, sexist attitudes were common among male gang members. Moore also uncovered evidence of the sexual exploitation of females by males within the gang, some of which was actively supported by female gang members. The continuing salience of gender inequality and oppression was also highlighted in the work of Karen Joe and Meda Chesney-Lind (1995: 428), who explained girls' participation in gangs as 'a consequence of and a response to the abuse, both physical and sexual, that characterises their lives at home'. Three-quarters of the girls interviewed as part of their Hawaiian study reported physical abuse in their families; 62 per cent stated that they had been sexually abused. The gang was thought to help young women survive such circumstances by providing a place to escape to, as well as the means to fight back against violence and abuse: 'For girls, fighting and violence is part of their life in the gang – but not something they necessary seek out. Instead, protection from neighbourhood and family violence is a major theme in girls' interviews' (ibid. 425). As one young woman explained, 'You gotta be part of the gang or else you're the one who's gonna get beat up' (ibid. 425). Statements such as this led Joe and Chesney-Lind to conclude that: 'The violations of traditional norms of femininity, particularly the "unacceptable" displays of toughness and independence, are hardly a reflection of their liberation from patriarchal controls' (ibid. 427), but rather represent young women's last-ditch attempts to cope with physical and sexual victimisation within their families and the wider community.

More recently, US researchers have sought to provide a more nuanced account of girls' experiences in gangs by demonstrating both the benefits and the drawbacks of membership (cf. Joe-Laidler and Hunt, 2001; Miller, 2001; Miller and Decker, 2001; Nurge, 2003; Schalet et al., 2003). Perhaps the best illustration of such work can be found in Jody Miller's (2001) analysis of African-American female gang involvement in Columbus and St Louis. Comparing gang versus non-gang girls, Miller found that gang members were significantly more likely to have witnessed physical violence between adults in their homes and to have been abused by family members. In addition, they were more likely to report familial drug use. Most significantly, however, they were much more likely to have experienced multiple family problems – with 60 per cent (vs. 24 per cent of non-gang girls) describing three or more of the following problems: being the victim of abuse; witnessing physical violence between adults; alcohol abuse within the family; familial drug abuse and/or the incarceration of a family member. As a result, and following the findings of Moore (1991) and Joe and Chesney-Lind (1995), Miller concluded that many girls joined gangs as a means of escaping chaotic family environments and for protection from abuse. Thus, it was somewhat paradoxical that gang involvement itself made them vulnerable to further victimisation, particularly sexual victimisation from fellow (male) gang members. Gang girls tolerated this higher degree of (predictable) risk by known gang members, Miller claimed, in implicit exchange for protection from (unpredictable) sexual risk from unknown individuals.

Miller's key contribution to the literature on girls and gangs (and female offenders more broadly) lay in her discussion of female gang members' contradictory attitudes toward gender equality (ibid. 197). The young women in her study placed great importance on seeing themselves as equal partners with young men in gangs, yet simultaneously colluded with gang males to uphold a distinct gender hierarchy that included: male leadership; a double standard with regard to sexual activities; the sexual exploitation of some girls and most girls' exclusion from serious gang crime. In other words, she demonstrated that gang girls were not merely the passive victims of gender oppression but rather actively participated in its perpetuation through the labelling of other young women as 'hoodrats' and 'hos'. By designating girls who were sexed-in to the gang as somehow 'deserving' of male violence and mistreatment, Miller's respondents positioned themselves as 'different from' and 'better than' other girls. In doing so, they struck a 'patriarchal bargain' (Kandiyoti, 1988) where the primary goal was to increase their status among male gang members and be accepted as 'one of the guys'. Of course, their participation in, and support of, an oppressive gender structure ultimately served to maintain their inequality, assuring that their power and options remained less than those open to male gang members.

Emerging empirical accounts of girls, groups and gangs in the UK

Compared to the US, the UK literature on girls and gangs is much less well developed. This is due in large part to a long-standing rejection of the 'gang paradigm' by British researchers and associated difficulties in defining what exactly constitutes a 'gang' (Aldridge et al., 2008). Early attempts to apply North American gang theory failed to find evidence of structured street gangs in the UK (Scott, 1956; Downes, 1966; Parker, 1974), leading to a shift in focus, from a concern with delinquent *gangs* towards the study of youth *subcultures* (where offending was one of a number of areas of investigation) (Hall and Jefferson, 1976; Muncie, 2009). As Hallsworth and Young (2008: 177) have observed, British resistance towards the gang paradigm has meant 'data on gangs have not been routinely collected or disseminated as they are in the USA . . . In other words, in the UK there is no sound evidential base to prove the case [for the proliferation of violent street gangs] one way or the other'. Recent research is expanding our knowledge about UK gangs, but the majority of studies emphasise gangs as a male phenomenon with little or no attention paid to girls or young women. Perhaps the two most high-profile studies of recent years are Judith Aldridge's and Juanjo Medina's (2007; this volume) account of youth gangs in an English city and John Pitts' (2007; this volume) study of armed gangs in the Waltham Forest area of London. Other qualitative studies include Kintrea et al.'s (2008; this volume) study of young people and territoriality in Bradford, Bristol, Glasgow, Peterborough, Sunderland and Tower Hamlets and Young et al.'s (2007; this volume) interviews with young people involved in group offending in five towns and cities in England and Wales. As will become apparent, only the latter account includes any detailed consideration of the views and experiences of girls and young women, but it remains theoretically undeveloped and, therefore, fails to provide the depth of understanding and level of explanation evident in the US literature.

In their end-of-award report for the Economic and Social Research Council, Aldridge and Medina (2007) devote just one paragraph to a discussion of gender. In it, they highlight the difficulties associated with identifying and accessing gang-involved girls: 'Our ethnographic data . . . indicate that females are *seen* as playing a secondary role in most of the gangs we had access to. In one of the gangs . . . we gathered reports of a greater involvement but were unsuccessful in talking to female members' (ibid. 7, emphasis added). A subsequent journal article – focusing upon the importance of place for young people living in known gang areas (Ralphs et al., 2009) – makes no reference to girls, women or gender. Keith Kintrea and colleagues (2008) dedicate two paragraphs to girls and young women in their Joseph Rowntree Foundation report, but all of the quotations used to back up the claims made are drawn from interviews with (male) adult practitioners, thus perpetuating the stereotype of girls as auxiliary members:

> Most participants who were reported to be involved in territoriality were boys or young men . . . Girls and young women took a more minor part; they were less often involved in gang conflict and they were less constrained by territoriality in their personal dealings, and it was believed that the impact on their life chances was much less than for boys . . . A typical comment about girls' role was: 'The girls play a background role to the gang. They are there, and they are there for their boys but they are not as territorial as the boys are. They are proud of their areas and they are proud of where they come from and they stick by their lads, but they are not as visible . . . for the girls it's part of hanging out with the lads'.
>
> (Kintrea et al., 2008: 25)

In line with the classic US studies discussed above, the report also portrays girls as relegated to gender-specific crimes, claiming that girls 'play an important role in encouraging gang activity' through 'wanting to have a boyfriend who is the biggest, baddest guy in their scheme' and '[making] boys in their area jealous by deliberately cultivating friendships with guys from other areas' (ibid. 25). This is a view reiterated by the male gang members and adult practitioners interviewed by Pitts (2007), who allots one paragraph of his report to a discussion of gender. Girls, his interviewees claim, 'play an ancillary role, sometimes carrying or hiding guns or drugs for the boys' (ibid. 40). They are apparently 'attracted to the "glamour" and "celebrity" of gang members' but often find themselves being sexually exploited, sometimes in exchange for drugs:

> The relationship [between gang members and their girlfriends] tends to be abusive; one of dominance and submission. Some senior gang members pass their girlfriends around to lower ranking members and sometimes to the whole group at the same time. Unreported rape by gang members, as a form of

reprisal or just because they can, is said to occur fairly frequently and reports to the police are rare.

(Pitts, 2007: 40)

'There are other girls,' Pitts claims, who 'do not perform the same sexual role as the "girlfriends" of gang members'. They 'regard themselves as "soldiers" and concentrate on violent street crime' (ibid. 40).

To date, the only published UK study to include a detailed consideration of the views and experiences of girls and young women is the work of Tara Young and colleagues (2007; this volume), commissioned by the Youth Justice Board in England and Wales. Unlike the other UK research referenced above – which portrays girls and young women in terms of their status as 'girlfriends' – Young et al.'s female interviewees reported that the mixed-sex groups they belonged to were composed of peers whose principal relation to each other was friendship. All denied that their group was a 'gang'. Sometimes the young women went out with older group members, some of whom were abusive, but this was said to be uncommon. Unlike in the US literature, the young women did not 'join' the group as a matter of ritual (the group emerged from friendships forged at schools, in the public care system, or in the estates where they lived) and there was no evidence to suggest that they were subject to initiation rites (such as being 'jumped in' or 'sexed in'). What's more, far from playing a minor role in group violence, the female interviewees claimed that young women 'were more likely to pursue thrills, engage in fights and cause trouble than their male counterparts' (ibid. 151) and were equally capable of instrumental violence, for example street robbery to fund a drug habit.

Young et al.'s study is methodologically important because it demonstrates that when researchers engage directly with girls and young women, a different picture emerges of their 'gang' involvement. Empirically, their findings challenge the claims made by Pitts (2007) and Kintrea et al. (2008) through demonstrating the active and assertive role that young women can play within their peer networks. Theoretically, however, their analysis remains at the level of description, with minimal discursive commentary or analytical interpretation. Whilst this ordered, descriptive detail is both legitimate and effectively pre-determined given its primary purposes and the format of its presentation – a research report com-missioned by the Youth Justice Board to inform the development of policy – it means that the authors are unable to explain *why* girls' gang involvement takes the forms that it does and, therefore, it leaves their findings open to interpretation by those who claim to detect the emergence of a 'new breed' of 'girl gangsters' who are 'just as bad as the boys' (Chesney-Lind and Irwin, 2008).

As the US literature reviewed above makes clear, gender inequality – not equality – is central to an understanding of the causes and consequences of girls' gang involvement. This is not to imply that research and theory on gangs should concentrate solely on gender difference but rather the goal should be to examine and explain convergence and divergence within, between and across gender

(Messerschmidt, 2005; Miller and Mullins, 2006). The remainder of this chapter attempts to move beyond over-simplified stereotypes of dichotomous difference, therefore – by drawing upon empirical research undertaken in Scotland – in an attempt to develop a more theoretically informed analysis of the ways in which gender shapes young women's participation in gangs and violence.

Exploring young women's involvement in violent street gangs in Scotland

The data presented here derive from in-depth oral-history interviews with 21 young women sentenced to custody for violent offending. The interviews were conducted as part of a doctoral thesis that examined the social meanings attached to violence committed by young women (Batchelor, 2007a). The key question addressed was: how do young women construct and recount subjectively meaningful explanations of their involvement in violent offending? In order to explore this question, fieldwork was undertaken in Cornton Vale prison, which at that time was used to detain nearly all of the young female prisoners in Scotland. All of the interviewees were single and all were white. Ages ranged from 16 to 24 years.

The findings suggested a pattern of offending that began with economic marginalisation, family problems and experiences of abuse. Approximately half of the young women lived with their parents prior to custody, all of whom rented properties from the local authority; a quarter resided in hostels, supported accommodation or were formerly homeless. Only one young woman was employed prior to custody but even she was reliant on benefits because she worked part-time. The only respondent who did not claim benefits was still at school and, therefore, financially supported by her mother. More than half of the young women had experienced significant family disruption as a result of parental separation, divorce and/or changes to their main caregiver. Three-quarters reported previous social work involvement and involvement in the Children's Hearing System and more than half had been 'looked after' by the local authority. Two-fifths had been sexually abused (usually by maternal grandfathers and paternal uncles), two-fifths had been victimised physically (usually by their parents) and two-fifths described witnessing regular incidents of 'serious' domestic violence, usually directed toward their mothers by their fathers (or another 'father figure').

Seventeen of the young women reported participation in delinquent peer groups consistent with the Eurogang definition of a 'gang', namely: 'any durable, street-oriented youth group whose identity includes involvement in illegal activity' (Weerman et al., 2009: 20). On the weekends these groups could be fairly large, consisting of 20 to 30 boys, girls and young adults aged between 11 and 28 years. During the week, however, the groups tended to be smaller – comprising six or seven core young people – and were much more male dominated. Interviewees conceptualised these groups differently, according to the region in which they lived. For example, interviewees from Glasgow and the West of Scotland (including Lanarkshire, Dunbartonshire and Inverclyde) commonly referred to 'gangs' engaged in organised fighting against groups from different areas. Young women from the East of Scotland (Perth, Dundee and Aberdeen), however, referred to the people they 'hung about' with in terms of a 'team' or 'group' not a 'gang'. The latter reported involvement in organised group fights less frequently than the former, but young women from across the complete sample described involvement in group offending, particularly underage drinking, drug taking and territorial violence, but also robbery, domestic burglary and car theft. The discussion that follows focuses on the participants' roles within these groups and their subsequent experiences of peer violence. As will become apparent, the findings suggest that whilst dichotomous 'tomboy'/'sex object' characterisations are present in young women's accounts, these categories fail to capture and/or explain the variation in their relationships to 'gangs'.

'Jist wan o' the troops'? Gender relations in street-orientated youth groups

The young women who reported involvement in delinquent youth groups generally started 'hanging around' on the street at age 13 or 14. Nineteen-year-old Joanne's experience was fairly typical:

> I started drinkin' when I was 13 or some'hin. Like at nights after school, hanging round. That was just like bottles o' cider, 'hings like that, ken, a bottle o' Buckfast. Then it was like I was runnin' aboot wi' ma pals all during the day and drinkin' wi' these aulder folk. And they're drinkin' bottles o' vodka and I would drink it as well. And that's when I started offending real bad. Like gettin' intae fights and goin' intae shops and goin' behind the counters and just lifting bottles o' drinks and sayin' cheers and just walkin' oot and just pure crazy 'hings [. . .] I just thought it was cool tae be hangin' aboot wi' all the big boys.

The research found no evidence of 'initiation ceremonies', but rather the young women characterised their groups as friendship- and/or family-based. As Jay, a 23-year-old young woman explained, 'We kent each other fae school. Just from where we stayed and through other people that we hung aboot wi'. We just all ended up thegither.' Likewise, Angela, a 24-year-old woman said, 'It was people I grew up wi'. Roond oor bit everybody just kent everybody, ken what I mean? Ma cousin, he stayed roond the corner and ma other cousin lived roond the other corner. A' oor family's there.'

The physical proximity of kith and kin often led to a strong sense of neighbourhood allegiance and affiliation. As the following dialogue with Stephanie – an 18-year-old from Dundee – illustrates, many of the young women understood their social worlds in terms of 'territories' and 'boundaries' and categorised other young people in terms of where they were from.

SB: 'Tell me what it's like in Hilltown.'
Stephanie: 'A rough area, a wild place. Just full o' young boys and lassies and that, just rogues.'
SB: 'What do you mean "rogues"?'
Stephanie: 'Going aboot spray painting, putting windaes in, just daein every'hing, eh? Fighting wi' people, battering wi' hammers, every'hing. People that comes in the scheme, they're no welcome, and they just get slung back oot the scheme. They're no welcome.'
SB: 'Do you mean new people moving in? Like, families?'
Stephanie: 'Mmm hmm. And young folk, they're no welcome in. Just dinnae like them. They're fae a different scheme an' they come into our scheme. We dinnae want them in our scheme, so they get put back out our scheme.'

During the interviews the young women drew upon the notion of territorial affinity and identity as a means of differentiating their own peer networks from 'regular' groups of friends. Members of the former, it was claimed, 'stuck up for' each other and their area, even if it meant being physically hurt. Very few participants reported any form of hierarchy or formal group structure. Instead, they said that 'We're all thegither, all a team . . . Everybody [i.e. anybody] could be the leader at whatever stage . . . It's whoever starts the fight, basically.' Zoë, a 20-year-old young woman from a peripheral housing scheme in Glasgow, expressed this territorial affiliation and group solidarity as follows:

> I come fae Strathfield, the roughest part you could come fae. It's where all the junkies and a' the alchies and all that kind o' live. [. . .] If you come fae a scheme, you don't forget your roots. Your're wan o' the troops, sort o' 'hing. They're always behind you. If somebody fucks wi' them then you've got tae do some'hin' aboot it.

Despite these protestations of sameness and solidarity, the young women's peer groups were male-dominated associations that upheld traditional gender hierarchies privileging maleness/masculinity and devaluing femaleness/femininity. In order to be respected and accepted as 'wan o' the troops', young women often had to prove themselves through participation in violence and other stereotypically masculine criminal pursuits. Eighteen-year-old Karen, for example, had status in her group because of her reputation as 'the only female housebreaker in Midvale' and her ability to 'hold [her] own' with the boys when it came to fighting:

> Some of the best fun I have had is being with my [male] friends doing what they do, ken? Like, see on a school night, when a' the other lassies used tae get thegither, we used to get thegither at the park, ken, and get drunk. There was six of us and we used to have wrestling competitions. Like we would take it in turns and whoever wasn't wrestling was drinking, eh? It started off quite

mild but by the end of the night we would have black eyes and we would basically be battered to death. And not one of them made an allowance for me being a female, not one of them.

Karen said she saw herself as 'one of the guys, always the tomboy' and valued what she and her peers considered to be traditionally masculine traits, including bravery, physical strength, toughness, risk-taking and emotional stoicism. She identified more with boys, she said, because they were less emotional and less 'bitchy' than girls: 'I dae [don't] like the company of lassies [. . .] They just come oot wi' all this psycho crap [. . .] they're all into meanings and stuff. Me and ma [male] friends think it is a lot of bullshit.'

Being accepted as 'one of the guys', then, involved not behaving 'like a girl'. This in turn meant not showing any signs of weakness (for example, crying or sulking) and – most importantly – not 'sleeping around'. This latter point is illustrated in the following extract from an interview with Zoë, who explained that she was often party to conversations in which her male friends disparaged other young women sexually – both those they had slept with and those they wanted to sleep with – and that this was something that she herself was careful to avoid, in order to be accepted by the group:

SB: 'Why are you accepted by the lads in a way that, like, other girls that you know aren't?'

Zoë: 'I don't sleep aboot. I don't put masel' aboot. [My male pals] a' dae it but I don't. They're like that, "I'm goin' to shag her the night." They don't think like that aboot me. I'd kill them if they thought aboot me like that! [. . .] I don't like sleepin' aboot. I'm quite prudish fer ma age. I think it's 'cause I hang aboot wi' boys and I hear them talkin' aboot birds: "Aw naw, you want tae hae seen her by the way. D'ye know what she was daein last night?"'

Comments such as these demonstrate that, despite significant changes in the social landscape, the sexual double standard remains relatively stable in street-orientated youth groups. Fear of being labelled a 'slag' or 'slut' operated as a potent force that served to contain and control the young women's sexual behaviour and self-presentation. As Sue Lees' research (1997) confirms, to speak of a woman's reputation still invokes her sexual experiences. Within the sample, young women were careful to make a distinction between having a 'name' for violence (which, as we shall see, was regarded as an important source of self-esteem) and being known for sexual promiscuity (regarded as damaging to self-esteem). Given the varying connotations and consequences of these inevitably gendered reputations, it was somewhat unsurprising to find that that while most of the young women were keen to portray themselves as 'wan of the troops' and were able to identify other girls in their group who were 'used' for sex, none admitted that they themselves had been taken advantage of in this way.

In light of the findings presented in the North American literature, the levels of peer-based physical and sexual victimisation reported in the current study were surprisingly low. None of the young women identified themselves as a victim of physical or sexual violence from their male friends, although one young woman did disclose that she had been raped by an ex-boyfriend (who was not a member of her friendship group) and a number of the older respondents described violent male partners (whom they had generally met outwith the group). Of course, reporting that young women didn't identify themselves as *victims* of peer violence is not to say that they didn't *experience* violence at the hands of their peers. As the section that follows demonstrates, the young women were actively involved in violence, both group fights and interpersonal fights. Fighting between 'friends', however, wasn't commonly defined as 'violent', no matter how physically damaging. Instead, such incidents were conceptualised as 'wee stupid fights', 'just a bit o' fun' or 'normal teenage stuff'. This playing down of peer violence can partly be explained by the high levels of 'serious' violence young women were exposed to within their homes and their wider communities. Another possible explanation is participants' adherence to subcultural norms of honour and respect which, as the section below demonstrates, require projecting an image of invincibility and invulnerability.

Different for girls? The motives and rewards of violence

When questioned about the motivations behind violence, three key themes emerged: excitement, status and protection. In relation to the former, respondents claimed to engage in violence as a means to counteract boredom and as a source of exhilaration, pleasure and power (Batchelor, 2007b). As 22-year-old Annie put it, 'I wasnae wanting to hurt anybody, it was just *boredom*'. Likewise, Kelly, a 21-year-old convicted for robbery and assault, said 'It was fun . . . jist some'hin tae break up the day. It gied us something to pass the time.' She gave the following example:

> When we was drinkin' we used to go to the Arch – that's a big bit in ma bit – jist tae cause a fight wi' somebody, lassies that never even done nothing to us, jist for the sake ay it. One night it was me and ma pals, and there was this lassie sittin' on the grass, an' they were all like pushin' me an' sayin' like, 'Go on, go on', makin' oot she'd took the cunt oot me an' all that when she hudnae. So, jist for the sake ay it, I went an' done it. Even though I knew it was wrong, I jist went up an' battered her for nae reason. Nothin'. Jist fer some'hin tae dae.

Stephanie expressed this quest for excitement more forcefully:

> When we were a' drinking at the weekend, we just used to go mental and every'hing. It was mad. We'd sit out, drink, go oot, look fer a fight, em,

any'hing that came in wer mind, we used tae go and dae. When I was 11 I
started daein all-nighters and walking aboot the streets at night. If I seen a man
come past and he was drunk, we used to go and batter 'im. Because we used
to get a rush oot it. We used to get a giggle, a buzz.

Many of the young women appeared to take pleasure from remembering and
describing their violent escapades and became visibly agitated when recounting
stories of fights between groups of young people from different areas. Such
violence was considered deeply meaningful; it served to maintain group solidarity,
reinforce kinship ties, affirm allegiances and enhance personal status within the
group.

Although the interviewees agreed that group fighting was a male-dominated
activity and that in general the young men in their group were 'mair gallus' or
'gemme' than the young women, females were still reported as playing an active
role. This is illustrated in the following two excerpts from interviews with Zoë and
Stephanie, both of whom fought alongside their male 'cousins' as members of
their local 'young teams'.

SB: 'Tell me about some of the other things you have been involved in.'
Zoë: 'Gang fights.'
SB: 'When you say "gang fights", what do you mean? Who between?'
Zoë: 'Wan end of Strathfield and the other end of Strathfield. Or Northwood
       against Strathfield, Churchill against Strathfield, Westport against
       Strathfield.'
SB: 'So it was between areas, different areas?'
Zoë: 'Aye, areas.'
SB: 'And would that involve boys and girls?'
Zoë: 'Mostly boys, but some lassies. The lassies used tae fight wi' each other, but
       I was in among the boys. [Laughs] I fight wi' boys. Lassies pull hair and all
       that and scratch. I *hate* any'hing like that. I stick the heid in them, a few rapid
       [motions punching] Aw naw! [Embarrassed] Heid them, kick, punch, stab,
       know what I mean? Hit them wi' something.'
SB: 'Are there any other ways in which you think boys and girls are different in
       the ways they use violence?'
Zoë: 'Boys get tore right in. [Laughs] They bite noses aff and a'thing, so they do!
       Well that's what some o' ma [male] pals dae, take chunks oot o' people's
       ears and all that. I don't dae 'hings like that.'

SB: 'Who did the Huntingtoon Huns used to fight with?'
Stephanie: 'Fairhill, Hillside, a' different schemes.'
SB: 'Can you give me an example of one time you had a fight with another
           scheme?'
Stephanie: 'I remember we were at the carnival, eh? And I walked oot the gates
           and a' the family and that was there and they were a' fighting, eh?

Next thing ma brother pulled an axe oot and starting hitting the boy over the heid wi' it and I was like that, trying to pull ma brother – 'cause I was getting feart a wee bit, I'll tell the truth, I was getting feart, eh? 'Cause I saw him an' he near killt the boy – an' the next minute a' the family, the rest o' them, just jumped up and started battering the boy wi' the hammers. It was mad. Scary.'

SB: 'Is it quite common for people to carry weapons?'
Stephanie: 'Mmm hmm.'
SB: 'Girls as well as boys?'
Stephanie: 'Naw, lassies don't carry weapons or that.'
SB: 'Why is that, that the boys do and the girls don't?'
Stephanie: 'Because boys are mair gemmer, I 'hink. I mean I'd go- I'd go wi' ma brothers and that. I'd be out fighting and that, eh? But the boys are just wilder.'
SB: 'So, what's the most serious thing . . .'
Stephanie: [Interrupts] 'The most serious thing is when I've thingied the boy wi' the hammer, at the carnival. I've done a few o' them, eh?'

Both of these extracts illustrate the young women's tendency to distinguish between both boys' and girls' use of violence, but also their own violence and that of *other* young women. So for example, whilst they claimed that young women *in general* were less likely to use weapons than were young men, more than half of the participants reported that they had themselves assaulted people using bottles, bricks, bats and, although less commonly, knives. Likewise, whereas the majority of the young women said that they themselves engaged in 'proper' – serious and rule-governed – violent behaviour, they thought that *in general* men were 'mair violent' and women were 'mair bitchy'. The notion of 'bitchiness' generally referred to verbal abuse, talking behind backs and so on. When used to describe physical violence, however, it signified the use of stereotypically female fighting techniques, such as scratching, slapping, hair pulling and biting. Most of the young women regarded such techniques with contempt. For these interviewees, status was gained by emulating male fighting techniques as closely as possible. Another group, however, claimed that women could be as violent as men, and dismissed 'bitch fighting' as a myth. In response to a question about the relative seriousness of male and female violence, for example 19-year-old Judy replied:

Judy: 'Lassies in here have done 'hings that guys in jail have done tae. It all depends on what situation you're in, but [women] can be [as violent as men].'
SB: 'A lot of folk, when they talk about lassies fighting, say that they just scratch with their nails and pull hair . . .'
Judy: [Interrupts] 'Naw! [Laughs] You're in the real world noo! You need tae open your eyes! [. . .] Young lassies are oot stabbing each other. Not just lassies stabbing lassies, lassies goin' ahead wi' guys. I've seen a guid few

of that. Like it use tae be you would 'hink guys would be the wan that would pick up the blades and fight with each other and use this and use that and lassies would be pulling each other's hair and all that. But it's no that, it's no that at all. Folk that 'hink that are walking aboot with their eyes shut or no living in schemes where it's all goin' on.'

What all of the young women interviewees agreed upon, however, was that men and women generally had different motivations for engaging in violence. In line with gender norms regarding feminine emotionality and masculine stoicism, they reported that: 'Women are more emotional and they put more emotion into their fights than guys do.' According to 21-year-old Lesley, the reason for this was that: 'Lassies are more protective than men are. They care.' In other words, women were considered to be motivated by emotional and/or relational concerns, for example, because they felt emotionally hurt or in order to protect a loved one, whereas men were considered more likely to 'just go oot there and hit anybody fer no reason'.

The majority of fights young women were involved in took place between individual young women and arose over issues of personal integrity or 'saving face'. Like male street youth (Bourgois, 2002), the young women placed a high premium on being treated with 'respect', defined as being treated right or granted the deference one deserves (Anderson, 1999). One way to acquire 'respect' was by developing a reputation as someone 'not to be messed wi'', who would 'step up' in response to any perceived slight or pejorative comment. Almost without exception, the young women expressed the importance of being seen to 'stand up for yourself', repeating the mantra: 'Better a sair face than a red face.' In other words, it is better to fight and lose than have the embarrassment of backing down. As Kelly remarked: 'You need to keep yer guard up all the time, or people will just take the cunt.' Likewise, Lesley explained: 'If everybody sees that you're just gonna take it, then everybody's gonna try and have a shot.' Adopting a tough, aggressive approach was regarded as an *unavoidable* aspect of life growing up in a 'rough' area and was something that many of the young women said that they were taught by their parents explicitly and, by example, from a very early age. As Joanne explained: 'I was brought up no tae let people boss me around or pick on me. Ken, if somebody hit me, then I've tae hit them back; if I disagree wi' some'hing, I've tae express the fact that I dinnae agree, 'hings like that.' Rather than being positively reinforced for demonstrating passivity, such young women were socialised to stand up to anyone who 'disrespects' them and to be able to 'hold their ain' (Batchelor, 2005; see also Ness, 2004).

In some ways, then, the motivations of the young women were similar to those of young men who engage in violence: they fought because it was fun, to gain respect and status, and to prevent (re)victimisation. That said, there were also some important differences. Fights over issues of public status, for example, were often highly gendered, involving assaults on the young women's personal integrity *as women*, in particular their sexual reputation, their ability to get a man and their competence as a mother. The role of girls and young women in enforcing the sexual double standard is well documented (Artz, 1998; Campbell, 1990; Miller, 2001). Within the current sample, respondents often disparaged other young women who were 'used' sexually by male peers for 'not respecting themselves' (that is, by not thwarting male advances). Against this backdrop, it is unsurprising that accusations of sexual promiscuity – or indeed 'frigidity' or 'perversion' (in the form of lesbianism) – were cited as common causes of fights between young women (see also Batchelor et al., 2001). As stated previously, a number of young women in the study identified themselves as 'one of the guys' as a means of resistance to the confines of emphasised femininity. This was an identity that had to be carefully managed, however, so as to avoid being labelled 'a dyke'. For example Zoë made repeated assertions throughout her interview that she was not 'a dyke' and could be 'girly' *when she wanted to be* (for example, wearing make-up when she went out to the dancing). In this way, whilst aligning herself against a (rather stereotyped) version of traditional femininity (huffy, bitchy, tarty, shallow), Zoë stressed that she was 'feminine' nonetheless. Like Karen, she explained that, generally speaking, she preferred 'daein the 'hings that boys dae' ('having a laugh', looking after herself, being able to dress casually and not worry about her appearance), but that there were still times when she enjoyed doing 'girly 'hings' too. This complex and seemingly contradictory relationship demonstrates how young women can 'do' femininity at the same time as they are attempting to resist it.

Discussion

The failure to fully incorporate gender into examinations of UK gangs, accompanied by an absence of critical theory, has led to analyses of young women's role that are partial, superficial and naïve. Much existing work relies on interviews with adult practitioners and male gang members, perpetuating unquestioned stereotypes about street-orientated young women. Gang-involved girls are depicted either as sexually exploited victims – a portrayal that confuses victimisation with victim identity and thereby denies young women's agency – or they are cast as mean and menacing 'bad girls'; active, autonomous agents, freed from patriarchal ties of family and gender. The findings reported here take issue with these overly simplistic and static categorisations and demonstrate a more complex understanding of the articulation and constitution of gender identity among young women involved in violent street 'gangs'. The central argument developed in the analysis of the interview data is that young women's accounts embody some persistent conflicts and tensions, including contradictory views about whether violence is essentially masculine or whether it can be used to express a particular form of 'bad girl femininity'.

Study participants grew up in family and peer contexts characterised by male domination (especially physical domination) and pervasive control over girls and women (particularly over their sexuality). These contexts severely limit young women's choices and options and contribute to rigid, stereotypical views about women and women's role. One way in which young women seek to resist negative gender stereotyping and thereby avoid feelings of vulnerability and powerlessness, is by taking up a subject position as 'one of the lads'. This involves adhering to subcultural norms of solidarity, solidity and the sexual double standard. By appropriating dominant masculine gender performances, young women gain some of the credibility and power associated with hegemonic masculinity. However, they also sustain gender boundaries, for example by distinguishing themselves from their male peers through affirmations that they are 'prudish' or 'proper' in their sexual behaviour. Young women also draw on feminine gender norms to justify their use of violence (as caring or self-sacrificing) and stress that, despite being 'one of the guys', they 'could be girly' when they wanted to be. In this way they negotiate gender identities that allow them to engage in gang activities and violence without being positioned as entirely unfeminine.

Whilst stereotypes of 'sex objects' and 'tomboys' are apparent in young women's interview accounts, a careful and critical reading of the data indicates that these should not be taken at face value as incontrovertible 'facts'. This is because interview accounts are not only socially constructed products, but also 'cultural products that combine memory, learned conventions, and narrative models for telling one's story' (Sandelowski, 2002: 106). Given that issues of identity are inextricably linked to issues of power, young women's investment in gender-stereotypical discourses can be read as the complex outcome of a gender hierarchy that celebrates males/masculinity and devalues females/femininity. Respondents in the current study make a distinction between their own behaviour and that of 'other' young women because of the power and status that taking on an identity as 'wan of the lads' provided. The flip side of this, of course, is that such young women lack ways to gain status and rewards on their own terms.

References

Aldridge, J. and Medina, J. (2007) *Youth Gangs in an English City: Social Exclusion, Drugs and Violence*. Swindon: Economic and Social Research Council.

Aldridge, J., Medina, J. and Ralphs, R. (2008) 'The Problems and Dangers of Doing Gang Research', in F. van Gemert, D. Peterson and I-L. Lien (eds) *Youth Gangs, Ethnicity and Migration*. Cullompton: Willan.

Anderson, E. (1999) *Code of the Street: Decency, Violence, and the Moral Life of the Inner City*. New York: W.W. Norton and Company.

Artz, S. (1998) *Sex, Power and the Violent School Girl*. Toronto: Trifolium Books.

Batchelor, S. (2005) '"Prove me the Bam!" Victimisation and Agency in the Lives of Young Women Who Commit Violent Offences', *Probation Journal*, 52(4): 358–75.

—— (2007a) '"Prove me the Bam!" Victimisation and Agency in the Lives of Young Women Who Commit Violent Offences', unpublished PhD thesis, University of Glasgow.

—— (2007b) '"Getting Mad Wi' It": Risk-seeking by Young Women', in K. Hannah-Moffat and P. O'Malley (eds) *Gendered Risks*. London: Glasshouse Press.

—— (2009) 'Girls, Gangs and Violence: Assessing the Evidence', *Probation Journal*, 56(4): 399–414.

Batchelor, S., Burman, M. and Brown, J. (2001) 'Discussing Violence: Let's Hear it for the Girls', *Probation Journal*, 48(2): 125–34.

Bourgois, P. (2002) *In Search of Respect: Selling Crack in El Barrio*, second edition. Cambridge: Cambridge University Press.

Campbell, A. (1984/1991) *The Girls in the Gang*. Oxford: Basil Blackwell.

—— (1987/1999) 'Self Definition by Rejection: The Case of Gang Girls', *Social Problems*, 34(5): 451–66. Reprinted in M. Chesney-Lind and J.M. Hagedorn (eds) (1999) *Female Gangs in America: Essays on Girls, Gangs and Gender*. Chicago: Lake View Press.

—— (1990) 'Female Participation in Gangs', in C.R. Huff (ed.) *Gangs in America*. Newbury Park, CA: Sage.

Chesney-Lind, M. and Irwin, K. (2008) *Beyond Bad Girls: Gender, Violence and Hype*. London: Routledge.

Downes, D. (1966) *The Delinquent Solution: A Study in Subcultural Theory*. London: Routledge & Kegan Paul.

Hall, S. and Jefferson, T. (eds) (1976) *Resistance through Rituals: Youth Subcultures in Post-war Britain*. London: Hutchinson.

Hallsworth, S. and Young, T. (2008) 'Gang Talk and Gang Talkers: A Critique', *Crime Media Culture*, 4(2): 175–95.

Joe, K. and Chesney-Lind, M. (1995) '"Just Every Mother's Angel": An Analysis of Gender and Ethnic Variations in Youth Gang Membership', *Gender & Society*, 9(4): 408–30.

Joe-Laidler, K. and Hunt, G. (2001) 'Accomplishing Femininity Among the Girls in the Gang', *British Journal of Criminology*, 41: 656–78.

Kandiyoti, D. (1988) 'Bargaining with Patriarchy', *Gender & Society*, 2(3): 274–90.

Kintrea, K., Bannister, J., Pickering, J., Reid, M. and Suzuki, N. (2008) *Young People and Territoriality in British Cities*. York: Joseph Rowntree Foundation.

Lees, S. (1997) *Ruling Passions*. Buckingham: Open University Press.

Messerschmidt, J.W. (2005) 'Men, Masculinities, and Crime', in M.S. Kimmel, J. Hearn, and R.W. Connell (eds) *Handbook of Studies on Men and Masculinities*. Thousand Oaks, CA: Sage.

Miller, J. (2001) *One of the Guys: Girls, Gangs and Gender*. New York: Oxford University Press.

Miller, J. and Decker, S.H. (2001) 'Young Women and Gang Violence: Gender, Street Offending and Violent Victimization in Gangs', *Justice Quarterly*, 18(1): 115–40.

Miller, J. and Mullins, C.W. (2006) 'Stuck Up, Telling Lies, and Talking Too Much: The Gendered Context of Young Women's Violence', in K. Heimer and C. Kruttschnitt (eds) *Gender and Crime: Patterns in Victimisation and Offending*. New York: New York University Press.

Millman, M. (1975) 'A Feminist View of the Sociology of Deviance', *Sociological Inquiry*, 45(3): 251–77.

Moore, J. (1991) *Going Down to the Barrio: Homeboys and Homegirls in Change*. Philadelphia, PA: Temple University Press.

Muncie, J. (2009) *Youth and Crime*, third edition. London: Sage.

Ness, C. (2004) 'Why Girls Fight: Female Youth Violence in the Inner City', *The ANNALS of the American Academy of Political and Social Science*, 595: 32–48.

Nurge, D. (2003) 'Liberating Yet Limiting: The Paradox of Female Gang Membership', in D. Brotherton and L. Barrios (eds) *The Almighty Latin King and Queen Nation: Street Politics and the Transformation of a New York City Gang*. New York: Columbia University Press.

Parker, H. (1974) *View from the Boys: A Sociology of Down-town Adolescents*. Newton Abbot, Devon: David & Charles.

Pitts, J. (2007) *Reluctant Gangsters: Youth Gangs in Waltham Forest*. Luton: University of Bedfordshire.

Ralphs, R., Medina, J. and Aldridge, J. (2009) 'Who Needs Enemies with Friends Like These? The Importance of Place for Young People Living in Known Gang Areas', *Journal of Youth Studies*, 12(5): 483–500.

Sandelowski, M. (2002) 'Reembodying Qualitative Inquiry', *Qualitative Health Research*, 12(1): 104–15.

Schalet, A., Hunt, G. and Joe-Laidler, K. (2003) 'Respectability and Autonomy: The Articulation and Meaning of Sexuality Among the Girls in the Gang', *Journal of Contemporary Ethnography*, 31(1): 108–43.

Scott, P. (1956) 'Gangs and Delinquent Groups in London', *British Journal of Delinquency*, 7: 4–24.

Spergel, I.A. (1964) *Racketville, Slumtown, Haulburg*. Chicago, IL: University of Chicago Press.

Thrasher, F.M. (1927) *The Gang: A Study of 1313 Gangs*. Chicago, IL: University of Chicago Press.

Weerman, F.M., Maxson, C.L, Esbensen, F-A., Aldridge, J., Medina, J. and van Gemert, F. (2009) *Eurogang Program Manual*. Online report, University of Missouri-St. Louis.

Young, T., Fitzgerald, M., Hallsworth, S. and Joseph, I. (2007) *Guns, Gangs and Weapons*. London: Youth Justice Board.

Chapter 7

In search of the 'shemale' gangster

Tara Young

Introduction

Serious crime perpetrated by young women is rare. Official statistics on female criminality have continuously shown that girls and young women are more likely to be the victims rather than the perpetrators of violent crime and, if they offend, they normally engage low-level, non-serious, criminal damage and/or summary offences. However, since 2003, national figures on female offending in general, and youth crime in particular, appear to signal a change in the offending profiles of young women and this has given rise to significant concern. According to statistics covering the period 2003–7 (Ministry of Justice, 2008): unprecedented numbers of women are being arrested and detained by the police; more young women are reported to be involved in aggressive and violent behaviour (traditionally the preserve of men) and, for the first time in recorded history, the proportion of women arrested for crimes classified as 'violence against the person' (35 per cent) outweighs arrests for 'theft and handling stolen goods' (32 per cent). Furthermore, there is a tendency to associate the apparent increase in the anti-social and violent activity of young women to a rise in female gangs and female gang membership. Arguably, this association is driven, in part, by dominant discourses relating to male gangs and the assumed and much maligned proliferation of youth 'gang culture' in the UK and the threat that violent street gangs (real or imagined) are said to pose to the wider society. The association between rising levels of female violence on the one hand and concerns about growing numbers of female gang members on the other is, on the face of it, understandable, since gangs are inextricably linked with delinquency and violent crime (Yablonsky, 1962; Klein, 1995; Jankowski, 1991; Decker and Van Winkle, 1997; Thornberry et al., 2003). The equation is conceived as both simple and causal: a rise in female violence is directly attributable to a rise in female gang membership.

Concern about the female gangster is not new of course. In the early 1980s Anne Campbell investigated the phenomenon of violence amongst girls and young women (Campbell, 1981) and female gang membership (Campbell, 1984). Although Campbell's work was situated within a context of rising concern about female offending, she concluded that dominant conceptualizations of female (gang) violence were exaggerated, effectively comprising a 'moral panic' (Cohen, 1980). Indeed, Campbell argued that the female gang phenomenon in the UK was, in essence, a social construction. She observed that male gangs were rare in Britain and since female gangs tend to follow (rather than precede) male gangs – as her research on gang girls in New York, USA illustrated – it was very unlikely that young women in the UK were organizing into gangs in any great numbers (Campbell, 1995). A decade on and a further 'panic' ensued, centred this time on the 'yob woman' and 'tank girl'. In a similar critique to Campbell's, Anne Worrall (1995) argued persuasively that the furore that surrounded 'tank girl'[1] was under-pinned by occasional atypical events as distinct from a sustained rise in the incidence of female violence. Notwithstanding such evidence-based critique, over the last decade authoritative sources have increasingly argued that there is a rise in female violence in general and a growing girl gang problem in particular. The former Metropolitan Police Chief Commissioner, Sir Ian Blair, for example, has suggested that the gang situation in the UK is the second most pressing policing issue after terrorism (*The London Paper*, 3 January 2008). Similarly, the Mayor of London, Boris Johnson, has referred to a 'culture of stabbing' that exists amongst young people in the capital and the 'gang culture' in which some young people are caught up (*The London Paper*, 16 June 2008).

Equally, (particular readings of) a growing body of statistical data deriving from research on gang membership in the UK also suggests a burgeoning problem. Bennett and Holloway (2004) – on the basis of their analysis of quanti-tative data – estimated gang membership in England and Wales to be around 20,000 and suggested that, if anything, this figure is likely to be an under-estimation. The Metropolitan Police estimate that there are 171 gangs operating in London alone and Strathclyde Police claim to have identified 170 gangs in Glasgow (Centre for Social Justice, 2009). The Home Office Offending, Crime and Justice Survey (Sharp et al., 2006), revealed that 3,827 10- to 19-year-olds (or 6 per cent of those surveyed) were members of delinquent youth groups or 'gangs' and, drawing on findings from the Edinburgh Study of Youth Transitions and Crime, Smith and Bradshaw's (2005) 'Gang Membership and Teenage Offending' study found that 20 per cent (846 out of a cohort of 4,300) 13-year-olds had been members of a gang in the 12 months prior to the survey. Similarly, a survey of 11,400 young people conducted as part of the Safer London Survey Youth Survey (Communities that Care, 2005) estimated that 2 per cent (228) of the total sample were gang members and a piece of research conducted in a single outer London borough (Waltham Forest) estimated that 600–700 young people in this area alone were involved in gangs (Pitts, 2008). The truth of the matter, however, is that the actual numbers of gangs and gang members in the UK are largely unknown and, for some social commentators, this paucity of knowledge is indicative of negligence, thus creating a situation where, in the last ten years, 'the failure of national and local government to act decisively has allowed gangs to become entrenched in some of our most disadvantaged neighbourhoods' (Centre for Social Justice, 2009: 20).

It follows, therefore, that concern with the question of youth gangs *per se* has raised corresponding anxieties pertaining to female gang members. Indeed, once again the violent female – especially in the form of the 'female gangster' – has (re)entered public consciousness and a series of high-profile 'news' reports have 'revealed' the violent capacities of young women, implying that they are as vindictive, cruel and callous as men. The unequivocal impression generated by these stories is that girls and young women are more readily engaging in violent crime, they are more likely to be involved in street gangs and the offences they commit are more serious than hitherto.

This chapter critically reviews evidence relating to the 'girl gangster' in the UK. I will argue that whilst there is some evidence to suggest a rise in violent crime committed by women, there is no substantial evidence of either a rise in female gangs or a gang–violence correlation. The media portrayal of the girl gangster ultimately comprises a crude caricature. The question at the core of the chapter is: why, despite the absence of empirical evidence, does the construction of the girl gangster endure within popular consciousness?

What is the problem?

In 2009, a 16-year-old girl was abducted at knife point, taken to an alleyway, stripped naked and whipped with belts by several members of a street gang. The incident, captured on a mobile phone and distributed to absent friends, was reputed to be a revenge attack and punishment for 'disrespect' shown to the gang leader's mother. It was reported that the gang leader held such vengeful and hateful feelings towards the victim, that they had wanted to arrange for her to be gang raped (Wright, 2009). Heinous crimes involving gang members are reported in the press with increasing frequency. Since 1997, there has been veritable surge in the number of reports on gangs and the offence profiles of their members. In the period 1997 to 2008, for example, the term 'gang' featured in the *Guardian* 'news section' 5,467 times (Fitzgerald, 2008). Whilst it is likely that many of these reports are repeat stories involving a myriad of groups engaged in a range of offending behaviours, the victimization of young women is a regular feature – particularly cases of serious violence against women committed by male gang members.[2] Perhaps what makes the case (above) more chilling, however, is that the perpetrators were not men but teenage girls, reputed to be members of a notorious London-based girl gang known as 'Girls Over Men'.

The violence displayed by 'Girls Over Men' is similar to that in other reports that have appeared in the media over the last decade. Over this period, a succession of reports has highlighted the violent capacity of girl gang members, thus contributing to wider fears about the gang 'epidemic' and consolidating the construction of the violent gang girl in British consciousness. Indeed, identifiable high-profile cases have seemingly come to epitomize girl gang members. One such case involves 16-year-old Toni Blankson who, in 2000, was convicted of the murder of Timothy Baxter and the attempted murder of his friend Gabriel Cornish in what was reported as a 'deliberate, gratuitous act of violence' (BBC News, 19 May 2000). Toni, the only girl in the gang, was reported to be an integral part of the incident, shouting encouragement to fellow gang members as they kicked the two men unconscious. When Baxter's body was thrown over Hungerford Bridge, into the River Thames, remorseless Toni 'celebrated' by engaging in a passionate kiss with her co-offending boyfriend. A second case, reported approximately one year later, involved Claire Marsh, who became the youngest female to be convicted of rape. Seventeen-year-old Marsh, was one of a number of young people involved in the canal-side rape of a 37-year-old woman and was reported to have instigated the incident; ripping clothing from the victim, holding her down and shouting encouragement to her male counterparts (Pook, 2001). In a third case, 14-year-old 'happy slap murderer' Chelsea O'Mahoney, dubbed 'a natural born killer' by the press, was reported to have instigated a flurry of violence against eight strangers in the London area which culminated in the death of David Morley. O'Mahoney's gang, known as the 'Sergeant Crew', apparently kicked Morley to death in a frenzied attack and, according to the national press, filmed the incident using mobile phones, retaining the footage as a 'trophy' (Laville, 2005). Finally, by way of illustrating media reporting girl gangsters, 15-year-old Samantha Joseph – labelled the 'honey-trap' killer – reportedly lured love-struck Shakilus Townsend to his death at the hands of her ex-partner Danny McClean and his gang, the 'Shine my Nine Crew'. It was widely reported that Samantha, who was secretly dating Shakilus, 'sacrificed' him in order to reclaim the affections of her ex-boyfriend who had found out about her infidelity (Bird, 2009).

Media reporting of extraordinary cases such as these adds weight to the girl gang thesis and invokes the impression that young women are in crisis. The discourse is commonly presented through two interconnected forms. The first, and arguably most prevalent, is the masculinized construction of the female gangster whereby she is conceived as an immoral rational actor; as aggressive and violent as any male counterpart. For social commentators they are Lombrosian women, atavistic throwbacks, out of control and capable of gratuitous brutality (Widdecombe, 2008). Such girls not only mete out violence directly but, indirectly, they also 'aggravate the violence of young boys' (Razaq, 2008: 6) and initiate 'inter-gang' violence by facilitating 'shootings and deaths' when 'dissed' (disrespected by others) (Centre for Social Justice, 2009: 74–5).

The second, and less pronounced, narrative presents the female gangster as a victim, whereby the young women are propelled towards gangs as a result of the neglect, brutality and trauma they have suffered. They are supposedly attracted to gangs in their search for respect, acceptance, company and escape from their abusers. Paradoxically, such young women are thought to assume subordinate positions within the gang, beholden to the men around them and compelled to respond to their whims and obey orders, sometimes imposed forcefully (Pitts, 2008). In fact, previously traumatized 'gang girls' are often considered more dangerous owing to the combination of chronic low self-esteem and shame and a hyper-inflated sense of self-respect, forming a retaliative fighter capable of giving and receiving 'man-licks' (Razaq, 2008).

How many girl gangsters?

As stated, the exact number of gangs in Britain is unknown and even less information is available on the number of young women involved in street gangs. This lack of knowledge is, in part, because there is no established database on which to frame current intelligence and no benchmark figures from which to draw conclusions about an increase or decrease in gang membership (Hallsworth and Young, 2008). To further complicate matters, there is no universally recognized definition of 'gang' in use in Britain, so invariably studies are often measuring different things. Moreover, US literature reveals a distinct difference in the composition and offending behaviours of male-only, mixed and female-only street-based gangs and/or groups (Taylor, 1993). Despite this, various attempts have been made to quantify the girl gangster phenomenon. A Channel 4 *Dispatches* documentary in 2003, for example, highlighted the extent of the [alleged] gang problem by stating that as many as 30,000 gangs were operational in the UK of which over half (57 per cent) included females (Thompson, 2003). Furthermore, in 2006, the Metropolitan Police Service claimed that 5 per cent (or 2,500) of the estimated 50,000 gang members in London were girls and women, most of whom were thought to belong to mixed or predominantly male gangs, with only three gangs exclusively comprising girls and young women.

Survey data such as the Offending, Crime and Justice Survey (OCJS) 2003 (Budd et al., 2005), the Delinquent Youth Groups and Offending Behaviour Survey (Sharp et al., 2006)[3] and Youth Justice Board MORI survey (MORI, 2004), estimate much lower numbers than the Metropolitan Police and it is important to note that these studies do not report on gang membership in itself, rather they derive from data on patterns of 'co-offending' and delinquent youth groups. The OCJS found that 'co-offenders' were primarily male (81 per cent of incidents involved men only); only one in five offences (17 per cent) involved male and female co-offenders. Co-offending amongst female-only groups accounted for a very small percentage (2 per cent) of the total number of offences (Budd et al., 2005: 60). Analysis of the 2004 Offending, Crime and Justice Survey (Sharp et al., 2006) examined the prevalence of young people's involvement in what the authors term 'delinquent youth groups' (DYGs)[4] and found 6 per cent (229) DYG membership amongst the 10–19-year-olds sampled (3,827), with equal membership (6 per cent) for young women and men. The total number of young women in the sample equalled 1,843, which puts the number of young women involved in DYGs at 110. If the variable: 'The group has at least one structural feature' (either a name, an area, or rules) is removed from the analysis – which would bring the definition closer to the Eurogang definition[5] – then level of gang membership drops by half to 3 per cent and actual female gang membership to 55 (or 0.4 per cent of the overall total sampled).

The validity and reliability of centrally generated statistical data has long been contested of course and, as Box (1971) notes, only a proportion of the population is incorporated into 'official' knowledge. Many self-report studies are conducted with pre-selected samples, especially school samples, which exclude specific groups from the research process. The Offending, Crime and Justice Survey, for example, only surveys individuals from private households in England and Wales, thus excluding young people in local authority care and penal institutions. Clearly this points to a significant deficiency in such statistics, not least because common-sense reasoning implies that young people in 'care' and/or custody are amongst the most likely to be involved in gangs.

Trevor Bennett and Katy Holloway (2004) attempt to tackle the issue of representativeness by analysing data gathered from the New English and Welsh Arrestee Drug Abuse Monitoring Programme (NEW-ADAM). From an examination of 2,725 interviews (conducted across 14 sites) they found that 15 per cent of arrestees had experience of gang life; 4 per cent claimed to be current members of a gang while 11 per cent claimed to have been a member in the past. Less than 5 per cent of gang members (current and past) were female, however, amounting to 18 women in total and suggesting that female gang membership is less common than media reports indicate (Bennett and Holloway, 2004: 314).[6] The seemingly low number of young women could be the result of the age population sampled, however. In Bennett and Holloway's study respondents were typically aged 17 or over whereas other studies show that female gang membership tends to be higher at a younger age (with a peak around 13–15 years old) and tails off considerably during their late teens (Esbensen and Lynskey, 2001; Sharp et al., 2006; Smith and Bradshaw, 2005).

The Safer London Youth Survey (Communities that Care, 2005) canvassed responses from 11,400 school-aged young people (11–15 years old) across six London boroughs as part of a neighbourhood prevention programme funded by Government Office for London (GOL). The respondents were asked to report on a range of topics including 'gang activity'. The schools involved in the survey were located in areas identified by 'Operation Trident' as having a growing or significant gang problem. Despite this, and even taking account of the broad definitions of 'gang' that were used, a relatively small number of young people – approximately 4 per cent, or 465 of the total sample – classified themselves as gang members, a figure commensurate with similar studies (Sharp et al., 2006; Klein and Maxson, 2006). Extrapolating the number of *female* gang members from the Safer London Youth Survey (Communities that Care, 2005) was problematic since the study did not adequately differentiate by gender, reporting simply that boys are more likely to report being involved in a (self-defined) gang than girls.

Another self-report survey by Smith and Bradshaw (2005) did quantify female gang membership as part of the Edinburgh Youth Transitions and Crime Study. Utilizing similar self-definition techniques as the Communities that Care survey, at 'Sweep 2' of the longitudinal study – at which point children were aged 13 and at the highest peak of gang membership[7] – the level of female gang membership

(21.5 per cent) was higher than for males (18.8 per cent). However, by 'Sweep 5' (when the young people were aged 16) the trend had reversed and the proportion of girls reporting to be gang involved was 10.8 per cent in comparison to 15.6 per cent of boys (Smith and Bradshaw, 2005: 11). In sum, current quantitative data on girl gang membership in the UK is sketchy, making it difficult to gauge precise numbers and draw adequate conclusions. Variations in definition and the inherent methodological biases within and between different studies only add to such sketchiness. Nevertheless, the available data suggest that limited numbers of girls and young women are involved in co-offending, DYGs or 'gangs'. However, research also suggests that violence – and sometimes serious violence – is closely associated with gang membership (Esbensen and Huizinga, 1993; Thornberry et al., 1995). Whilst overall numbers might be small, therefore, they might still represent a significant problem.

An abundance of female violence?

According to Government Office figures, violent crime committed by young women in London rose 15 per cent over the period 2003–4, with the rate of increase attributed to 15-year-old girls standing at 38 per cent (Smith, 2005). Similarly, the Offending, Crime and Justice Survey 2003 (Budd et al., 2005) also suggests that females are committing a larger proportion of the total number of violent crimes, a trend that is apparently replicated in Scotland (Batchelor, 2005 and this volume). Inevitably, perhaps, such apparent increases are frequently linked to debates associated with female gang affiliation. Recent arrest data for England and Wales also indicates an increase in the number of females apprehended for – traditionally male – 'violence against the person' offences,[8] implying that young women are becoming more violent. For the first time in recorded history 'more females were arrested for offences of violence against the person (35 per cent) than for theft and handling stolen goods (32 per cent)' (Ministry of Justice, 2008: 7). This represents a 135 per cent increase since 1999/00 and an 11 per cent increase on the year 2005/06 (2008: 5). Although more women were arrested for 'violence against the person', however, the figures show that adult women (aged 18+) represented a larger proportion of the increase than girls aged 10–17 (67 per cent compared to 25 per cent) and the most common offence type for the younger age group continues to be theft and handling stolen goods followed by criminal damage (2008: 6).

Findings presented in a Youth Justice Board (2009) report on patterns of offending by girls, echo the above figures. Whilst the report highlights a year-on-year increase in a range of offences committed by girls and young women during the period 2000–6 (including violence against the person, robbery, criminal damage and arson, public order and breach), it states that a greater number of girls, aged 10–17, engage in acquisitive crimes (such as 'theft and handling stolen goods' and fraud) rather than 'violence against the person'. This suggests that, despite the apparent rise in violent crime amongst girls and young women, the majority of young female offenders are still significantly more likely to engage in traditionally 'female' crimes (Youth Justice Board, 2009: 46). Furthermore, closer examination of such data reveals that the majority of 'violence against the person' offences are likely to be low-level in nature, normally comprising domestic assaults against partners and relatives (Budd et al., 2005). Equally, drawing upon the offence profiles of girls and young women presented in the Youth Justice Board (2009) report, only 11 per cent of juvenile 'violent crimes' were committed against strangers and the substantial majority of assaults involved victims known to the offender (36 per cent), with previous infraction or provocation comprising the most common motivational factor. Such findings are congruent with other research (Young, 2009; Batchelor, 2005; Budd et al., 2005; Phillips, 2003).

Violence by girls and young women in groups

Official statistics presented on female offending appear, in large part, to relate to lone offending females and adult women, as distinct from girls and young women in groups. As Gelsthorpe and Sharpe (2006) note, attempting to extrapolate figures and analyse offence trends amongst the female population is difficult, particularly so when attempting to assess the evidence on female offending in groups. The available empirical research is profoundly limited in the UK, which adds significantly to the difficulty of coming to any reliable conclusions about the extent of girls' and young women's gang involvement and/or their offending profiles. The situation is made all the more problematic by the wide variation found in definitions of 'gang'. As discussed, for example, the findings on group related offending recorded as part of the Offending, Crime and Justice Survey 2003 (Budd et al., 2005) refers to 'co-offenders', the MORI Youth Survey (MORI, 2004) to 'partners in crime' and the Delinquent Youth Groups and Offending Behaviour Survey (Sharp et al., 2006) to 'delinquent youth groups'.

One of the enduring images of the female gangster is that she is often a lone female within an all-male group, albeit armed and dangerous. Whilst this salacious image might serve to sell newspapers the actual evidence paints a different picture. In fact, female offenders are most likely to offend together (rather than with males) and are least likely to use a weapon in the commission of offending, thus rendering the recurring image of the solitary offending girl within a male gang and/or the knife-wielding, gun-toting murderess little more than media fiction at best and exceptional aberration at worse. Indeed, despite growing hysteria surrounding female gang violence in the media, young women rarely engage in violent crime and, on the relatively rare occasions when they do, it is almost exclusively restricted to assault of a non-injurious nature against intimate others. This is entirely consistent with earlier studies of female criminality (Smart and Smart, 1978; Chesney-Lind 1997) that have repeatedly shown that women commit far less violent crime than is implied by media coverage. This is not to suggest that young women do not instigate and participate in violent crime but rather that such offending needs to be contextualized, including, in part, an appreciation of the normalization of violence within their biographies and their attempts to exert some control over their lives, to (re)gain the power and self-affirmation lost as a result of victimization (Young, 2009).

Studies on the prevalence and experience of violence in gang girls' lives reveal that it is often conceived as a 'normal' and everyday part of life. North American studies consistently show that gang girls are likely to come from families experiencing multiple difficulties and to be exposed to high levels of verbal, physical and sexual violence prior to becoming part of a street-based group (Chesney-Lind, 1997; Moore, 1991; Miller, 2001; Taylor, 1993; Gover et al., 2009). Within a context of potential and actual violence, young women learn the 'value' of violence, how to marshal its power for themselves (Batchelor, 2001; Young, 2009) and, as noted by Miller (2001), to behave like 'one of the guys'.

Gangs are traditionally beholden to male norms, values and expectations (Thrasher, 1927; Cohen, 1955; Cloward and Ohlin, 1960). As members of such predominantly male groups, girls are more likely to be exposed to aggression from male members and to act to protect themselves from further victimization. Within these groups, research indicates that they are often actively excluded from engaging in violent altercation or serious criminality by male peers (Miller, 2001) and that young women in gangs use their femininity to negotiate and temper involvement in gang crime (Miller and Decker, 2001). As a result, girls' violence and aggression arises within the context of the peer group, principally amongst friends when 'hanging out' and ''aving fun' (Young, 2009) as distinct from targeting strangers through premeditated acts of gratuitous violence:

> 'Hanging out', however, was a tenuous and fragile activity with potential to tip from a playful occasion into an anti-social one – especially with the addition of alcohol which, as some young women highlighted, could transform a relatively peaceful social situation into a combative one. Most social situations did not end with a fight and the young women congregated together not to cause trouble but to experience the pleasure of each other's company.
>
> (Young, 2009: 234)

Indeed, the research consistently reports that gang girls do not conventionally go looking for violence, rather they engage in violence when directly challenged or in need. Such violence, therefore, is shown to be: expressive and linked to the threat of attack (from within or outside of the group); the experience of disrespect or injustice (Nurge, 2003; Miller, 2001; Young, 2009); a reaction to past incidences (Young, 2009); an attempt to defend reputation (including sexual reputation) (Phillips, 2003); and/or for male attention (Young, 2009). Far less commonly, female gang members are known to engage in street robbery often linked to economic necessity, alcohol consumption and/or drug dependency (Young et al., 2007; Taylor, 1993).

Explaining the 'hyper-violent "shemale" gangster'

Prolonged exposure to violence and neglect can result in neurological and psychological problems. One consequence noted by psychologist Camilla Batmanghelidjh (2007) is the emotional 'shutdown' of individuals from which they enter a destructive state of emergency. As Batmanghelidjh (2008) found in her study of 400 alone young people 'on the road', the consequences of over-exposure to violence and consistent neglect and rejection essentially creates two 'types' of young people: the 'initiators' and the 'imitators'.

The *initiators* are young people who, as a consequence of sustained abuse, have little or no empathetic tendencies and/or regulatory control mechanisms. Consequently they can't slow down, they can't show compassion and they can't 'self-soothe' (except in violent situations where, paradoxically, they report to being 'calmed' or 'relieved'). Such young people are consistently anxious and live in a 'state of emergency', where they exist and survive on wit, adrenaline and instinct (Batmanghelidjh, 2007; 2008) and exhibit a 'hood mentality' or a form of semi-controlled insanity that Vigil (2003) terms 'locura'. According to Batmanghelidjh (2007; 2008), such vulnerable young children 'store' their victimization and 'bank' their pain until such a time as they are physically strong enough to avenge the wrongdoing that they have experienced directly. In essence, they switch from the victimized to the victimizer and because many are homeless – 83 per cent of Batmanghelidjh's sample – they often seek and find opportunities for revenge 'on the road'. They set the tempo, the yardstick and the rules for violence on the road and, in doing so, they become the 'badass' as Katz (1988) might have it.

The *imitators* are normally young people from more stable backgrounds who are not compelled to violence in quite the same way but who have to be aggressive (or at least be seen to be competent in violence) in order to stave off and deal with potential threats from the initiators. According to Batmanghelidjh (2007; 2008), the imitators are often intensely bullied or humiliated by the initiators or are witness to their violent capacities. However, they are no match for the initiators and so are forced into imitating their violence and to arm themselves with weapons for protection.

Within a gang context it is likely that the relations between the 'initiators' (often males) and the 'imitators' (often females) are largely gendered. Recall how 15-year-old Samantha Joseph reportedly led Shakilus Townsend to his death. In her defence, Samantha apparently stated that she had been beaten repeatedly by her former boyfriend. On the day of the offence she was seemingly given an ultimatum: to 'deliver' Shakilus for what she thought would be a beating or to be beaten herself (BBC News, 2009). Similarly, 16-year-old Toni Blankson and 14-year-old Chelsea O'Mahoney both reportedly 'encouraged' or 'instigated' male violence without actually delivering it. Whilst their actions are deeply problematic they played little direct part in the violence – it was the males who battered, kicked or stabbed the victims to death.

The 'shemale' gangster as moral panic

The nuanced representation of the girl gangster and her engagement in violent crime presented here offers an alternative picture to the stereotypical image commonly found in the media and challenges popular notions that: violence by females is 'getting worse'; gang girls are habitually violent; and shemale gangsters increasingly engage in serious violence in the same way as males. It suggests that, despite concerns about the link between rising violence and girl gangs, there is very little 'evidence' in the UK to substantiate them. What is deducible from the available – if limited – research evidence is that, on the whole, extreme violence by young women is rare. Yet in the relative absence of empirical data the 'panic' around the shemale gangster persists. Why is this the case?

If we consider populist conceptualizations of female violence and the shemale gangster two key themes dominate. The first, and most persistent, theme links increasing (violent) criminality to female emancipation. The construction of the young woman as a 'liberated crook' (Chesney-Lind, 1997) is illuminated by the work of Freda Adler (1975), who attributed the rise of female criminality to the increase of women in the workplace. According to Adler, as women become more prominent in the workforce they appropriate masculine roles and characteristics and engage in 'masculine' aggressive criminal activity to a greater extent. Whilst Adler's thesis has been persuasively critiqued (Carlen, 1988; Naffine and Gale, 1989), her 'explanation' for female aggression and violence remains popular amongst the media and some sections of the academy (Chesney-Lind, 1997). When explaining the current rise in female violence, for example, academics such as Henry (2008), blame 'Britain's "ladette" culture'. Indeed, sociologist Barbara Littlewood of Glasgow University appears to have embraced the emancipation thesis when commenting on a rise in female violence by stating:

> Women are far more visible than ever before in all sections of society, and so perhaps female violent behaviour is also simply more visible. A certain number of boys have always created trouble on the streets and so if we accept that girls are now out there socialising with them, in a sense it should be no surprise if they behave like their brothers. Violence could be just a simple consequence of women spreading their wings now they are no longer trapped in their bedrooms.
>
> (Littlewood cited in Macaskill and Goodwin, 2004: 8)

The second theme stems from particular readings of gender-role theory. Traditional gendered stereotypes provide that men are by nature aggressive and women are largely law-abiding, nurturing, passive, caring, temperate and sub-missive (Adler, 1975). Within this binary, women are narrowly cast in the role of either the 'Madonna' or the 'whore' (Feinman, 1980; Batchelor, this volume). The 'whore' (the violent woman) is the antithesis of female, of femininity, of womanhood because she no longer adheres to the socially prescribed, 'natural' characteristics and is, therefore, more readily conceptualized as mad, bad, sad, or overly masculine if she transgresses traditional gendered role ascriptions (Smart, 1976; Heidensohn, 1996). The violent female and the shemale gangster have – by allegedly becoming more indistinguishable in their actions from male gangsters – 'betrayed' femininity and such transgression is vilified in the media. Orr (2001), for example, described the offending of 17-year-old Claire Marsh as 'inhumane' and argued that such a 'wretched creature' was undeserving of any compassion, preferring to speculate that early sexual relations, the desire to be one of the boys and female jealousies are pivotal motivational drivers of violent offending by young women.

In direct contrast to such vacuous populist conceptualizations (feminist) criminologists have repeatedly argued that the increase in recorded violent crime by girls and young women reflects (in large part) the responses of criminal justice agencies; consolidating intolerance towards particular forms of female behaviour and the increasing criminalization of women (Chesney-Lind, 1997; Worrall, 2004).[9] Indeed, a report published by the Youth Justice Board (2009) on patterns of girls' offending suggests that the increase is largely due to girls being arrested and prosecuted for behaviour that was previously tolerated and not considered serious enough to warrant legal sanction and prosecution. Thus it is – as repeatedly argued by academics – the response to female behaviour that has changed rather than the actual behaviour itself (Chesney-Lind, 2001).

Similarly, historians have highlighted the extent to which the street presence of young people has been problematized. Davies (2008; this volume), for example, draws attention to the participation of young women in Manchester gangs in the late nineteenth century. These female 'rippers' or 'scuttleresses', were reportedly engaged in anti-social behaviour, street fighting, robbery, aiding and abetting and fencing stolen goods. Media reporters – chagrined at the disrespectful and 'unlady-like' ways in which such girls and young women behaved – claimed to identify the existence of a 'gang of female scuttlers' who 'actively incited conflicts between the gangs and were thus responsible for the *majority* of scuttling affrays' (Davies, 2008: 241). Indeed, girls and young women were deemed to be just as bad as the boys: the 'viragoes are no less cruel and violent than the lads' (Davies, 2008: 248).

The behaviour of the 'girl rippers' resembled the types of anti-social behaviour, disorder and crime that contemporary girls and young women are being arrested for today. Then, as now, a minority of young women occasioned drunkenness, disorderly behaviour, violence and aggression. Then as now, young women were held responsible for inciting violence amongst men, stashing their weapons, tending their wounds and providing shelter and alibis should the need arise (Davies, 2008: 241). Then as now, grave concerns were expressed over the moral degradation of the street girl and her seemingly virtue-free existence. Then as now, there was a tendency to reconstruct old phenomena as new problems and find ever more solutions to tackle it.

Notes

1　Described in an article published in the *Sunday Times* as 'the shaven-head feminist, beer swilling, cocky and aggressive female who is politically savvy and exploitative' (Brinkworth, 1994).
2　See, for example, the case of Mary-Ann Leneghan who was tortured, raped and murdered by a group of five young men in Reading, Berkshire in 2006.
3　The findings were based upon findings from the 2004 Offending Crime and Justice Survey.
4　A group was defined as a DYG and young people as 'gang members' if respondents declared that: they hung out in groups of three or more (including themselves) and spent a lot of time together; the group spent a lot of time in public places; the group had existed for three months or more; the group had engaged in delinquent or criminal behaviour together in the last 12 months and the group had at least one structural feature (either a name, an area, or rules) (Sharp et al., 2006: 2).
5　The Eurogang Network define the street gang (or Troublesome Youth Group) as 'any durable, street-oriented youth group whose involvement in illegal activity is part of its group identity' (see Klein and Maxson, 2006: 4).
6　This is in contrast to a study by Esbensen and Lynskey (2001), who found a larger proportion of female gang members in their sample.
7　The study involved six sweeps in consecutive years.
8　'Violence against the person' includes a number of offences ranging from 'common assault' to 'murder'.
9　For a detailed discussion see the special issue of *Youth Justice: An International Journal* (2009, volume 9, number 3) on 'Girls, Young Women and Youth Justice'.

References

Adler, F. (1975) 'The Rise of the Female Crook', *Psychology Today*, 9: 42–6.
Batchelor, S. (2001) 'The Myth of Girl Gangs', *Criminal Justice Matters*, 43: 26–7.
—— (2005) '"Prove Me the Bam!" Victimization and Agency in the Lives of Young Women who Commit Violent Offences', *Probation Journal*, 52(4): 358–75.
Batmanghelidjh, C. (2007) 'Demons and Angels: Who Cares? Poor Care Structures and Moral Breakdown', in G. Walker (ed.) *The Science of Morality*. London: Royal College of Physicians.
—— (2008) 'Ways to be Sure the Kids are Alright: Zero Tolerance for Violence Against Children Will Result in No Violence from Children', *The Times*, 2 June.
BBC News (2009) 'Honey Trap Girl Guilty of Murder'. Retrieved 8 July 2009 (http://news.bbc.co.uk/1/hi/8116380.stm).
Bennett, T. and Holloway, K. (2004) 'Gang Membership, Drugs and Crime in the UK', *The British Journal of Criminology*, 44: 305–23.
Bird, S. (2009) 'Honeytrap Teen Samantha Joseph Jailed for 10 Years over Murder of Shakilus Townsend', *The Times*, 5 September.
Box, S. (1971) *Deviance, Reality and Society*. London: Holt, Rinehart and Winston Ltd.
Brinkworth, L. (1994) 'Sugar and Spice But Not All Nice', *The Sunday Times*, 27 November.
Budd, T., Sharp, C. and Mayhew, P. (2005) *Offending in England and Wales: First Results from the 2003 Crime and Justice Survey*. Home Office Research Study 275. London: Home Office.

Carlen, P. (1988) *Women, Crime and Poverty*. Milton Keynes: Open University Press.

Campbell, A. (1981) *Girl Delinquents*. Oxford: Basil Blackwell.

—— (1984) *The Girls in the Gang: A Report from New York City*. Oxford and New York: Basil Blackwell.

—— (1995) 'Media Myth Making: Creating a Girl Gang Problem', *Criminal Justice Matters* 19 (spring): 8–9.

Centre for Social Justice (2009) *Dying to Belong: An In-depth Review of Street Gangs in Britain*. A Policy Report by the Gangs Working Group. London: Centre for Social Justice.

Chesney-Lind, M. (1997) *The Female Offender: Girls, Women, and Crime*. Thousand Oaks, CA: Sage.

—— (2001) 'Are Girls Closing the Gender Gap in Violence?', *Criminal Justice*, spring: 18–23.

Cloward, R. and Ohlin, L. (1960) *Delinquency and Opportunity: A Theory of Delinquent Gangs*. Glencoe, IL: Free Press.

Cohen, A.K. (1955) *Delinquent Boys: The Culture of the Gang*. Glencoe, IL: Free Press.

Cohen, S. (1980) *Folk Devils and Moral Panics*. London: Martin Robertson.

Communities that Care (2005) *Findings from the Safer London Youth Survey 2004*. London: Communities that Care.

Davies, A. (2008) *The Gangs of Manchester*. Preston: Milo Books.

Decker, S.H. and Van Winkle, B. (1997) *Life in the Gang: Family, Friends and Violence*. Cambridge: Cambridge University Press.

Esbensen, F-A. and Huizinga, D. (1993) 'Gangs, Drugs, and Delinquency in a Survey of Urban Youth', *Criminology*, 31(4): 565–89.

Esbensen, F-A. and Lynskey, D.P. (2001) 'Young Gang Members in a School Survey', in M.W. Klein, H-J. Kerner, C.L. Maxson and E.G.M. Weitekamp (eds) *The Eurogang Paradox: Street Gangs and Youth Groups in the U.S. and Europe*. Amsterdam: Kluwer Academic Publishers.

Feinman, C. (1980) *Women in the Criminal Justice System*. New York Praeger Publishers.

Fitzgerald, M. (2008) 'Gangs: A UK Perspective'. Public lecture delivered at Middlesex University (unpublished).

Gelsthorpe, L. and Sharpe, G. (2006) 'Gender, Youth Crime and Justice', in B. Goldson and J. Muncie (eds) *Youth Crime and Justice*. London: Sage.

Gover, A.R., Jennings, W.G. and Tewksbury, R (2009) 'Adolescent Male and Female Gang Members' Experiences with Violent Victimization, Dating Violence, and Sexual Assault', *American Journal of Criminal Justice*, 34:103–15.

Hallsworth, S. and Young, T. (2008) 'Gang Talk and Gang Talkers: A Critique', *Crime, Media, Culture*, 4(2): 175–195.

Heidensohn, F. (1996) *Women and Crime*. Basingstoke: Macmillan.

Henry, S. (2008) *Bullying as a Social Pathology: A Peer Group Analysis*. Lampeter: Edwin Mellen Press.

Jankowski, M.S. (1991) *Islands in the Street: Gangs and American Urban Society*. Berkeley and Los Angeles: University of California Press.

Katz, J. (1988) *Seductions of Crime: Moral and Sensual Attractions in Doing Evil*. New York: Basic Books.

Klein, M.W. (1995) *The American Street Gang*. New York: Oxford University Press.

Klein, M.W. and Maxson, C.L. (2006) *Street Gang Patterns and Policies*. Oxford: Oxford University Press.

Laville, S. (2005) 'Happy Slap Gang Guilty of Killing Barman in Clockwork Orange-style Violent Spree', *Guardian*, 15 December: 6.

Macaskill, M. and Goodwin, K. (2004) 'Women Behaving Badly: Is the Female Crime Wave the Dark Side of "Ladette" Culture?' *The Sunday Times*, 2 May: 8.

Metropolitan Police Service (2006) *MPS Pan-London Gang Profile*. London: Metropolitan Police Service.

Miller, J. (2001) *One of the Guys: Girls, Gangs, and Gender*. New York: Oxford University Press.

Miller, J. and Decker, S.H. (2001) 'Young Women and Gang Violence: Gender, Street Offending and Violent Victimisation in Gangs', *Justice Quarterly*, 18(1): 115–40.

Ministry of Justice (2008) *Arrests for Recorded Crime (Notifiable Offences) and the Operation of Certain Police Powers Under PACE England and Wales 2006/7*. London: Ministry of Justice.

Moore, J. (1991) *Going Down to the Barrio: Homeboys and Homegirls in Change*. Philadelphia: Temple University Press.

MORI (2004) *MORI Youth Survey*. London: Youth Justice Board.

Naffine, N. and Gale, F. (1989) 'Testing the Nexus: Crime, Gender and Unemployment', *British Journal of Criminology*, 29(2): 144–56.

Nurge, D. (2003) 'Liberating yet Limiting: The Paradox of Female Gang Membership', in D. Brotherton and L. Barrios (eds) *The Almighty Latin King and Queen Nation: Street Politics and the Transformation of a New York City Gang*. New York: Columbia University Press.

Orr, D. (2001) 'Gangs, Girlfriends and a Rising Tide of Violence', *Independent*, 11 May.

Phillips, C. (2003) 'Who's Who in the Pecking Order? Aggression and "Normal Violence" in the Lives of Girls and Boys', *The British Journal of Criminology*, 43: 710–28.

Pitts, J. (2008) *Reluctant Gangsters: The Changing Face of Youth Crime*. Cullompton: Willan.

Pook, S. (2001) 'Girl, 18, Guilty of Towpath Rape', *Telegraph*, 17 March.

Razaq, R. (2008) 'Girls are Becoming as Violent as Boys', *Evening Standard*, 14 May.

Sharp, C., Aldridge, J. and Medina, J. (2006) *Delinquent Youth Groups and Offending Behaviour: Findings from the 2004 Offending, Crime and Justice Survey*. London: Home Office.

Smart, C. (1976) *Women, Crime and Criminology: A Feminist Critique*. London: Routledge & Kegan Paul.

Smart, C. and Smart, B. (1978). *Women, Sexuality and Social Control*. London: Routledge & Kegan Paul.

Smith, D.J. (2005) 'Deadlier than the Male?', *The Sunday Times*, 17 April.

Smith, D.J. and Bradshaw, P. (2005) *Gang Membership and Teenage Offending*. The Edinburgh Study of Youth Transitions and Crime Number 8. Edinburgh: Centre for Law and Society, The University of Edinburgh.

Taylor, C.S. (1993) *Girls, Gangs, Women and Drugs*. East Lansing, MI: Michigan State University Press.

Thompson, T. (2003) 'Girls in Half of Crime Gangs', *Observer*, 8 June.

Thornberry, T.P., Krohn, M.D., Lizotte, A.J. and Chand-Wieschem, D. (1995) 'The Role of Juvenile Gangs in Facilitating Delinquent Behaviour', in M.W. Klein, C.L. Maxson and J. Miller (eds) *The Modern Gang Reader*. Los Angeles: Roxbury.

Thornberry, T.P., Krohn, M.D., Smith, C.A. and Tobin, K. (2003) *Gangs and Delinquency in Developmental Perspective*. Cambridge: Cambridge University Press.

Thrasher, F.M. (1927) *The Gang: A Study of 1,313 Gangs in Chicago*. Chicago, IL: University of Chicago Press.

Vigil, J.D. (2003) 'Urban Violence and Street Gangs', *Annual Review of Anthropology*, 32: 225–42.

Widdecombe, A. (2008) 'Help Stop Gang Girls Terrorising our Streets', *Sun*, 18 September.

Worrall, A. (1995) 'Troublesome Young Women', *Criminal Justice Matters*, 19: 6–7.

—— (2004) 'Twisted Sisters, Ladettes, and the New Penology: The Social Construction of Violent Girls', in C. Adler and A. Worrall (eds) *Girls' Violence: Myths and Realities*. New York: SUNY.

Wright, S. (2009) '"We Should Have Had the Victim Raped", said Girl Gang Thug after Stripping and Whipping Rival, 16, in the Street', *Daily Mail Online*. Retrieved 30 August 2010 (http://www.dailymail.co.uk/news/article-1193109/We-victim-raped-said-girl-gang-thug-stripping-whipping-rival-16-street.html).

Yablonsky, L. (1962) *The Violent Gang*. New York: Macmillan.

Young, T., Fitzgerald, M., Hallsworth, S. and Joseph, I. (2007) *Groups, Gangs and Weapons*. London: Youth Justice Board.

Young, T. (2009) 'Girls and Gangs: "Shemale" Gangsters in the UK?', *Youth Justice*, 9(3): 224–38.

Youth Justice Board (2009) *Girls and Offending: Patterns, Perceptions and Interventions*. London: Youth Justice Board.

Chapter 8

Young people and 'weaponisation'

Peter Squires

Introduction

The principal aim of this chapter is to critically explore and engage with the debates concerning 'weaponisation' and youth violence. It begins by analysing evidence relating to weapon-involved victimisation in the UK together with key government responses. The chapter then turns to research into young people's use of weapons, the ways in which this is understood and interpreted and the related processes of criminalisation and 'gangsterisation'. Finally, the core issues are contextualised politically by exploring the key law and order interventions to which they have given rise.

Recent trends

In June 2009, the House of Commons Home Affairs Select Committee published its report on *Knife Crime* (House of Commons Home Affairs Select Committee, 2009) followed, less than two months later, by the Home Office monitoring report on 'Phase I' of the *Tackling Knives Action Programme* (TKAP) (Ward and Diamond, 2009). The particular clustering of such official reports on 'knife crime' is attributable to four key developments.

First, a growing perception that serious knife and stab injuries are bucking a general trend for falling levels of overall criminal violence (Home Office, 2008).

Second, a series of high-profile knife-related and/or stabbing murders – including black teenager Stephen Lawrence, the head teacher Philip Lawrence (no relation) and 10-year-old schoolboy Damilola Taylor – that, taken together, served to keep the issue of 'knife crime' in the public eye.

Third, between 2003 and 2007 the number of serious 'knife-enabled' injuries of young people aged under 18 increased by 78 per cent, from 524 incidents to 931 (see Figure 8.1). Furthermore, although knife-related violence is often conceptualised and presented as if it were primarily a youthful phenomenon, in absolute terms there are significantly more casualties aged *over* 18. Equally, whilst the same data (see Figure 8.2) show an overall *decrease* in gunshot injuries to young people aged under 18 during the past five years, the over 18 rate has risen

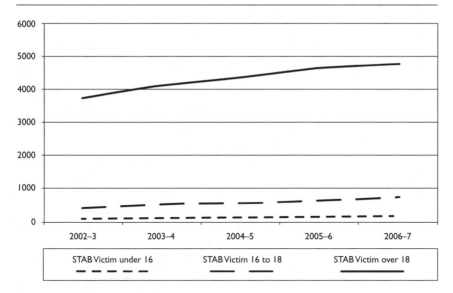

Figure 8.1 Stabbing victims aged under 18 reporting to accident and emergency departments 2002–7.

Source: Department of Health (2008)

slightly. The data has to be interpreted carefully, however. On the one hand, for example, since 2002 medical practitioners working in hospital accident and emergency (A&E) departments have been required to notify the police of gunshot injuries and this may have deterred some victims of non-serious/non-life-threatening gun-related injuries from attending A&E (Fallouh et al., 2009). On the other hand, an analysis of civilian firearm injuries by the Trauma Audit and Research Network shows a five-fold increase between 1995 and 2007 in the number of persons presenting at A&E departments with gunshot injuries (Davies and Lecky, forthcoming).

Fourth, during the first half of 2008, considerable media attention was devoted to a series of particularly brutal and fatal knife-related incidents, most occurring in London and many involving young people either as perpetrators, victims or both (Squires, 2009a; 2009b). Marfleet's (2008) report on weapon carrying by young people, for example, identified 36 teenagers who had been fatally stabbed in London during the period of her research. Between 2006 and 2007, the number of murder victims aged under 18 in London more than doubled, 70 per cent having been stabbed to death (Centre for Crime and Justice Studies, 2008: 34).

These four inter-related issues are illustrative of wider concerns pertaining to patterns of youth violence and apparently mushrooming 'weaponisation'. Both gun- and knife-related offences share a similar age profile and are concentrated in the same areas: particularly parts of London, Manchester, Merseyside and the West Midlands. Likewise, despite the trends showing that the number of victims aged

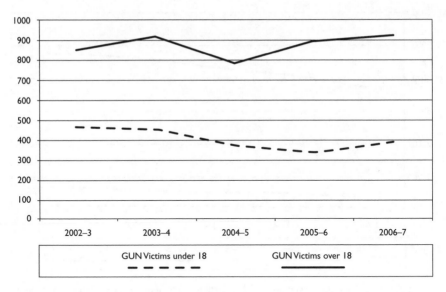

Figure 8.2 Gunshot victims reporting to accident and emergency departments 2002–7.

Source: Department of Health (2008)

under 18 are substantially outnumbered by older victims, media reporting has tended to focus upon youth. This has been as true of gun-involved homicides (where the murder of Rhys Jones in Liverpool in 2007 served as a focus of concern), as of knife crime (with the series of fatal stabbings of children and young people in London during the first part of 2008 drawing particular attention to the youth of both perpetrators and victims). The impact of media reporting of such cases will be considered later in the discussion. Furthermore, the Parliamentary Home Affairs Select Committee has observed that London has the greatest *volume* of knife crime (just over a third of the national total) and that a far greater *proportion* of murders are committed with knives (50 per cent) in the capital city, compared with the national average (House of Commons Home Affairs Select Committee, 2009). Accounting for these 'London factors', the Select Committee referred, on the one hand, to 'gangs' or youth groups, peer pressure and youthful 'territorialism' and, on the other, to increasing weapon availability and use (2009: 20–1). As with media reporting, such issues are reviewed later.

The 'Tackling Knives Action Programme'

The Tackling Knives Action Programme (TKAP) comprised a major practical response to the related questions of youth violence and 'weaponisation' (Ward and Diamond, 2009). Targeting the 13–19 age group, the initiative ran from July 2008 to March 2009 in 10 police force areas (selected for their relatively high rates of knife-involved offending). The TKAP exercise built upon the perceived success of Operation Blunt in London and involved a range of police-led interventions including: the utilisation of 1,150 mobile search arches and weapon detection wands; the targeting of local 'gangs'; the intelligence-led policing of so-called 'hot-spots' (where weapon-involved violence was known to occur) and, finally, intensive after-school patrolling. Concerted efforts were made to engage young people in the TKAP initiative and each of the participating police forces delivered 'weapon-awareness courses' in schools, youth clubs, focus groups and youth conferences. Further, each dimension of the TKAP built upon and extended a wide range of additional initiatives – introduced since 2007–8 – to tackle the possession and use of weapons by young people, including: a national media advertising campaign; Safer Schools Partnerships; 'test-purchase' operations (checking for retailers selling knives to those aged under 18); the introduction of a series of specialist Knife (offender) Possession Programmes developed and implemented by the Youth Justice Board;[1] improved data-sharing between health professionals (including A&E departments in hospitals) and local Crime and Disorder Reduction Partnerships;[2] the Tackling Gangs Action Programme (TGAP); and, finally, a range of 'tougher penalties' and new sentencing arrangements for young people and others found to be in possession of a knife.

The TKAP relied heavily upon labour-intensive police stop-and-search operations. There were some 220,000 TKAP searches between July 2008 and March 2009, almost three times the number in the comparable period of the previous year (such searches are allowed under Section 1 of the Police and Criminal Evidence Act 1984 or Section 60 of the Criminal Justice and Public Order Act 1994). At the commencement of the programme approximately four weapons were being found for every 100 searches (4 per cent), whereas, by the end of the operation only 2 per cent of searches were producing a weapon (which could indicate either some deterrent impact upon weapon carrying and/or that over 95 per cent of searches were misdirected). In terms of the TKAP's impact upon the target age group, a 13 per cent reduction in the number of weapon offences was recorded for those aged 13–19 years compared with an 8 per cent *increase* for those aged 20 and over. Relating these figures to the relative proportions of knife crime involving the under 18s – as compared with the over 20s as evidenced in Figure 8.1 – a 13 per cent reduction in stabbings for the 13–19 age group might represent a decrease in the order of 130–50 offences, whereas an 8 per cent increase for the older group approximates 350–70 *additional* offences, hardly a positive overall outcome. Furthermore, whilst there was no change in the number of stabbing homicide victims aged 13–19 years in the TKAP areas, a slight increase in homicide victims was recorded with regard to people aged 20 and over (Ward and Diamond, 2009: ii–iii). Interpreting such seemingly equivocal trends requires great care, therefore, as does the data pertaining to the patterning of hospital admissions in respect of stabbing incidents (see Figure 8.3). Ward and Diamond (2009: iii) note:

> building on earlier reductions, there was a provisional 32 per cent decrease in admissions to hospitals for assault with a sharp object among victims aged 19

and under in English TKAP areas, compared with an 18 per cent drop in non-TKAP areas.

In other words, whilst the fall in hospital admissions relating to knife-induced wounds clearly predates the launch of the TKAP initiative – and such patterns can also be seen to apply beyond the 10 TKAP pilot sites – the rate of decline is greatest in the TKAP areas. Furthermore, at the point of cessation of the TKAP initiative patterns of knife-related crime returned to and, in some cases, exceeded their previous levels. Despite difficulties of interpretation, therefore, questions about the appropriateness and sustainability of intensive police-led stop-and-search operations such as the TKAP are uppermost.

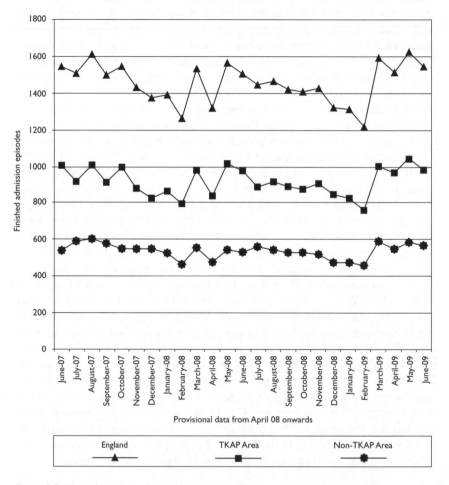

Figure 8.3 Monthly activity: hospital admissions for assault (13–24 years old).

Source: Hospital Episode Statistics (2010)

The effect of the TKAP initiative on prosecution and sentencing outcomes is less equivocal. Consistent with the tougher targeted sentencing emphasis, cautions and discharges fell by around 30 per cent each, while the proportion of knife-offenders sentenced to immediate custody rose by 37 per cent (compared with 19 per cent increase in the non-TKAP areas). Average custodial sentence lengths also increased (by a third for adults and a fifth for juveniles) (Ward and Diamond, 2009: 8). There was a 12 per cent increase in the number of community penalties imposed and suspended prison sentences also increased by 44 per cent. Perhaps the most enduring impact of the TKAP initiative, therefore, is the introduction and consolidation of a more punitive sentencing regime.

The weapon or the violence?

Any discussion of youth violence and 'weaponisation' has to take into account how such phenomena are represented and understood and, in this respect, two 'watershed' incidents are particularly noteworthy. The first occurred in the small Scottish town of Dunblane where, in March 1996, Thomas Hamilton, aged 43, entered a primary school and, with one of four guns, opened fire on a class of children in the school's gymnasium. In total, 16 children aged 5 and 6, together with their teacher, lost their lives. The public inquiry that followed the 'Dunblane Massacre' (Cullen, 1996) recommended, amongst other things, the tighter control of handguns and, in 1998, legislation was introduced to ban their ownership. The second key incident comprised a 'drive-by shooting' in the city of Birmingham in 2003. Charlene Ellis, aged 18, and Latisha Shakespear, aged 17, both died at the scene outside a hairdressing salon in the Aston area of the city. The young women were caught within a hail of approximately 30 bullets and two other girls were also injured: Charlene's twin sister Sophie, who underwent emergency surgery, and 17-year-old Cheryl Shaw. Apparently, the young women were not the intended victims but the shooting, with an automatic weapon from a moving vehicle, was recklessly indiscriminate. Such incidents appeared to fix popular attention on the *means* by which violence was dispensed rather than the actual violence itself. In other words, the fact that firearms are both illegal and relatively scarce (Squires, 2000) – together with the horrific and atypical nature of the above 'incidents' – meant that such weapons attracted inflated levels of attention as a distinctive form of criminality. In turn, all 'gun crime' – ranging from armed robberies and attempted murders to criminal damage with an air weapon and even public misuse of an imitation pistol – has come to be misleadingly conflated in the public debate (Squires, 2008). The same principles manifestly do not apply to knife crime, however. In general, knives are not illegal (with the exception of certain specific types): every household will contain numerous knives of different forms for perfectly legitimate uses. Yet because a seemingly unitary category of 'gun crime' has consolidated, a similar construction of 'knife crime' has emerged as if to imply homogeneity. Two core consequences follow from this tendency to focus upon weapons as the *means* of violence and although they might, in one sense, be seen as contradictory, they contribute significantly to contemporary discourse on street violence and youth 'weaponisation'.

First, the focus upon weapons detracts from the wider 'social relations' or 'social ecology' (Fagan and Wilkinson, 2000) of violence, within which *some* young people in *some* urban areas become enmeshed. This requires more than simply attempting to account for the supposed 'causes' of street violence. It is also necessary: to embrace cultural and psycho-social criminologies; address the function of violence in the performance of masculinity in street cultures; examine complex negotiations around conceptualisations of 'respect' – street currency (Sandberg, 2008) – and take account of both the projection and defence of personal identity. The lack of attention afforded to such crucial issues has tended to mean that common understandings of youth and weaponisation become detached from their contexts and meanings and are (mis)represented instead as the 'mindless' violence of the semi-human 'other'; the viciousness of the 'depraved' and 'evil'.

A second key consequence of focusing narrowly upon the weapon concerns the ways in which meanings are attributed to the violent act itself. In this respect the shift from 'gun' to 'knife' violence is read as a descent into even greater visceral brutality. More significantly, however, gun violence has come to be closely associated with 'gangs' in particular cities and urban areas, in ways that both draw parallels with the USA and 'racialise' the phenomenon. It follows that gun crime is often conceived as 'new' within a UK context and profoundly 'un-British'.[3] It is also presented and responded to, explicitly or implicitly, through racialised lenses.[4] Furthermore, while gun violence is commonly represented as violent, brutal and irresponsible – part of the disorganised criminal chaos of youthful street life – closer analysis reveals greater levels of organisation and more nuanced meaning. In other words, whilst a propensity for intimidating people with guns or, more problematically, the frequent discharging of firearms, certainly invokes a degree of irresponsibility and even a casual disregard for life, weapon 'use' (including: carriage and possession; display; brandishing and threatening) entails far more than simple intimidation and/or discharge.

Harcourt's (2006) fascinating study *Language of the Gun* – based upon interviews with persistent gun-carrying offenders – explores the wide variety of meanings, emotions and relations (of empowerment, 'manliness', respect and protection) that gun possession and use entails. Gun carrying/use – and the violence associated with it – was full of meaning even if, from the outside, it appeared chaotic and disorganised. This serves to contextualise the symbolic significance of weaponisation. Furthermore, once the 'shock of the new' is digested, it soon becomes apparent that – contrary to much media reporting – gun crime is not 'spinning out of control', the streets are not 'awash with blood', 'shootouts' are relatively uncommon and gun-enabled offences constitute no more than 0.2 per cent of recorded crime or the equivalent of 1 in 600 offences (Association of Chief Police Officers, 2007).[5] Equally, evidence from the Greater Manchester Police Operation Xcalibre – the dedicated intelligence-led gun and gang crime operation and the equivalent to the Metropolitan Police Operation

Trident – reveals many police records relate to shootings where cars, buildings, doors and windows – rather than people – comprise principal targets. Such incidents also include so-called 'drive-by shootings', which – notwithstanding the reckless irresponsibility with which they are often carried out – are manifestly not intended to take life. Rather, as Sanders' (1994) pioneering American study shows, such actions communicate a number of meanings including: sending out messages; issuing warnings; making territorial claims and presenting challenges. Similarly, during autumn 2009 the Metropolitan Police (Davenport, 2009) released figures revealing that of 985 firearms seized in London between January and July 2009, less than a quarter (22 per cent) were 'live-firing' weapons, the others were air weapons, BB guns, replica pistols or other non-firing guns. The publication of this data was accompanied by a statement to the effect that 'young gang members were carrying out non-fatal shootings to inflict "war wounds" on their rivals'. In other words, although undoubtedly violent, firearm attacks were often ambiguously motivated and cannot adequately be conceptualised as attempts to kill (Davenport, 2009). Unearthing otherwise hidden layers of meaning concerning youth violence and weaponisation, therefore, comprises an important corrective to oversimplified and amplified media hype, even if the true 'story' is not entirely reassuring.

Furthermore, if we move from the specifics of gun possession and use amongst identifiable constituencies of urban youth, to the wider social contexts and relations in which they negotiate landscapes of risk and danger, a number of crucially important additional issues come into play. The first and almost universal explanation is that the carrying of a weapon is motivated by considerations of personal protection – both literally and symbolically (Harcourt, 2006; Marfleet, 2008). At the literal level, defence – or at least the capacity to retaliate – are key. At the symbolic level, carrying a weapon speaks to reputation and street credibility. Ultimately, the two dimensions – literal self-defence and symbolic 'defence of the self' – walk hand-in-hand. As Harcourt (2006) and others (Fagan and Wilkinson, 2000; Mullins, 2006) have noted, people with poor reputations – 'punks' or 'pussies' – can find themselves relentlessly bullied and victimised, ultimately having to defend themselves physically.

This takes us to the debate surrounding the so-called 'code of the street'. Some commentators, Anderson (1999) prominent amongst them, have argued that a knowledge of the street – including its hierarchy and associated relations of deference and respect – equips those who 'know the codes' with the means to negotiate their way relatively safely around their neighbourhoods. Yet the 'codes' are neither clear nor consistently followed and/or applied. Stewart et al. (2006), in an article revealingly titled 'I Ain't Gonna Let No-one Disrespect Me', for example, reveal how street behaviour codes are just as likely to *provoke* violent challenges and altercations as they are to *forestall* them. The very attitudes, demeanours, behaviours and steely glares ('ice grills' or 'eye fucks') that were intended to convey the status of not being 'messed with' were just as likely to be perceived as a *challenge* by others. Respect, therefore, was not something fixed and constant but a relation that needed to be renewed and reinvested constantly.

Indeed, constructions of identity and status – within which the notion of 'respect' is pivotal – are key to understanding the cultural realities, social capital and political economy of the street (Squires, 2009a). Anderson (cited in Short, 1997: 65) notes that:

> the seemingly inordinate concern with 'respect' – resulting in a low threshold for being 'dissed' (disrespected) – can be traced to the profound alienation from mainstream American society felt by many inner city blacks, particularly the poorest.

Furthermore, as Short (1997: 65) observes:

> out of concern for being disrespected, respect is easily violated. Because status problems are mixed with extreme resource limitations, people – especially young people – exaggerate the importance of symbols, often with life-threatening consequences.

Analyses of the violent habitus of inner-urban street life have been further developed by Fagan and Wilkinson (1998; 2000), who interviewed over 300 actively violent street youth in two New York suburbs. The research centred on the social dynamics of violent encounters in which their interviewees had been personally involved. Fagan and Wilkinson (1998) argue that obtaining and using a gun becomes part of a (masculine) 'rite of passage' within contexts in which 'processes of *anticipatory socialisation*' are underpinned by shortened life expectations and the perceived likelihood of threats, risks, victimisation and, ultimately, lethal violence. In such environments, 'carrying firearms seem[s] to enhance feelings of safety and personal efficacy among teenagers' socialised within an '*ecology of violence*', within which 'beliefs about guns and the dangers of everyday life' are internalised in early childhood and come to shape young people's cognitive frameworks, their interpretations of events and their actions throughout adolescence (1998). Thus, experiences (direct or indirect) of violence fuel expectations of violence and this leads young people to both anticipate and prepare for violent encounters, necessitating acquiring, carrying and using weapons. Weapon carrying is normalised and a 'shoot or be shot' mentality prevails in which even trivial precipitating incidents can result in fatal exchanges. In this way, Fagan and Wilkinson (1998) found that over two-thirds of violent incidents in their US research derived from 'identity/status/respect' conflicts. Hales and colleagues (2006: 82–3) also found that anticipation of violence was common amongst their interviewees, comprising convicted firearms offenders in the UK:

> you just have to bust [shoot] in their face before they bust at you.

and

> If you actually know someone's out there to kill you, what choice [have] you got?

It remains an open question as to how far knives perpetuate similar violence dynamics as guns. Firearms are conceived of as the supreme instrument of lethal inter-personal violence: portable, concealable and relatively easy to use. A simple pull of the trigger by reckless and impetuous youth can end a life. To kill with a knife, by contrast, generally demands closer contact, more explicit force and a more clearly defined intention. It is important to be clear about this. By adopting a 'signal' perspective (Innes, 2004), the shift to knife violence represents a kind of 'signal displacement' or a 'signal shift', specifically with regard to the meanings attributed to knife violence. Knife crime is normally construed as worse by virtue of the meanings associated with – and the motives attributed to – the deliberate, up close, personal, forceful and visceral brutality involved in thrusting a blade into another person. While shooting might seem remote and detached, knife crime appears as immediate and connected. Thus a new low in youth violence is apparently signalled. But knife-enabled assault can be just as ambiguously motivated as any other violence including, of course, appeals to 'self-protection' and/or 'defence'.[6] In this light it is important to explore the contexts, causes and drivers of knife-related weaponisation and to begin to address some of the crucial questions that the Government's Tackling Knives Action Programme (Ward and Diamond, 2009) omitted.

Violent contexts for 'weaponisation': marginality, anticipation and protection

Rather than emphasise spurious and decontextualised conceptions of youthful brutality, it is important to seek understanding of how 'choices' are made and the conditions in which they are located. In some respects the late modern 'delinquent solutions' echo those adopted in earlier times. In other ways it is imperative to engage with the concept of 'advanced urban marginality' (Wacquant, 2006) and the wider 'de-civilisation' thesis to glean understanding. Harris (2006: x), for instance, endeavours to explain why 'community' matters by imagining its nightmarish alternative: 'we would gradually become less inclined to venture out unless armed and protected, we would move in fear of others'. In a more direct reference to the dynamics of class, 'race' and social exclusion Lee Jasper, the former Mayor of London's 'Race Relations Advisor' – in giving evidence to the Parliamentary Home Affairs Select Committee inquiry into Young Black People and the Criminal Justice System (House of Commons Home Affairs Select Committee, 2007: 20) – referred to a 'specific crisis' in urban black communities in respect of the levels of violence in general and the number of fatalities attributable to guns and knives in particular. The Committee itself went on to note how:

Social exclusion is a key underlying cause of young black people's over-representation as both victims and suspects. Not only does it fuel involvement in crime directly, it makes young people vulnerable to a host of other risk factors, such as living in neighbourhoods where crime is high and [so is] underachieving at school.

(House of Commons Home Affairs Select Committee, 2007: 29)

The point to be made is that, in such communities, for many young people Harris's (2006) imagined 'nightmare' has become, or is fast becoming, a reality. A toxic mix of social exclusion and violence directly frames the social relations negotiated by young people in the poorest areas. As Wacquant (2006: 54 and 69) puts it: 'an extraordinary prevalence of physical danger and [an] acute sense of insecurity pervades the streets . . . everyone must protect themselves from violence by being ready to wield it at any time'.

A report by Golding, McClory and Lockhart (2008) emphasises the large numbers of young people affected by weapon-involved crime. Over half of young offenders 'have had a gun or knife used against them or been threatened with a gun or knife in the past 12 months'. Furthermore:

> more than 1 in 4 of those surveyed (27 per cent) have either been the victim of a violent crime committed by children or young people, have had a gun or knife used against them, have been threatened with one or know a friend or relative who has had a gun or knife used against them or who has been threatened with one in the past 12 months.

> (Golding et al., 2008: 5)

As stated, this can produce 'anticipatory' and 'protective' responses. A survey conducted by Broadhurst, Duffin and Taylor (2008) on behalf of the teacher's union NASUWT revealed the extent to which young people emphasise self-defence:

> It's not a bad thing to bring a weapon into school. You might get attacked on the way to school, or on the way back. It's protection.

> I can protect myself with a knife or a gun. I would rather be arrested than dead.

> It's not a bad thing to bring weapons into school because of the area you are going to on the way to school.

> (Broadhurst et al., 2008: 15–16)

Equally, Marfleet (2008) noted how a large proportion of her interviewees spoke of anticipating unprovoked attacks because of where they lived, who they were or where they went. One young man described how he had to travel through part of the Wood Green area in London:

> to see my girl . . . and I've got beef with Wood Green, man. I get shot at, or like if I don't have a strap then they chasing me up trying to move me up. I'd rather have a shank and flick it out and start wetting man than get stabbed myself. Cos if you have a shank and they haven't, they gonna back off.

> (Marfleet, 2008: 77–8)

When the same young man was asked about his mother's attitude to his carrying a knife, he added, 'she wasn't happy but she knows how the area is. People dying and shit like that. She would rather me have a knife on me to protect myself' (2008: 75).

In the face of such attitudes Government marketing campaigns to achieve attitude change are seemingly doomed to fail.[7] Sensationalised media reporting – nationally and locally – is likely to prompt more young people, living in areas perceived to be dangerous, to seek their own 'protection' solutions. A vicious circle is at work and it may not be operating in isolation.

Weaponisation, criminalisation and gangsterisation?

Zimring (1998) has explored the means by which hostile and increasingly intolerant perspectives on particular groups of young people developed and consolidated in the USA. Violence and disorder became the primary lenses through which contemporary youth was perceived. This, he argues, distorted public policy and encouraged the projection of 'negative stereotypes and cartoon superficiality onto the motives and character of young people' (1998: 181). Perhaps inevitably, it was primarily around the issues of gangs, weapon use and violence that the most pressing concerns were focused. In the UK similar processes are evident, including the more generic emphasis on 'antisocial behaviour'; the Pandora's Box that has opened up an entirely new range of fears and concerns about youth and has facilitated a virtual paradigm shift in the seriousness with which such 'antisocial' behaviours are conceptualised and responded to (Squires and Stephen, 2005).

The problems of social and 'racial' exclusion, gang formation and violence in the UK may be far removed from the scale reported in US cities, but transatlantic echoes are discernible in young people's accounts regarding the urban 'ecologies of violence' in which they have to adapt and survive by associating with peer groups ('gangs') and carrying weapons. But these are contextually driven 'choices' and, as Sandberg (2008) has argued, the 'street' behaviours and identities that specific groups of young people adopt represent the resources to which they turn in order to negotiate the risks that they face. Heale's (2008) recent discussion of 'gangland rules' brings these issues to life and, by illuminating how young people live, feel, dress, think, walk, talk and respond, a further vicious circle is revealed, whereby cultivating a violent identity and/carrying a weapon may *seem* like a sensible precaution/

Just as the 'delinquent solutions' adopted by 'gang-members' and street youth attracted the censure of their communities and the attention of the police in the USA (Hagedorn, 1988), so it is in London, Manchester and other British cities. Furthermore, as in the USA, conflict, police enforcement and processes of criminalisation – not least the police-led application of the 'gang' label and specialist, heavy-handed 'gang suppression' tactics and intelligence-led targeting including 'task forces' and specialist 'gang units' – tend to have a self-fulfilling effect on the 'gang problem' (Squires and Kennison, 2010; Hallsworth, this volume). Malcolm Klein (1995: 7–8), one of the USA's leading gang researchers, has concluded:

> Most gang intervention programs can be shown to increase gang cohesiveness . . . increasing gang cohesiveness also increases group morale and productivity. One of the products of gangs is crime . . . Most gang intervention programmes, without meaning to, have the net effect of increasing gang crime.

A US Justice Policy Institute study arrived at similar conclusions (Greene and Pranis, 2007: 7). Whilst observing that gang suppression 'remains an enormously popular response to gang activity', it also acknowledges that 'such tactics can strengthen gang cohesion and increase community tension . . . heavy-handed suppression efforts can increase gang cohesion and police-community tensions, and they have a poor track record when it comes to reducing crime and violence'.

The furore that greeted the news that in October 2009, in the wake of a series of gang-related shootings, the Metropolitan Police had (apparently) decided to routinely deploy armed patrol officers in certain areas of London is a case in point. Armed patrols are *not* a new departure in policing responses of course, but opinion is seemingly divided. On one hand, the Metropolitan Police Commissioner was severely criticised for taking such a step without consulting partner agencies, advisors and stakeholders. On the other hand a sizeable proportion of Londoners apparently felt that armed police patrols were a good idea ('If armed patrols work – let's keep them'; 'Gun patrols could have stopped my son from being shot', *Evening Standard,* 27 and 28 October 2009). No similar 'debate' accompanied the launch of the Government's Tackling Gangs, and Tackling Knives Action Programmes, even though the thinly veiled 'racialised' (racist) focus of the former[8] and the dubious legality of the mass 'stop and search' operations of the latter,[9] are deeply problematic. Such 'exceptionalising' of the law and order response to youth – predicated upon a police-constructed notion of 'gangsterised' violence – extends and deepens processes of criminalisation (more enforcement, tougher sentences, more and longer custodial penalties) and echoes experimentation in the USA that has been seen to fail. But just as the Tacking Knives Action Programme monitoring report admits to having no real grasp of the 'underlying causes' of weapon-involved youth crime (Ward and Diamond, 2009), policy makers apparently have little appetite for examining its complex 'drivers' beyond attributing it to an essentialised antisocial 'culture of violence', symptomatic of a demoralised and 'broken' society.

If the focus for policy and action has shifted from 'broken windows' (Wilson and Kelling, 1982) to the 'broken society' (Centre for Social Justice, 2009), and if restoring neighbourhoods and communities by building social capital is seen as the way forward, it is important to consider what this will mean for excluded and demonised youth. Such young people are not only structurally located *outside* the protections otherwise offered by the adult community and its forms of authority (perhaps, in the first instance, the police), they have also increasingly become the *objects* of local crime and disorder governance processes. Criminal justice interventions have become heavily implicated in sustaining the predicament of marginalised youth as their socially excluded status and identity is reinforced and recycled through increasingly frequent encounters with the police, new tiers of community justice agents, criminal justice disposals and an intolerant climate of public fear and alarm. These are precisely the conditions that fostered the weaponisation of American youth. The real danger is that similar processes are increasingly evident in the UK too.

Notes

1   The executive non-departmental public body established by the first New Labour administration with a statutory function to advise the Secretary of State on matters of youth justice policy and practice.

2   The Crime and Disorder Act 1998 established these 'partnerships' comprising the police, local authorities, probation service, health authorities, the voluntary sector and local residents and businesses.

3   For example the comment, in the House of Commons, of David Mellor MP that, if we sought to embrace the 'American way of life', we must also accept the American way of death.

4   Thus Operation Trident in London was detailed to tackle 'black on black' crime and, as a policing response, was soon reproduced in a number of other areas. Similarly, the Tackling Gangs Action Programme (TGAP) that was implemented during 2007–8 comprised a markedly racialised pattern of policing. Seventy-five per cent of TGAP targets were African-Caribbean – a proportion significantly higher than the ethnic profiles in any of the four cities in which the TGAP operated (see Dawson, 2008; Squires et al., 2008).

5   It should be noted that the 0.2 per cent figure relates to firearms excluding air weapons and the Association of Chief Police Officers acknowledges that many firearms incidents, especially those involving no injury, or only minor injuries, may go unreported. Furthermore, there are important misgivings about the definition of 'recorded' firearm crimes. A *Sunday Telegraph* survey of police forces (Barrett, 2008) found that around 5,600 additional gun crimes (a 60 per cent increase) would be recorded if illegal possession and trafficking offences were also counted.

6   A series of youth surveys confirm that young people identify 'self-protection' as their main reason for carrying a knife including: Wilson et al., 2006; National Youth Agency, 2006; Firmin et al., 2007; NCH Action for Children, 2008; Marfleet, 2008; Hayden, 2008; Broadhurst et al., 2008.

7   'TKAP 2', the second phase of the Government's Tackling Knives Action Programme, broadened to encompass both the 13–24 age group and 'all serious youth violence', involves a significant media marketing/advertising campaign – co-ordinated through an initiative entitled 'It doesn't have to happen' – that aims to 'convince young people at risk of carrying [weapons] that it is never a safe or acceptable option' (Home Office, 2009–10).

8   See note 4.

9   Section 60 of the Criminal Justice and Public Order Act 1994 provides police with powers to search people in a defined area at a specific time when they believe, with good reason, that there is a possibility of serious violence or that a person (or persons)

is carrying a dangerous object or offensive weapon. Use of the power has to be 'reasonable' and 'proportionate', authorised by a senior officer and specifically time-limited. Concern has arisen that the use of this power in London – and elsewhere – has become routine, excessive and protracted.

References

Association of Chief Police Officers (2007) *Gun Crime and Gangs: A Reponse to the Home Secretary*. London: Association of Chief Police Officers, September.

Anderson, E. (1999) *Code of the Street: Decency, Violence and the Moral Life of the Inner City*. New York: W.W. Norton & Co.

Barrett, D. (2008) 'Gun Crime 60 Per Cent Higher than Official Figures', *Sunday Telegraph*, 19 October.

Broadhurst, K., Duffin, M. and Taylor, E. (2008) *Gangs and Schools: Interim Report: An Interim Report for NASUWT*. Birmingham: Perpetuity Group and NASUWT.

Centre for Crime and Justice Studies (2008) *Street Weapons Commission Evidence: Guns, Knives and Street Violence*. London: Centre for Crime and Justice Studies, Kings College.

Centre for Social Justice (2009) *Dying to Belong: A Policy Report by the Gangs Working Group*. London: Centre for Social Justice.

Cullen, Lord (1996) *The Public Inquiry into the Shootings at Dunblane Primary School on 13 March 1996*. London: The Stationery Office.

Davenport, J. (2009) 'Teenage "Respect" Shootings Sends Gun Crime Soaring', *Evening Standard*, 19 October.

Davies, M.J. and Lecky, F.E. (forthcoming) *Civilian Firearm Injury in England and Wales*, Trauma Audit and Research Network. Manchester: University of Manchester.

Dawson, P. (2008) *Monitoring Data from the Tackling Gangs Action Programme*. London: Home Office.

Department of Health (2008) *Hospital Accident and Emergency Admissions for Gunshot Wounds and Stab Injuries by Age*. Placed in the House of Commons Library 25 June. London: House of Commons.

Fagan, J. and Wilkinson, D. (1998) 'Guns, Youth Violence and Social Identity in Inner Cities', *Youth Violence*, 24: 105–88.

—— (2000) *Situational Contexts of Gun Use by Young Males in Inner Cities*. Rockville, MD: US Department of Justice, National Criminal Justice Reference Service.

Fallouh, H.B., Venugopal, P.S. and Newton, A. (2009) 'Occult Gunshot Wounds in the Emergency Room', *The Lancet*, 373(9664): 631–2.

Firmin, C., Turner, R. and Gavrielides, T. (2007) *Empowering Young People Through Human Rights Values: Fighting the Knife Culture*. London: Esmee Fairbairn Foundation.

Golding, B., McClory, J. and Lockhart, G. (2008) *Going Ballistic: Dealing with Guns, Gangs and Knives*. London: The Policy Exchange.

Greene, J. and Pranis, K. (2007) *Gang Wars: The Failure of Enforcement Tactics and the Need for Effective Public Safety Strategies*. Washington, DC: Justice Policy Institute.

Hagedorn, J.M. (1988) *People and Folks: Gangs, Crime and the Underclass in Rustbelt City*. Chicago: Lakeview Press.

Hales, G., Lewis, C. and Silverstone, D. (2006) *Gun Crime: The Market in and Use of Illegal Firearms*. Home Office Research Study 298. London: Home Office.

Harcourt, B.E. (2006) *Language of the Gun: Youth Crime and Public Policy*. Chicago: University of Chicago Press.

Harris, K. (2006) 'Introduction', in K. Harris (ed.) *Respect in the Neighbourhood: Why Neighbourliness Matters*. Lyme Regis: Russell House Publishing.

Hayden, C. (2008) *Staying Safe and Out of Trouble: A Survey of Young People's Perceptions and Experiences*. Portsmouth: Institute for Criminal Justice Studies, University of Portsmouth.

Heale, J. (2008) *One Blood: Inside Britain's New Street Gangs*. London: Simon & Schuster.

Home Office (2008) *Saving Lives. Reducing Harm. Protecting the Public: An Action Plan for Tackling Violence 2008–11*. London: The Home Office.

—— (2009–10) *Anti-Knife Communication Campaign*. Retrieved 30 August 2010 (http://www.crimereduction.homeoffice.gov.uk/stopknifecrime/).

Hospital Episode Statistics (2010) *Monthly Activity: Hospital Admissions for Assault (13–24 years old)*. Retrieved 30 August 2010 (http://www.hesonline.nhs.uk/Ease/servlet/ContentServer?siteID=1937&categoryID=1131).

House of Commons Home Affairs Select Committee (2007) *Young Black People and the Criminal Justice System*. Second Report of Session 2006–7. London: The Stationery Office.

—— (2009) *Knife Crime*. Seventh Report of Session 2008–9. London: The Stationery Office.

Innes, M. (2004), 'Signal Crimes and Signal Disorders: Notes on Deviance as Communicative Action', *British Journal of Sociology*, 55: 335–55.

Klein, M. (1995) *The American Street Gang: Its Nature, Prevalence and Control*. Oxford, Oxford University Press.

Marfleet, N. (2008) *Why Carry a Weapon? A Study of Knife Crime Amongst 15–17 Year Old Males in London*. London: The Howard League for Penal Reform.

Mullins, C.W. (2006) *Holding Your Square: Masculinities, Streetlife and Violence*. Cullompton: Willan.

NCH Action for Children (2008) *'Step Inside Our Shoes': Young People's Views on Gun and Knife Crime*. London: NCH Action for Children.

National Youth Agency (2006) *Knives, Guns and Gangs*, 'Spotlight' Issue 37. Leicester: National Youth Agency.

Sandberg, S. (2008) 'Street Capital: Ethnicity and Violence on the Streets of Oslo', *Theoretical Criminology*, 12(2): 153–71.

Sanders, W.B. (1994) *Gang-bangs and Drive-bys: Grounded Culture and Juvenile Gang Violence*. New York: De Gruyter.

Short, J.R.F. (1997) *Poverty, Ethnicity and Violent Crime*. Boulder: Westview Press/Harper Collins.

Squires, P. (2000) *Gun Culture or Gun Control?: Firearms, Violence and Society*. London: Routledge.

—— (2008) *Gun Crime: A Review of Evidence and Policy*. London: Kings Centre for Crime and Justice Studies, Kings College.

—— (2009a) '"You Lookin' at Me?" Discourses of Respect and Disrespect, Identity and Violence', in A. Millie (ed.) *Securing Respect: Behaviour Expectations and Anti-Social Behaviour in the UK*. Bristol: The Policy Press.

—— (2009b) 'The Knife Crime "Epidemic" and British Politics', *British Politics*, 4: 127–57.

Squires, P. and Stephen, D.E. (2005) *Rougher Justice: Anti-Social Behaviour and Young People*. Cullompton: Willan.

Squires, P. and Kennison, P. (2010) *Shooting to Kill: Policing, Firearms and Armed Response*. Oxford: Wiley/Blackwell.

Stewart, E.A., Schreck, C.J. and Simons, R.L. (2006) '"I Ain't Gonna Let No-One Disrespect Me": Does the Code of the Street Reduce or Increase Violent Victimisation Among African American Adolescents?', *Journal of Research in Crime and Delinquency*, 43(4): 427–58.

Wacquant, L. (2006) *Urban Outcasts: A Comparative Sociology of Advanced Marginality*. Cambridge, Polity Press.

Ward, L. and Diamond, A. (2009) *Tackling Knives Action Programme (TKAP) Phase 1: Overview of Key Trends From a Monitoring Programme*. Home Office Research and Statistics Directorate, Research Report 18. London: Home Office.

Wilson, D., Sharp, C. and Patterson, A. (2006), *Young People and Crime: Findings from the 2005 Offending, Crime and Justice Survey*. London: Home Office.

Wilson, J.Q. and Kelling, G.L. (1982) 'Broken Windows', *Atlantic Monthly*, 249: 29–38.

Zimring, F. (1998) *American Youth Violence*. Oxford: Oxford University Press.

Chapter 9

Mercenary territory

Are youth gangs really a problem?

John Pitts

> First the killing was about drugs, then it was about territory, now it is about postcodes, respect . . . anything.
>
> (Daniel, aged 18, 2007)

> Yes, so far as the individual is concerned . . . it may very well be true that character is destiny. And the other way round. But on the larger scale, destiny is demographics; and demographics is a monster.
>
> (Martin Amis, *House of Meetings*, 2007)

Introduction

This chapter draws upon research undertaken in London, England, over a four-year period, together with current research into the impact of gang desistance programmes.[1] It first addresses the thorny academic debate about whether or not 'youth gangs' actually exist and, if they do, whether or not we should be worried about them. It concludes that they do and we should. It then examines why, when and where these violent youth gangs emerged and developed.

So do they exist?

Although police officers, professionals, adults, children and young people appear to believe that violent youth gangs exist in 'gang-affected' neighbourhoods (Pitts 2007, 2008a, 2008b; Palmer, 2009), some academics remain sceptical. They tend to argue that the contemporary furore surrounding violent youth gangs is akin to the 'moral panics' which attended the 'teddy boys' in the 1950s, the 'mods and rockers' in the 1960s, the punks in the 1970s, the lager louts in the 1980s and so on. They contend that these periodic expressions of popular outrage tell us more about the anxieties of an adult public, 'opinion formers' and the media than the behaviour of young people. For them, the most important task is to allay popular anxieties by pointing to historical continuities between contemporary youth cultures and those of yesteryear (Young et al., 2007). Simon Hallsworth and Tara Young (2008: 175), for example, argue that:

This anxiety has coalesced in a perception that the gang is a serious and growing problem, that the rise in lethal violence, as seen recently in inner cities such as London, Birmingham, Manchester and Liverpool, is connected to the proliferation of the gang, and that the solution to the problem of urban gang violence lies in its suppression.

In this critique, allegedly exaggerated portrayals of violent youth gangs are presented as a product of 'moral entrepreneurism' (Becker, 1963), wherein criminal justice agencies dramatise a problem and stoke popular anxieties in order to gain increased resources and greater political influence. Other academics believe that this demonisation has a more sinister purpose, however, arguing that current concerns about violent youth gangs are orchestrated by the state, its agencies and the media in order to justify ever deeper incursions into our freedoms and ever greater control over our lives (Rose, 2000; Muncie and Hughes 2002; Simon 2007).

Academics associated with the Eurogang project,[2] by contrast, hold that youth gangs exist throughout the UK but, unlike popular North American portrayals, they have a fluid membership, porous boundaries and are, for the most part, engaged in only relatively innocuous adolescent offending (Klein, 2008; Aldridge et al., 2008). For them, the academic task consists of demolishing unhelpful stereotypes (Aldridge et al., 2008) and identifying those personal, familial and environmental characteristics of gang-involved young people that set them apart from others, in order to develop targeted intervention programmes (Klein, 2008).

This chapter acknowledges historical continuities between youth subcultures past and present and the, sometimes misplaced, social anxieties they engender (Pearson, 1983 and this volume; Davies, this volume). It accepts that there are many adolescent groups in the UK, characterised by fluid membership and porous boundaries, engaged in relatively innocuous adolescent misbehaviour that are identified as 'gangs' (Klein, 2008). It concurs with the view that although the term 'gang' is used indiscriminately in popular discourse, the media and the criminal justice system, all too often, its use is stigmatising and racist (Alexander, 2008). And while it recognises that since the late 1970s, UK governments have exploited the fear of crime for electoral advantage (Pitts, 2003), it nonetheless maintains that violent youth gangs exist and that their existence poses a serious threat to the safety and well-being, and in some cases the lives, of the children, young people and adults who live in gang-affected neighbourhoods (Bullock and Tilley, 2002; Palmer and Pitts, 2006; Pitts, 2008b; Matthews and Pitts, 2007; Palmer, 2009; Centre for Social Justice, 2009, Balasunderam, 2009).

What should we call them?

In 2006, in Waltham Forest, 54 respondents (gang-involved young people, non-gang-involved young people, local residents, youth workers, social workers, school teachers/heads, street wardens, youth justice and community safety professionals and police officers) were asked the following questions:

- What do you mean by a 'youth gang'?
- Are there youth gangs in this area? (*and, if the answer was yes*)
- How long have they been here?

Their responses indicated that they believed that youth gangs existed and that they were characterised by:

- a shared name or designation that is recognised by both affiliated and non-affiliated children and young people, local adults and local criminal justice, educational and social welfare personnel;
- a discernible structure characterised by hierarchical role differentiation (a 'pecking order') and, in some cases, links into upper echelon organised crime;
- the influence they exerted over the neighbourhood, drug dealing or institutional territory by dint of local loyalties or the threat or imposition of (sometimes lethal) violence;
- a paramount concern with the illicit acquisition of wealth and the maintenance of 'respect' in the territories where they have their influence; and
- conflictual relationships with other, similar, groups or networks and the police (Pitts, 2007).

While Claire Alexander (2008) is undoubtedly right that the media should be far more circumspect in its use of the word 'gang', we nonetheless need a term that describes these groupings because, as Ludwig Wittgenstein (1921/1971) observed: 'whereof we cannot speak thereof we must pass over in silence'. Robert Gordon (2000) distinguishes between conventional adolescent 'youth movements', 'youth groups', 'criminal groups', 'wannabe groups', 'street gangs' and 'criminal business organisations'. The groups I am concerned with here fall somewhere along a continuum from 'wannabe groups', to 'street gangs' and 'criminal business organisations' but, for the most part, I am concerned with what, for the sake of brevity, I shall call violent youth gangs.

Are they a new phenomenon?

Respondents in Waltham Forest reported that they had been aware of violent youth gangs in the neighbourhood for between five and eight years. A similar sample of respondents was asked the same questions in Lambeth in 2008. They offered a similar definition and explained that although in the 1990s they had been aware of only one named gang in the area – 'The 28s' – in 2008 there were many more. In fact, the research identified 40 such gangs (Pitts, 2008a). Suzella Palmer (2009: 41), whose research was based on a public housing estate in North West London, gives an indication of the pace of change when she writes:

This research was initiated in 2003, and at that time there was no clear evidence to suggest the existence of structured, territorial, criminal gangs, which currently exist in some communities across Britain today ... in the neighbourhood in which my study is based. Yet by August 2007, the Metropolitan Police had identified twenty-five gangs in the Borough and at least three of these were based in the neighbourhood where this research was conducted.

In the mid 1990s, Peter Stelfox (1998) a senior police officer from Lancashire, having undertaken preliminary research in the United States, embarked upon a national gang survey for the Home Office. Although he elicited a remarkable 91.45 per cent response rate to his questionnaire, only 16 police services were able to identify gangs in their area, yielding a national total of 72. The majority of the UK gangs identified by Stelfox were composed of adult males aged between 25 and 29. Some gangs spanned a broader age range with a few gang members below the age of 16. These gangs were predominantly White, only 25 per cent had members described as 'Black Caribbean', and only 7 per cent had members who were predominantly from ethnic minority groups. This led Stelfox (1998: 399) to conclude that:

> These figures challenge the perception that violent gangs are primarily either a youth problem or one which occurs mainly within ethnic communities. Organisationally the majority of gangs tended towards a loose structure.

Yet, within nine years, the Metropolitan Police (2007) had identified 172 named youth gangs in London alone, many using firearms, estimated to have been responsible for around 28 knife and gun murders. Clearly, things had changed. While 'youth gangs' are not a new phenomenon in the UK (Pearson, 1983 and this volume; Davies, 2008 and this volume), the kinds of violent youth gangs discussed in this chapter are, and one that is evolving and spreading rapidly.

Is the concern with violent youth gangs overblown?

Are these anxieties well-founded or are they a product of popular anxieties and governmental hype? In April 2009 at Liverpool Crown Court, 11 members of the South Manchester 'Gooch Gang' were convicted of 154 shootings, including 23 murders, and 94 serious woundings. On the basis of evidence from 'gang members' and an elaborate 'wire tap', the Greater Manchester Police identified these men as key figures in the Class A drug trade in Manchester. Drug-related gang violence in Manchester has its origins in the struggles between criminal cliques in the Cheetham Hill and Moss Side districts for control of the city centre drugs market in the 1980s. Later, the Moss Side gangs split into the Gooch Close Gang and the neighbouring Doddington Gang. In 1995, Raymond Pitt was killed by members of the Doddington Gang (to which he belonged) and his assassins and their associates founded a new gang, the Pit Bull Crew. The Pit Bull Crew then entered an uneasy alliance with the Gooch Close Gang, but the killing continued unabated. In 1996, the murder of 17-year-old Orville Bell by the Young Gooch was the catalyst for the formation of the Longsight. A series of tit-for-tat shootings ensued and, as a result, in June 1997, five members of the Young Gooch were sentenced to 43 years in prison for firearms-related offences. Nonetheless, the violent conflict between the Young Gooch, Doddington and Longsight gangs continued into the twenty-first century, culminating in the Crown Court trial in 2009.

Research undertaken in South Manchester by Karen Bullock and Nick Tilley (2002) – based on intelligence compiled by Greater Manchester Police and interviews with former and current 'gang members' – confirmed that much of this armed violence was, in the first instance at least, designed to ensure that the street dealers and the night club security firms the gangs were supplying, were protected from rival gangs. The study revealed that between April 2001 and March 2002, South Manchester gangs were responsible for 11 fatal shootings, 84 serious woundings and 639 other incidents of violence involving firearms. It also showed that many of the perpetrators and victims were in their early teens. These shootings were highly localised. Of those recorded in 1999, for example, 68 per cent were in the two main gang-affected areas in South Manchester.

Bullock and Tilley (2002) found that for every shooting in other parts of Greater Manchester, there were 35 in the two main gang-affected neighbourhoods, meaning that people living there were 140 times more likely to be shot than residents elsewhere. The 92 per cent fall in firearms crime in Manchester between February 2008 and July 2009 following the arrests of the 11 members of the Young Gooch calls into question the assertion that the recent rise in lethal violence in London, Birmingham, Manchester and Liverpool is unrelated to the pro-liferation of violent gang crime (Hallsworth and Young, 2008). Indeed, in 2008, prior to the arrests of members of the Young Gooch, Greater Manchester police had issued 225 'Osman warnings', alerting potential victims of gang-related crime that their lives were in danger. In recent years, Manchester has had the highest rate of 'Osman warnings' in the country; three times that of the Metropolitan Police (in London). Thus, on the face of it, Manchester has had, and may still have, a serious gang problem.

Nonetheless, some academics appear to believe that the anxieties expressed about Manchester gangs by the police the media, social welfare agencies, community groups and other academics are exaggerated. So how are we to account for the discrepancy between commentaries that seem to downplay the seriousness of the problem on the one hand, and, on the other hand, the findings of Bullock and Tilley (2002), Matthews and Pitts (2007), Pitts (2008a, 2008b) and Palmer (2009), together with the concerns repeatedly expressed by criminal justice, educational and social welfare professionals and residents in gang-affected neighbourhoods?

Conceptual difficulties

Dennis Mares (2001), who conducted his study in Manchester in the late 1990s –
the period when the shootings researched by Bullock and Tilley (2002) were
at their height – contends that youth gangs have been misunderstood and
misrepresented as more tightly structured, more criminally sophisticated and more
dangerous than they actually are. He writes:

> Compared with the Manchester gangs in the late 19th century the current
> gangs are small and probably less delinquent . . . This suggests that the gang
> problem in this Northern city is fairly limited.
>
> (Mares, 2001: 157)

In similarly reassuring vein, Judith Aldridge and colleagues (2008: 34) castigate
the press for presenting a:

> distorted view of gangs, gang members and their communities, through a
> sensationalised, skewed and superficial emphasis on crime and violence.
> Moreover some of these publications over-emphasise the relevance of
> ethnicity or immigration status as factors that explain or define gangs.

The researchers contrast this with their own portrayal of Manchester 'gangs' as
groups of young people with fluid memberships, porous boundaries and a messy
structure. However, the reference here to 'messiness', like Eurogang's similarly
porous gang definition, allows considerable space for equivocation about the
actual nature of the groupings under investigation.

This vagueness about the phenomenon to be investigated is not uncommon in
contemporary gang scholarship but for the social scientist, such 'messiness' should
be a starting point, not a conclusion, because 'messiness' is what social scientists
are required to explain. David Matza (1969) states the matter succinctly in his
critique of the Chicago School (see Park and Burgess, 1921), arguing that 'social
disorganisation' is a term used by social scientists who have failed to discern the
subtleties of the many modes of informal social organisation extant within an
apparently chaotic social milieu.

Political difficulties

As Aldridge and her colleagues (2008) note, in their attempts to establish links
with the 'community representatives' who ran 'projects' in gang-affected neighbourhoods they were sometimes met with scepticism and a concern that the
research would merely compound the negative stereotypes the groups were
struggling to combat. The researchers attempt to resolve this problem by:

> Attending community events and meetings and seeing the same faces that at
> first were suspicious of our motives enabled others to see the commitment and

community relationships we had built. The same people who were first wary were the same ones who introduced our fieldworkers as 'sound' and 'from the street' (sic). Even so, the generally negative view of researchers/academics remained evident as they described us as not like your typical academic.

(Aldridge et al., 2008: 41)

However, as Joan Bailey (2009) has observed, these 'community representatives' often have an investment in representing their communities in particular ways. Thus, in April 2009 the *Manchester Evening News* reported:

When most people think about Manchester's Moss Side area, the words 'notorious' and 'gun crime' spring to mind. In a recent interview for the Manchester Evening News, peace campaigner Erinma Bell MBE talked about the common misconception. 'Most people live their lives without any kind of trouble. They are genuinely shocked when they hear that someone here has been shot.' Erinma argues that the real Moss Side is far removed from its 'Gunchester' image: 'people want to live here because it's a great place to live in a great city'.

(Church Urban Fund, 2009)

Erinma Bell is chair of CARISMA, the Community Alliance for Renewal, Inner South Manchester Area, which is funded by the Church Urban Fund and works in partnership with the police and Manchester City Council. For the past decade or so the Manchester City Council has been making strenuous efforts to minimise the deleterious impact of the city's violent image on its urban renewal strategy.

Establishing close relationships with these community groups in order to gain access to respondents, therefore, poses a dilemma for researchers because, all too often, there will be a tacit expectation that the research findings will serve to dispel the unhelpful stereotypes against which these groups and their sponsors are battling.

Methodological difficulties

Beyond problems of conceptualisation and access, but related to them, lie questions concerning what constitutes valid data and the identification of relevant research subjects. Several recent studies suggest that, in some neighbourhoods, groups of local children and young people are linked into, and provide a street-level presence for, middle-level drug trafficking networks (see for example Young et al., 2007; Matthews and Pitts, 2007; Pitts, 2007, 2008a, 2008b; Palmer, 2009). However, it is usually very difficult to gain access to, and elicit accurate information from, people who are actively engaged in the middle and upper echelons of organised crime in general and class A drug distribution in particular. As Geoffrey Pearson and Dick Hobbs (2001: 4) have observed: 'the use of ethnographic methods is rarely feasible in the study of upper and middle level trafficking owing to the degrees of secrecy and security that are employed'. As a result, the few UK studies that exist have relied upon the testimony of convicted, and normally imprisoned, respondents.

It is, therefore, often the more peripheral young people who are most accessible to gang researchers, whereas those who are more central to the illicit activities of the gang tend, for obvious reasons, to be far more circumspect. This means that 'gang studies' in which the methodology determines that only the testimony of younger, street-level, respondents – either individually or in focus groups – constitutes legitimate data, risk giving a partial, and probably distorted, view of the gang phenomenon. Although discerning researchers may have intimations that 'there is more to this than meets the eye', the inaccessibility of any data to substantiate this hunch tends to lead to 'mission drift', a process in which the research comes to focus upon the characteristics and lifestyles of the children and young people associated with the disorganised, fluid, ephemeral street-level groups to which researchers are able to gain access, rather than the 'social fields' (see below) in which they are embedded. In consequence, such 'gang-related' offending as they are able to discover inevitably appears disorganised, random and only tenuously connected with the drugs business or other forms of organised crime (Young et al., 2007). But the absence of evidence gained through such restrictive research methodologies does not add up to evidence of absence.

In my study of youth gangs in Waltham Forest (Pitts, 2007), I eventually identified a social grouping which I described as an 'articulated super gang',[3] a network containing fairly tightly knit groups of older career criminals from four notorious local families and groups of younger adolescents involved in street crime and drug distribution. These families were what Pearson and Hobbs (2001: 9) have described as 'middle market multi-commodity drug brokers' who link the upper and lower levels of the market. They maintained strong links – based upon commercial interest and kinship – with younger, looser-knit, estate-based 'gangs', 'fams' and/or 'brerrs' that were, in turn, connected by propinquity, ethnicity and pragmatism to other, more fluid and volatile, 'crews' of younger children and adolescents. These kinds of networks are seldom the focus of analyses of the structure and functions of violent youth gangs, yet their influence on local crime patterns and their impact on local people in this part of North East London was profound.

Evidence for the existence of these networks was derived from interviews with adults who had once been affiliated with them, gang-involved and non-gang-involved young people, local adult residents on gang-affected estates, Youth Offending Team (YOT) and community safety personnel, police officers and youth workers. This data was triangulated with intelligence amassed by Metropolitan Police Source Units in relevant boroughs. These networks were characterised by the police as 'fairly organised at the top but chaotic at the bottom' and this seems a fair summation. This suggests that a research methodology designed to capture the nature, structure, function and impact of the violent youth gang must necessarily include the accounts offered by street-level respondents together with those of apprehended and imprisoned gang affiliates, triangulated with data held by relevant criminal justice and social welfare agencies (see for example Bullock and Tilley, 2002; Pitts, 2007; Matthews and Pitts, 2007).

The social field of the violent youth gang

In *Against Method* Paul Feyerabend (1975), echoing C. Wright Mills (1957), notes that in social science, everything we encounter in the social world is a potential data source and we must, therefore, beware that an uncritical commitment to a restrictive methodology does not blind us to this reality. During a visit to a youth project in South London in 2008, for example, I fell into conversation with a young film-maker from a local community group who was working with primary school children on a project about risk and safety in their neighborhood. He said:

> You wouldn't believe it. In some of them [primary schools], the kids know the names of all the guns the young guys on the estates are using – Glock 17s, Mach 10s, Hecklers, converted Brococks, all that. Now that really is scary, man.

This unsolicited observation, subsequently corroborated, was crucial to my understanding of the 'social field' inhabited by the gang (see below), yet inadmissible had I been constrained by an inflexible research methodology. Interestingly, erstwhile Home Secretary Jacqui Smith had a similar experience on a visit to primary schools in Moss Side and Hulme in Manchester in 2008, an encounter filmed by Granada News, where 6-, 7- and 8-year-old children spoke knowledgeably about gang names and locations, guns and drug-dealing territories.

The individualising tendencies of conventional, 'correctional' (Matza, 1969), UK gang research necessarily preclude investigation of the 'social fields' (Bourdieu, 1999) that shape and give meaning to the lives of the children, young people and adults who reside in gang-affected neighbourhoods. Yet, only by understanding the dynamics and dimensions of these social fields can we begin to make sense of what Frederic Thrasher (1927) called *Gangland*. Pierre Bourdieu (1999: 137) notes that actors in a 'social field' develop a distinctive habitus; a system of beliefs, values, attitudes and behavioural styles: 'habitus is evident in the most automatic gestures [and] the apparently most insignificant techniques of the body – ways of walking or blowing one's nose'.

This habitus is shaped by both the broad 'determining structures' of class, family and education, and the social, cultural and economic imperatives of a particular social field which, in the case of 'gangland', are established through often violent struggles for particular forms of financial, social or cultural capital: the domination of drug-dealing territory, for example, or the monopoly of violence within a given neighbourhood. The boundaries of these social fields are demarcated by the points at which their effects and their influence cease. Bullock and Tilley (2002) offer chilling testimony to the scope of this influence in South Manchester. In the 140 cases of gang-related firearms offences they researched,

125 witnesses made initial statements, but only one eventually appeared in Court. No victims of gang-related firearms offences testified in Court and, in consequence, convictions were secured in only 8 per cent of cases, and this despite the fact that the identities of the culprits were well known in the neighbourhood.

A housing officer interviewed in Waltham Forest in 2006 points to the ways in which the gang is able to silence would-be informers or witnesses trapped within their sphere of influence:

> For five or six years a group of 16 to 18 years olds was terrorising Shelley and Byron Towers. They would wait at the bottom of the lift and take money, mobile phones, clothes that they fancied, even a dog, from the residents. A younger sister also had these terrible parties in the foyer but nobody complained. The Police had been trying to prosecute for years but because of witness intimidation, residents stayed quiet. These kids came to believe they were untouchable.
>
> (Pitts, 2008a: 57)

A report from Manchester City Council's Children and Young People Overview and Scrutiny Committee (2009: 40) focuses upon the impact of this code of silence upon the lives of girls and young women who live in gang-affected neighbourhoods:

> 1.1 The safeguarding issues of young people involved in criminal gangs and subject to sexual exploitation are unfortunately not new concerns to Manchester. The issue of gun/gang violence has existed in the City for the past twenty or more years, with a growing trend of younger adults becoming active gang members. The issue of sexual exploitation of children by predominantly older men has also been a recognised child protection concern for many years.
>
> 1.5 It is within this context that we wish to focus on what is increasingly being reported as a growing child safeguarding concern; that is, involvement and association of young girls with gangs. This is a different type of sexual exploitation in that it is often the victim's peers through gang membership and association who exploit young girls under the threat and intimidation of reprisals by gang members.

Another approach to the question of the social field of the gang is to ask what 'manifest' and 'latent' 'functions' the gang performs and whether, and to what extent, it performs them successfully. Class A drugs distribution in the UK is estimated to constitute between 0.5 per cent and 1.1 per cent of GDP (United Nations, 2009), roughly equivalent to the yield from UK agriculture (1 per cent). If we consider class A drugs distribution in Manchester, from the 1980s to the present day, as a social system, constituted by interconnected roles, regulated by inter-related norms and performing a specific set of social functions (Parsons,

1937), we are drawn inexorably to the conclusion that a changing cast of around 400 to 500 young people, from a handful of Manchester neighbourhoods, functioned as the economic conduit whereby locally produced dance drugs, heroin from the poppy fields of Afghanistan and Cocaine from the coca farms of South America found their way to 'end-users' on the street corners and in the nightclubs of Manchester for over 20 years. The 'latent function' of the drugs business in Manchester was to create a status hierarchy, which offered social recognition to those who were denied it, and a career structure for a social group effectively excluded from the licit economy (cf. Young, 1999).

Some of those involved were very troubled young people, some were barely literate, hardly any understood the scope and complexity of the social system of which they were a part and, at the outset at least, few would have understood the formidable risks they ran (Bullock and Tilley, 2002). Their apparently chaotic lives notwithstanding, viewed systemically, the social organisation of street-level drug distribution in Manchester, with its attendant enforcement activities, has been and remains extraordinarily effective. Thus, when scholars tell us that these 'gangs' are simply fluid associations of younger adolescents, engaged in relatively innocuous behaviour, with porous boundaries, or that these days, young people are 'going it alone' in the drugs business, we must regard their claims with scepticism and ask instead about the social systems or social fields, of which they may be only partially aware, but in which they are profoundly implicated. But how did it come to this?

How did it come to this? Macro social change

Over the past three decades in the UK, the globalisation of neo-liberal economic regimes, de-industrialisation, financial de-regulation, income polarisation and welfare retrenchment have reversed the post-war tendency towards a narrowing of the gap between rich and poor and have created, in certain urban neighbourhoods, what Loïc Wacquant (1996, 2008) describes as a state of 'advanced marginality':

> The differential 'stitching together' of color, class, and place on both sides of the Atlantic does not, however, obviate the possibility that the recent transformations in the US ghetto the French Banlieue, and the British and Dutch 'inner cities' might herald the crystallisation of a novel, still inchoate, yet distinctive regime of urban marginality, different from both America's traditional ghetto and the twentieth century European worker's space. Viewed from this admittedly prospective angle, the 'return of the repressed' realities of extreme poverty and social destitution, ethno-racial divisions (linked to colonial history) and public violence, and their accumulation in the same distressed urban areas, suggests that First World cities are now confronted with what we may call advanced marginality.
>
> (Wacquant, 1996: 122–3)

Whereas at the beginning of the 1980s the average household income of council house tenants was 73 per cent of the national average, by the early 1990s this had fallen to 48 per cent. By 1995, over 50 per cent of what had been council households had no breadwinner (Power and Tunstall, 1995). By 1997, 25 per cent of the children and young people under 16 in the UK were living in these neighbourhoods (Pitts, 2008b). Moreover, until the 1980s 40 per cent of heads of households in social housing were aged 65 or over, by the 1990s, 75 per cent of newly formed households entering social housing were headed by someone aged between 16 and 29. A high proportion of these new residents were unemployed, not least because they included a heavy concentration of lone parents, the homeless, refugees and asylum seekers, ex-psychiatric patients and the addicted. This concentration of disadvantage is highlighted in a recent study, entitled *Growing Up in Social Housing*, in which Ruth Lupton and her colleagues (2009: 5) observe that:

> As the role of social housing changed for families, so its tenants became increasingly disadvantaged. When the 1946 cohort were aged four, 11% of the best-off fifth of families were in social housing, compared to 27% of the least well-off. By the time the 2000 cohort were aged five, the tenure gap had grown hugely: just two per cent of the best-off fifth were in social housing while 49% of the least well-off were.

Although the 1980s and 1990s comprised a period of considerable upward educational and social mobility within Britain's Black and Minority Ethnic (BME) communities, this was paralleled by a worsening of the predicament of large numbers of BME people at the other end of the social and economic scale (Robins 1992; Power and Tunstall, 1995; Pitts, 2003; Palmer and Pitts, 2006). By 1995, 40 per cent of African-Caribbeans and 59 per cent of Pakistanis and Bangladeshis in the UK were located in the poorest fifth of the population. This contrasts with only 18 per cent of the White population (Power and Tunstall, 1995). In London, by the mid-1990s, up to 70 per cent of the residents on the poorest housing estates were from ethnic minorities (Power and Tunstall, 1995)

The worsening fortunes of those at the bottom end of the social structure were compounded by changes in the UK labour market in the 1980s and 1990s. During this period, partly as a result of market deregulation, Britain lost over 20 per cent of its industrial base. One of the consequences of this contraction was that between 1984 and 1997, the numbers of 16- to 24-year-olds in the labour market shrank by almost 40 per cent. In the poorest neighbourhoods, levels of adult and youth unemployment were amongst the highest in Europe (Pitts, 2003). The poorest young people were further disadvantaged in the labour market by educational polarisation in which the growing number of young people achieving five A–C grades at GCSE was paralleled by a steady increase in those with low or no GCSEs. This polarisation was exacerbated by rising rates of school exclusion and truancy (Berridge et al., 2001). Moreover, as a result of the international migration of refugees and asylum seekers, and the internal migration of families deemed to be 'voluntarily homeless' because of failure to pay their rent and other tenancy violations, the inner cities saw growing numbers of 'invisible' children who were uninvolved in, and unknown to, the educational system, sometimes living with friends and family in private rented accommodation, or illegally occupying hard-to-let council properties.

How did it come to this? Micro social change

Some commentators present the gang as an ephemeral, possibly imaginary, social form, and its 'members' as essentially unproblematic young people in transition to adulthood. In support of this view they often cite Andrew Davies' nineteenth-century Manchester 'scuttlers' (2008 and this volume) and Geoffrey Pearson's London Hooligans (Pearson, 1983 and this volume), wartime Spivs (Taylor, 1981), 1950s Teddy Boys (Fyvel, 1961), 1960s Mods and Rockers (Cohen, 1972), 1970s Skinheads (Clarke, 1976), the Rude Boys and football hooligans of the 1980s (Hebdidge, 1991; Murphy et al., 1990) and so on. However, as Geoffrey Pearson pithily observed on the radio programme *Thinking Allowed* in February 2008, the big difference between these earlier manifestations of youth (sub)culture and today's violent youth gangs is that their adherents were, for the most part, 'gainfully employed' and, as a result, were 'just passing through' on their way to a more or less conventional working-class adulthood (Downes, 1966; Willis, 1977).

Far from 'just passing through', however, for many of the young people involved in violent youth gangs, this is their final destination. Moreover, whereas these earlier 'youth movements' (Gordon, 2000) were essentially a 'youthful' phenomenon, the 'violent youth gang' is something of a misnomer because gang-involved children and young people are sometimes seriously implicated in the same social fields and social networks as adult felons who are active within national and international criminal business organisations (Gordon, 2000; Pitts, 2008b).

However, this is not simply a case of children and adolescents being drawn into adult crime. Over the past decade, we have also witnessed the proliferation of younger 'crews', 'gangs' and 'fams' that, while only tangentially related to the drugs business, have nonetheless adopted the 'gangsta' style and modus operandi and are, if anything, more predatory and less measured in their violence than their drug-dealing elders (Stevens, 2007; Palmer, 2009).

The steady retrenchment of state welfare, educational and criminal justice institutions in the past two decades, referred to above, means that these 'discredited' neighbourhoods are gradually floating free from the socio-cultural and political mainstream. In consequence, traditional modes of informal social control and informal social support, rooted in common values and an expectation of local solidarity, have become untenable (Wilson, 1988; Steyaert, 2006). And so, as the state retreats, the power vacuum left by its departure is filled by new and more menacing actors exerting new forms of informal social control in the territories to which they lay claim. John Hagedorn (2008: 100), commenting on the findings of an international study of young people involved in armed violence, notes that: 'loss of faith in the state renders the armed gang a normal feature of what Davies calls the Planet of Slums'.

The enforced estrangement of these neighbourhoods from the mainstream calls into question the validity of those who populate them. Detlef Baum (1996: 15–21) writes:

> Young people sense this discreditation in their own environment, in school or in the cultural or leisure establishments. Through this they experience stigmatisation of their difference, of their actions, and the perceived incompetence of the people they live among. The options for action are limited and possibilities for gaining status-enhancing resources are made more difficult. At some stage the process becomes a self-fulfilling prophecy; young people and adults come to think that there must be 'something in it' when their characteristics and ways of behaving are stigmatised, and some become confirmed in this uncertainty.

Like Baum, Petonnet (1982: 148) sees that living in what she describes as the (sub) proletarian housing projects of the periphery of Paris 'creates a muted sentiment of guilt and shame whose unacknowledged weight warps human relations'. And yet these devalued and stigmatised actors must find ways to defend themselves against the corrosive impact of this discreditation. The excluded must, to borrow a term from Castells (1997: 8), develop 'resistance identities' to exclude the excluders who are the source of their discreditation: 'thus building trenches of resistance and survival on the basis of principles different from or opposed to, those permeating the institutions of society'. But in doing so, these actors become simultaneously excluded and self-excluding. While on the one hand they abhor the 'shit work' that is on offer, on the other they castigate those who endeavour to 'better themselves' via conventional educational or vocational means because, on the street, such striving is viewed as a form of capitulation to the logic of the excluders. As MacDonald and Marsh (2005), attest:

> Long-term participation by young men in street-corner society generated adherence to a particular form of (sub)culturally defined personal identity, values and lifestyle which became important in circumscribing broader career possibilities.

As their life-worlds shrink so their self-definitions narrow, setting in train a process in which the 'self' is stripped down to a simplified, unambiguous, essence that is 'then contrasted with "Others" (Catholics against Protestants, Islam against non-Islam, White against Black) and allows prejudice to be based on notions of fixed differences' (Young, 1999: 198).

Moreover, as Wacquant (1996, 2008) observes, this de-proletarianisation of what were once working-class neighbourhoods denies residents a common language and a shared vision of the future offered by the politics of social class. This absence of a common idiom threatens to fragment and erode a sense of solidarity amongst the urban poor. But as Hagedorn (2008: 88) contends, in its place we see the emergence of:

> Gangs and criminal cartels, narco trafficking networks, mini-mafias and favela bosses, through community, grassroots and non-governmental organisations, to secular cults and religious sects . . . [these] . . . are the alternative social forms that fill the void left behind as state powers, political parties, and other institutional forms are actively dismantled or simply wither away as centres of collective endeavour or social bonding.

Mercenary territory and reluctant gangsters

In 2008 a new West London gang emerged known as All Bout Money (ABM). Like the Love of Money Crew (LMC) (in the Borough of Hackney), the Get Money Daily Crew (MDC) (in the Borough of Waltham Forest) and the Poverty Driven Children/Peel Dem Crew (PDC) (in the Borough of Lambeth), their name crystallises their ambition. Clinton, a 15-year-old interviewed in North London in 2007, explained:

> People get money-addicted. It's getting much worse. All they ever think about is money. Now you've got 13-year-olds with guns going after the money.

David, a 16-year-old from South East London, made a similar point:

> Their lives revolve around money. Money gets you respect and being able to hang onto your money or take it off other people, violently, gets you even more respect . . . it was all just 'money' and 'respect'.

Marlon (17) echoed the observations of many other gang-involved young people when he said:

> It's OK for rich kids. They tell their mum and dad they want this and that and they give it to them, and then they come round here being all 'street'. My mum never had any money to give me and I can't get no job so how am I going to get my P's if I ain't taking it off them?

However, the idea of the poor ghetto child who grows up to become a local hero, an idea at the heart of street culture, makes it difficult to disentangle whether it is the actual experience of growing up poor or the social cachet attached to this sub-cultural persona that motivates these young men. It may also be that this rationale serves to 'neutralise' any culpability they might feel (Sykes and Matza, 1962). Whatever the explanation, 'making their Ps' (making money) is a major preoccupation of gang-involved young people.

In many ways, the violent youth gang is 'all about money' because the ability to amass, hold onto and take money from other people is the preeminent source of respect in gangland. In consumer society, real men make real money, even if it means 'channelling their consumer-inflated desires for social distinction into privatised, hostile and potentially criminal projects' (Hall et al., 2008: 150). Money represents 'recognition', it is the way they calculate how valuable they are; the way they keep score. The more tenuous their hold upon the 'glittering prizes' of conventional life, the more their validity as men is called into question:

> Young men facing such a denial of recognition turn . . . to the creation of cultures of machismo, [specifically] to the mobilisation of one of their only resources, physical strength, to the formation of gangs and to the defence of their own 'turf'. Being denied the respect of others they create a subculture that revolves around masculine powers and 'respect'.
>
> (Young, 1999: 12)

But this collective solution to their 'status frustration' (Cohen, 1955), powered by what Germaine Greer (2009) has described as 'toxic rage', engenders not solidarity, but a ruthless individualism. Ace, a 17-year-old interviewed in South East London, explained:

> It is not just people robbing any old women on the street, they are robbing their so-called friends or the so-called breddrins, the same people rob each other because they think 'we're in the same situation'.

Jason, a 16-year-old interviewed in North West London, makes a similar point:

> I've been set up a few times but I'm not watching no faces because that's life. You don't know the brers . . . face covered, it might be your own friends.

As Rodger (2008: 53) observes:

> Where marginality, social exclusion or sectarianism emerges, the sense of empathy for the other and the mutual restraint on behaviour . . . are absent. This tendency should be understood as a structural property of social systems where social polarisation and inequality are present or deepening and not as a property of pathological individuals.

In the dog-eat-dog world that is Gangland, few can remain neutral and for some the consequences are catastrophic. Christopher, an 18-year-old interviewed in North West London, is talking about a close friend:

> They're crouched up in the corner crying because they brought the gun out to protect themselves and they've been challenged so they've pulled the trigger. They haven't wanted to pull the trigger.

Indeed, while some young people embrace, and revel in, gang involvement, many are either ambivalent about or resigned to it, seeing few, if any, realistic alternatives. But this should not surprise us because the earliest US gang studies (Thrasher, 1927) found that gangs were brought together, and held together, by fear of other gangs. Seventy years later, Decker and Van Winkle (1996) describe how threats from the neighbourhood gang, and rival gangs, induce young people to affiliate. In my own research in London (Pitts 2007, 2008a, 2008b) it was evident that as the neighbourhood gangs grew larger, in the early years of the twenty-first century, and territorial disputes intensified, the numbers of protagonists increased and it was no longer easy to distinguish who, on any given estate, was or wasn't a gang member. This meant that, in effect, residence became synonymous with affiliation and young people with no prior gang involvement were restricted to their own estates because of the threat posed to them by rival gangs. In this situation of profound mutual fear and suspicion, rumours abound and respect-related attacks escalate. This increasingly dangerous environment serves as a stimulus for many previously unaffiliated young people to join their local gang as a means of self-defence, but also to arm themselves with knives and sometimes guns. David moved on to a gang-affected estate in South East London when he was 13:

I realised that if you lived there [on the estate] you couldn't ignore what was happening because they would turn against you. You had to be part of it. I reckon about 200 of the 300 kids on the estate were involved with the gang. It was like being in a family; you couldn't avoid being in it and if you were in it you had to contribute to it. Contributing to it meant either selling drugs or fighting. You could also contribute legally, like helping to promote the music that some of the kids made, if you had the skills, but most of these kids didn't have the skills and didn't earn any money. Mind you, three of them were at university. I think because they'd grown up there the culture was too strong for them to leave. Others were in school or college although most were out of school.

But the problem is, once you get in you can't get out, and if you live on one of the gang estates, you're in, full stop. This means that if you go to another gang area and they recognise you, you can be killed. If they don't recognise you you'd just be robbed. So it's not only pressure from your own gang but also the threat from the other gangs that means that if you are part of it you can't leave it. There really is no way out unless you go a long way away, like back to Jamaica with your parents or something.

Kids think guns, and shooting someone or being shot, are very glamorous. They don't have any sense of the future. They take every day as it comes; they're always ready for action. There are heartless people who might just shoot you for the 'rush'. But if the guy's got that mentality, you have to think like that too or you'd be dead. This is why it grows. Most people involved in gangs would rather be doing something else. A lot of the time they're just keeping the others sweet so they don't get hurt.

Being unable to 'escape' from these neighbourhoods, young people like David cannot afford to appear resistant or indifferent to the powerful cliques and individuals who are involved. In his *Atlantic Monthly* article, 'The Code of the Streets', published in May 1994, Elijah Anderson put the matter thus:

> The rules prescribe both a proper comportment and a proper way to respond if challenged. They regulate the use of violence and so allow those who are inclined to aggression to precipitate violent encounters in an approved way. The rules have been established and are enforced mainly by the street-oriented, but on the streets the distinction between street and decent is often irrelevant; everybody knows that if the rules are violated, there are penalties. Knowledge of the code is thus largely defensive; it is literally necessary for operating in public. Therefore, even though families with a decency orientation are usually opposed to the values of the code, they often reluctantly encourage their children's familiarity with it to enable them to negotiate the inner-city environment.
>
> (Anderson, 1994: 92)

Although Anderson is writing about life in the ghettoes of the United States, this describes fairly accurately the realities of life for growing numbers of children and young people in the UK's most impoverished urban neighbourhoods, particularly if they are Black African-Caribbean. And if, as C. Wright Mills (1957) suggests, our duty as social scientists is to strive to transform private troubles into public issues; to ignore this reality and perpetuate the sentimental fallacy that the profound social, economic and political changes described here have not changed and worsened the crime perpetrated against the urban poor, in the mistaken belief that in doing so we are in some way averting the 'demonisation' of young people, this is not only bad social science, it is also a dereliction of our professional duty.

Notes

1   In 2005 I undertook an evaluation of 'Lewisham Live', a music project targeting gang-involved and gang-affected young people in (North) Lewisham (a London Borough). The project involved interviews with 15 individual participants and a focus group with a further eight. In 2006 I undertook an evaluation of the 'X-It' gang desistance programme in the Borough of Lambeth that included interviews with 27 past and present gang-involved young people. Between 2006 and 2007 I directed a study of violent youth gangs in the Borough of Waltham Forest. This research included interviews with 15 gang-involved young people and ten non-gang-involved but gang-affected young people. The study also interviewed 29 other respondents including: local residents, youth workers, social workers, school teachers/heads, street wardens, youth justice and community safety professionals and police officers. The principal findings were published in a report entitled *Reluctant Gangsters: Youth Gangs in Waltham Forest* (2007). Between 2007 and 2008 I returned to Lewisham to work on a

study of street crime. This project involved interviews with 40 young people – in Young Offender Institutions and Youth Offending Teams – involved in street crime, together with interviews with their parents, staff and parent governors of the schools they attended. Between 2007 and 2008 I served as researcher for the Lambeth Executive Commission on Young People, Gangs and Violent Crime. The commission took evidence from 23 young people involved in, or directly affected by, inter-gang violence, together with 12 other respondents including: local residents, youth workers, social workers, school teachers/heads, youth justice and community safety professionals and police officers. My current research is focusing on eight experimental youth projects managed by the Brathay Trust in the North of England, the Midlands and London.

2   Eurogang is the brainchild of Malcolm W. Klein, a Californian academic who embarked upon the Eurogang project partly because street gangs were beginning to be recognised in Europe, but also because of the difficulties inherent in conducting systematic gang research in the USA. There, Klein notes, gang scholarship is uncoordinated, with researchers utilising different theoretical perspectives and different research methods. He argues that Eurogang should, therefore, develop a shared theoretical perspective, a shared gang definition and shared research instruments that will, in the fullness of time, enable *a series of prospective, multi-method, cross-national, comparative studies of street gangs.* Founded in 1997, by 2004 Eurogang had developed just such a definition: 'A street gang (or problematic youth group) is any durable street-oriented youth group whose involvement in illegal activity is part of their group identity'.

3   'Articulated' meaning a vehicle consisting of flexibly connected sections, and 'super' meaning over and above a single group or entity.

References

Aldridge, J., Medina, J. and Ralphs, R. (2008) 'Dangers and Problems of Doing Gang Research in the UK', in F. van Gemert, D. Peterson and I-L. Lien (eds) *Street Gangs, Migration and Ethnicity*. Cullompton: Willan.

Alexander, C. (2008) *(Re)thinking 'Gangs'*. London: Runnymede Trust.

Anderson, E. (1994) 'The Code of the Streets', *The Atlantic Monthly*, 273(12): 11–15.

Baum, D. (1996) 'Can Integration Succeed? Research into Urban Childhood and Youth in a Deprived Area of Koblenz', *Social Work in Europe*, 3(3): 14–21.

Bailey, J. (2009) 'Inter-racial Conflict and Identity Formation', *Youth and Policy*, 102: 81–99.

Balasunderam, A. (2009) 'Gang-related Violence Amongst Young People of the Tamil Refugee Diaspora in London', *Safer Communities*, 8(2): 34–41.

Becker, H. (1963) *Outsiders: Studies in the Sociology of Deviance*. New York: Free Press.

Berridge, D., Brodie, I., Pitts, J., Porteous, D. and Tarling, R. (2001) *The Independent Effects of Permanent Exclusion from School on the Offending Careers of Young People*. London: Home Office.

Bourdieu, P. (1999) *The Weight of the World*. Stanford: Stanford University Press.

Bullock, K. and Tilley, N. (2002) *Shooting, Gangs and Violent Incidents in Manchester: Developing a Crime Reduction Strategy*. London: Home Office.

Centre for Social Justice (2009) *Dying to Belong: An In-depth Review of Street Gangs in Britain*. London: Centre for Social Justice.

Castells, M. (1997) *The Power of Identity, The Information Age: Economy, Society and Culture Vol. II*. Cambridge, MA, Oxford: Blackwell.

Church Urban Fund (2009) 'Erinma Bell Interviewed by Manchester Evening News'. Retrieved 30 August 2009 (http://www.cuf.org.uk/page2503334.aspx).

Clarke, J. (1976) 'The Skinheads and the Magical Recovery of Community', in S. Hall and T. Jefferson (eds) *Resistance through Rituals: Youth Subcultures in Post-war Britain.* London: Hutchinson.

Cohen, A. (1955) *Delinquent Boys: The Culture of the Gang.* Chicago: Chicago Free Press.

Cohen, P. (1972) *Folk Devils and Moral Panics.* London: Paladin.

Davies, A. (2008) *The Gangs of Manchester.* Manchester: Milo Books.

Decker, S. and Van Winkle, B. (1996) *Life in the Gang: Family, Friends and Violence.* Cambridge: Cambridge University Press.

Downes, D. (1966) *The Delinquent Solution.* London: Routledge & Kegan Paul.

Feyerabend, P. (1975) *Against Method: Outline of an Anarchistic Theory of Knowledge.* London: New Left Books.

Fyvel, T. (1961) *The Insecure Offenders.* Harmondsworth: Penguin.

Gordon, R. (2000) 'Criminal Business Organisations, Street Gangs and "Wannabe" Groups: A Vancouver Perspective', *Canadian Journal of Criminology and Criminal Justice*, 42(1): 39–60.

Greer, G. (2009) 'Schoolboy Doodles? Hardly. These Cars are a Glimpse into the Male Psyche', *Guardian 2*, 26 October: 22.

Hagedorn, J. (2008) *A World of Gangs: Armed Young Men and Gangsta Culture.* Minneapolis: University of Minnesota Press.

Hall, S. and Jefferson, T. (1976) *Resistance through Rituals: Youth Subcultures in Post-War Britain.* London: Hutchinson.

Hall, S., Winlow, S. and Ancrum, C. (2008) *Criminal Identities and Consumer Culture: Crime, Exclusion and the New Culture of Narcissism.* Cullompton: Willan.

Hallsworth, S. and Young, T. (2008) 'Gang Talk and Gang Talkers: A Critique', *Crime, Media and Culture*, 4(2): 175–95.

Hebdidge, D. (1991) *Subculture: The Meaning of Style.* London: Routledge.

Klein, M. (2008) 'Foreword', in F. van Gemert, D. Peterson and I-L. Lien (eds) *Street Gangs, Migration and Ethnicity.* Cullompton: Willan.

Lupton, R., Hammond, C., Mujtaba, T., Salter, E. and Sorhaindo, A. (2009) *Growing Up in Social Housing: A Profile of Four Generations From 1946 to the Present Day.* York: Joseph Rowntree Foundation.

MacDonald, R. and Marsh, J. (2005) *Disconnected Youth: Growing up in Britain's Poor Neighbourhoods.* Basingstoke: Palgrave.

Manchester City Council Children and Young People Overview and Scrutiny Committee (2009) *Gang Related Violence.* Manchester: Manchester City Council.

Mares, D. (2001) 'Gangstas or Lager Louts? Working Class Street Gangs in Manchester', in M. Klein, H-J. Kerner, C.L. Maxson and E.G. Weitekamp (eds) *The Eurogang Paradox: Street Gangs and Youth Groups in the U.S. and Europe.* Dordrecht: Kluwer Academic Publishers.

Matthews, R. and Pitts, J. (2007) *An Examination of the Disproportionate Number of Young Black Men Involved in Street Robbery in Lewisham.* Lewisham: Children and Young People's Directorate and Lewisham's Youth Crime Group.

Matza, D. (1969) *Becoming Deviant.* Englewood Cliffs, NJ: Prentice Hall Inc.

Metropolitan Police (2007) *The Pan-London Gang Survey.* London: Metropolitan Police.

Muncie, J. and Hughes, G. (2002) 'Modes of Youth Governance, Political Rationalities,

Criminalisation and Resistance', in J. Muncie, G. Hughes and E. McLaughlin (eds) *Youth Justice: Critical Readings.* London: Sage.

Murphy, P., Williams, J. and Dunning, E. (1990) *Football on Trial: Spectator Violence and Development in the Football World.* London: Routledge.

Palmer, S. (2009) 'The Origins and Emergence of Youth Gangs in a British Inner City Neighbourhood', *Safer Communities*, 8(2): 17–26.

Palmer, S. and Pitts, J. (2006) 'Othering the Brothers: Black Youth, Racial Solidarity and Gun Crime', *Youth and Policy*, 91: 5–22.

Park, R. and Burgess, E. (1921) *Introduction to the Science of Sociology.* Chicago: University of Chicago Press.

Parsons, T. (1937) *The Structure of Social Action.* Cambridge, MA: Harvard University Press.

Pearson, G. (1983) *Hooligan: A History of Respectable Fears.* Basingstoke: Macmillan.

Pearson, G. and Hobbs, D. (2001) *Middle Market Drug Distribution.* London: Home Office.

Pétonnet, C. (1982) *Espace Habités. Ethnologie des Banlieues.* Paris: Galilée.

Pitts, J. (2003) *The New Politics of Youth Crime: Discipline or Solidarity.* Lyme Regis: Russell House Publishing.

—— (2007) *Reluctant Gangsters: Youth Gangs in Waltham Forest.* London: London Borough of Waltham Forest.

—— (2008a) *Young and Safe in Lambeth: The Deliberations of the Executive Commission on Young People, Gangs and Violent Crime.* London: London Borough of Lambeth.

—— (2008b) *Reluctant Gangsters: The Changing Face of Youth Crime.* Cullompton: Willan.

Power, A. and Tunstall, T. (1995) *Swimming Against the Tide: Polarisation or Progress.* York: Joseph Rowntree Foundation.

Robins, D. (1992) *Tarnished Vision: Crime and Conflict in the Inner Cities.* Oxford: Oxford University Press.

Rodger, J. (2008) *Criminalising Social Policy: Anti-social Behaviour and Welfare in a De-civilised Society.* Cullompton: Willan.

Rose, N. (2000) 'Government and Control', *British Journal of Criminology*, 40(2): 321–39.

Simon, J. (2007) 'Governing Through Crime', in I. Friedman and G. Fisher (eds) *The Crime Conundrum: Essays on Criminal Justice.* Boulder, CO: Westview Press.

Stelfox, P. (1998) 'Policing Lower Levels of Organised Crime in England and Wales', *The Howard Journal of Criminal Justice*, 37(4): 393–404.

Stevens, M. (2007) 'Review of the Histories of Young People Involved in the Fatal Stabbing of Kodjo Yenga on 14.03.07, and of the Role of Agencies Providing Services to Children and Young People for the London Borough of Hammersmith and Fulham' (unpublished). London: London Borough of Hammersmith and Fulham.

Steyaert, J. (2006) 'Respect in the Lowlands and in the UK: A Cultural Comparison of Policy and Practice', in K. Harris (ed.) *Respect in the Neighbourhood: Why Neighbourliness Matters.* Lyme Regis: Russell House Publishing.

Sykes, G. and Matza, D. (1962) 'Techniques of Neutralisation: A Theory of Delinquency', in M. Wolfgang, L. Savitz and N. Johnson (eds) *The Sociology of Crime and Delinquency.* London: Wiley.

Taylor, I. (1981) 'Crime Waves in Post-war Britain', *Crime, Law and Social Science*, 5(1): 43–62.

Thrasher, F. (1927) *The Gang*. Chicago: University of Chicago Press.

United Nations (2009) 'Office of Drug Control and Crime Prevention (ODCCP)', Vienna International Centre. Retrieved October 2009 (http://www.undcp.org).

Wacquant, L. (1996) 'The Rise of Advanced Marginality: Notes on its Nature and Implications', *Acta Sociologica*, 39(2): 121–39.

—— (2008) *Urban Outcasts: The Sociology of Advanced Marginality*. Cambridge: Polity Press.

Willis, P. (1977) *Learning to Labour How Working Class Kids Get Working Class Jobs*. London: Saxon House.

Wilson, W. J. (1988) *The Truly Disadvantaged: The Inner City, the Underclass and Public Policy*. Chicago: University of Chicago.

Wittgenstein, L. (1921/1971) *Tractatus Logico-Philosophicus*. London: Routledge and Kegan Paul.

Wright Mills, C. (1957) *The Sociological Imagination*. Harmondsworth: Penguin.

Young, J. (1999) *The Exclusive Society*. London: Sage.

Young, T., Fitzgerald, M., Hallsworth, S. and Joseph, I. (2007) *Groups, Gangs and Weapons*. London: Youth Justice Board.

angland Britain?

Realities, fantasies and industry

Simon Hallsworth

'Gangs' and 'gang industry'

Every age produces a 'public enemy' and such 'enemies' have a habit of changing. In 2002, public enemy number one in the UK was the 'street robber' (Hallsworth, 2005). Such 'folk devils' had, of course, always existed but, in 2002, they were re-profiled with a vengeance. As in the 1970s, the 'street robber' became the source of considerable anxiety and sensational media coverage (Hall et al., 1977). Fast forward eight years and haven't things changed? Nobody today is preoccupied with 'muggers', and 'street crime' is barely mentioned (despite the fact that there is still a fair bit of it around). If anxiety pertaining to 'muggers' once abounded, this has now been replaced by a burgeoning fear of youth 'gangs'. Indeed, according to the 'gangland Britain' thesis, youth 'gangs' are on the move every-where. Moreover, it is claimed that such 'gangs' are armed, organized, predatory and lethal.

What are we to make of this re-focusing? According to John Pitts (2008; this volume), we are looking at a society where 'street life' has changed – and is changing – dramatically; a society where, until recently, few if any 'gangs' existed, to a society where 'gangs' are mushrooming apace. Pitts (2008) is both unequiv-ocal and bold in his convictions. We are, he asserts, witnessing the 'changing face of youth crime' and many state agencies appear to agree. The UK government, for example, has identified the 'gang' as a primary target of its 'action plan' to tackle violent crime (Home Office, 2008). It identifies the 'gang' as a serious threat to public order and, accordingly, it has established designated 'task forces' (to address the threats that 'gangs' supposedly pose) and introduced 'tough' legislation (to suppress them). Nor are government ministries acting alone. Indeed, every major agency within the criminal justice system – including the Metropolitan Police, the Youth Justice Board (YJB), the National Offender Management Service (NOMS) and the Association of Chief Police Officers (ACPO) – has either commissioned research on 'gangs' or has commissioned research to find out what to do about them. Many of these agencies have estab-lished various committees to deliberate over 'gangs' and many others have created specialist positions with a dedicated 'anti-gang' remit. At the local level, Crime and Disorder Reduction Partnerships (CDRPs) have replicated such responses. Many CDRPs have identified the 'gang' as a primary 'public enemy' and have sought, and been granted, government funding/public money to help them tackle 'gang' activity in their respective areas. Accordingly, a growing 'industry' has emerged, populated by a multitude of organizations and consultants offering 'expert' opinion, guidance and advice, together with 'tailor-made' programmes in 'gang' suppression.

In the face of such 'industry' it is ostensibly difficult to question the 'gangland Britain' thesis. Surely, all we need to know is that 'gangs' have arrived and we need to 'get real' about this problematic phenomenon. Or do we? This chapter poses a 'heretical' counter-thesis by arguing that whilst social entities commonly termed 'gangs' (notwithstanding the problems of definition) certainly exist (as they always have done – see Davies and Pearson, this volume), there is no compelling evidence to suggest either that 'street violence' can be reduced to a problem of 'gangs' or that 'gangs' are the principal drivers of violent street crime. Indeed, the problem of the street is not primarily derivative of *organized* armed groups; rather social *disorganization* better explains the violence that is increasingly being attributed to 'gangs'. A central contention here is that the problem of the 'gang' is not the 'gang' itself, but the media-driven 'moral panic' and 'gang control industry' that surrounds it. The major problem, therefore, lies less in suppressing 'gangs' and more in addressing the 'industry' that has emerged to 'tackle' them.

The 'gangland Britain' thesis revisited

Given that the UK has no established record of conducting qualitative and quantitative 'gang' research (unlike the USA), there is no readily available data to verify, or not, whether the presence of 'gangs' has increased or decreased in recent years. What the limited number of existing surveys indicate is that the level of 'gang' membership is relatively low among the population at large (ranging between 2 per cent and 7 per cent depending upon the definition of 'gang' used). Given that such surveys typically focus upon the 'usual suspects' (young people in deprived areas and/or young offenders), this typically produces skewed results that artificially inflate and overstate the actual level of 'gang' membership (see, for example, Bennet and Holloway, 2004; Sharp et al., 2006).

On closer inspection, much of the violence that is often attributed to 'gangs' appears not to be specifically 'gang'-related. Even if 'gang' members commit offences, it is often not evident that the offence in question is motivated by 'gang' membership in and of itself. It is precisely because a significant volume of violent crime is routinely being defined as 'gang'-related – coupled with the tendency on the part of the media to apply the term permissively and arbitrarily to classify all and every group that occasions harm to others as a 'gang' – that has, at least in part, served to establish and consolidate the 'gang' as a new 'folk devil'.

Drawing on grounded research with young people in areas supposedly awash with 'gang' activity, it is certainly possible to identify some young people who might reasonably be classified as 'gang-affiliated', but many others typically labelled 'gang members' simply do not recognize and/or conceptualize the peer groups with whom they associate as 'gangs' (Hallsworth and Young, 2008). Indeed, far from the streets being overrun by 'gangs', the most pervasive street collectives appeared to comprise volatile peer groups randomly and erroneously labelled as 'gangs' by control agencies. If, in order to legitimately be classified as a 'gang', a group has to have some integral relation to crime and violence, then the overwhelming majority of young people involved in the research simply failed to qualify (Hallsworth and Young, 2008).

In interviews conducted with practitioners across a range of different UK cities we found few who believed that the problematic issues posed and experienced by young people are, in fact, derivative of 'gangs' (Young et al., 2007). Interestingly, many practitioners have minimal informed knowledge with regard to 'gangs' and the knowledge they do possess typically comes saturated with American stereotypes. Far from seeing the problems of the young people they dealt with as a problem posed by their involvement in gangs, the experience of many practitioners leads them to conclude that the principal problems of the street are more accurately understood in terms of young people's often chaotic and deeply distressed lives, coupled with endemic deprivation and structural marginalization. Few practitioners appeared to perceive the 'gang' to be a new or escalating phenomenon and, in an intriguing test of the proposition that young women were increasingly involved in 'gangs' (part of the current control fantasy), members of Youth Offending Teams were invited to identify girl 'gang' members. The exercise failed to generate anything like a substantive sample of 'shemale' gangsters. From interviews conducted with young women who were identified we found few committed gang girls (the 'shemale' gangsters of the populist imaginary) but mainly young women who had experienced deeply troubled and traumatic lives (see Batchelor and Young, both this volume).

Whilst it could be argued that this research focused upon areas without the same degree of 'gang' organization as those studied by protagonists of the 'gangland Britain' thesis (particularly Pitts, 2008), a better way of understanding the core discrepancies between the respective sets of research findings might more readily be understood in terms of the problematic assumptions that 'gang talkers' routinely make in conducting their inquiries.

The first thing to note is that the fundamental claims that Pitts (2008) makes about 'gangland Britain' derive from field research conducted in London. Quite how it is possible to generalize from such findings and argue that they reveal the 'changing face of youth crime' is open to question. Equally, the evidential basis upon which Pitts builds his case is also questionable. Indeed, the argument is principally rooted in the testimony of practitioners (interestingly referred to as 'informants' thus invoking policing discourse) whose narratives Pitts appears to accept at face value. Whilst it is, of course, possible to garner good evidence by talking with front-line practitioners working with young people at street level, it is equally important to acknowledge that the epistemological implications of such testimony need to be critically interrogated in ways that seem to be overlooked in Pitts' work. As we found in the course of conducting research into 'gangs', practitioners are inclined to project a level and degree of organization onto the street that best reflects the kind of organizations to which they belong (Hallsworth and Young, 2008). In this sense practitioners tend to see (and perhaps want to see) structures, hierarchical divisions of labour and organized entities that they can map and which chime with familiar agency discourses. In other words, they do 'gang talk' in a manner of 'tree thinking' and this arboreal way of seeing and interpreting the world leads them to misrepresent what are often fluid, amorphous and even rhizomatic street realities.

Young people often replicate the same conceptual errors. As the Norwegian anthropologist Giur Moshmus (2005) observed, they do not live their 'gang' realities in the way that they are typically invited (by researchers) to narrate them. Often, young people themselves revert to what we might call 'gang talk' which, in reality, is the de facto language of control agents. The problem with Pitts (2008) and most other 'gang talkers' in this respect, is that they fail to adequately address complex (and perhaps inconvenient) epistemological issues. Maybe they cannot, because they are 'tree thinkers' who (even despite themselves) ultimately inhabit the space of the control imaginary – constructing a fantasy of the contemporary street as a world dominated not only by 'gangs', but 'super gangs', that control all aspects of social life in the areas in which they operate. It makes for a good story but perhaps that is all.

Whilst Pitts (2008) is right to assert that street life is not totally disorganized and that, in response to globalization, new forms of criminal organization have appeared, he may well be wrong in supposing that organized 'gangs' define the adaptation and he is certainly mistaken in looking to Castells (1996) to support such a claim. Indeed, Castells is the consummate theorist of the network society and it is precisely through complex distributed networks – rather than the territorial 'gangs' that Pitts appears to situate at the heart of things – that organized crime evolves. Similarly, the 'reluctant gangster' thesis that Pitts develops – holding that young people are coerced into becoming members of 'gangs' – is also questionable. There is little disputing that relationships between organized criminals and their 'on road' brethren are frequently coercive and exploitative, but the relations between the *organized core* and the more *disorganized periphery* of the street world is characterized by a multifaceted complex. Such relationships can veer between support and help – provided to and from people who are kith and kin – to more calculated and instrumental business contracts between buyers and sellers in the drug economy. If contemporary youth 'gangs' amount to the 'changing face of youth crime', then what are we to make of a British history replete with stories of estates populated by young men and sometimes older and more professional criminals (see Aldridge et al., Davies and Pearson, all this volume)? In such estates, 'getting a good kicking' – if you are in the wrong place at the wrong time – is a longstanding risk many young men (in particular) have experienced whilst growing up. And how are we to conceptualize the longstanding traditions of collective violence that have always been a feature of street life in the UK (Patrick, 1973; Bean, 1981)? Indeed, the 'changing face' claim implies the negation of history and invokes the amnesia that Pearson charted many years ago in his seminal study of 'hooligans' and 'respectable fears' (Pearson, 1983; this volume).

Another critique that might be levelled at 'gang talkers' begins with their *a priori* assumption that the problem of the street is one of 'gangs'. Whilst not disputing that 'gangs' are certainly part of a complex – and sometimes deeply problematic – street tapestry, by focusing on 'gangs' alone, by reifying the 'gang' and constructing it as a kind of fetish, 'gang talkers' lose sight of the wider ecology of the street itself which, arguably, ought to be the real focus of any attempt to understand violent street worlds. But Pitts (2008) and other fellow travellers are not the only arborialists in the expanding 'gang' research community; many others advance similar claims. Figure 10.1, for example, invokes another fantasy of the street, this time taken from a publication produced by Jonathon Toy (2008), a leading practitioner in the 'War Against Gangs' in London.

To this we might also consider the totally 'evidence-free' New Labour 'action plan' to confront violence (Home Office, 2008). The document – without any evidence to support such a contentious claim – identifies the 'gang' as a major driver of lethal violence. Despite utter disregard for any notion of 'evidence-driven policy', the 'action plan' makes the case for 'gang' suppression as a solution to violent crime and a whole new paradigm of risk management is touted as the most effective response.

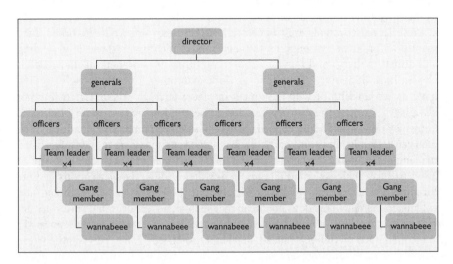

Figure 10.1 Fantasies of the street (1): 'business typical organizational gang structure'.
Source: Toy (2008: 31)

Rethinking violent street worlds

If the violence that occasions public concern cannot legitimately be attributed to organized 'gangs', how are we to make sense both of the violence itself and the anxiety and outrage that it tends to induce? Why do certain constituencies of young people (normally boys and young men) routinely carry knives (and sometimes guns) and use them against each other, sometimes with fatal consequences? I recently sought to address these questions with Daniel Silverstone, drawing upon a range of different research projects in which we had been involved (Hallsworth and Silverstone, 2009). Rather than begin (as is the tendency of 'gang talkers') with the presumption that the answer to the violence is to be found by looking for 'gangs', we found it more profitable to listen instead to what many young people – and, indeed, convicted adult criminals – had to say about the violent street worlds they inhabit(ed). Whilst such testimonies certainly feature 'gangs', few tend to conceptualize the 'gang' in quite the same ways that control agents are inclined to do. In other words, 'gangs' might – in certain circumstances – form an integral part of their street reality but they do not fully envelop or totalize this reality. Rather than impose a particular construction of the 'gang' (typical of control agents) upon complex street realities – what Katz and Jackson-Jacobs (2004) have appropriately termed 'the criminologists' gang' – we sought instead to understand what such testimonies told us about multi-dimensional street worlds and the violence that might characterize them (Hallsworth and Silverstone, 2009). This requires making a heuristic distinction between the lifeworld of more organized and professional criminals – the *organized core* of the street world where men 'do the business' and crime is a vocation – and what might better be understood as the more *disorganized periphery* termed by many of those we interviewed as 'on road'.

Professional criminals are 'successful' because they are well-networked, they manifest a pragmatic orientation to their work (typically mid-level drug dealing and armed robbery) and they are able to mobilize entrepreneurial flair in their chosen lines of activity. They tend to work with others, mostly those who they have grown up with or who they meet in places such as prison. Often (but not always) the groups they are part of have specified names or, more likely, are known by others (including control agents) by ascribed names and identities. Such men can certainly apply and/or mobilize violence and many are trained and skilled in using guns (unlike their 'on-road' brethren), but they are also acutely aware of how 'bad for business' (and dangerous for themselves) using weapons can be. Firearms are accordingly used sparingly and preferably in an organized and calculated manner. This does not mean that such men – the criminal core – are not violent but, arguably, they are not as problematic as others who operate 'on road', at the margins or periphery. Indeed, this latter group occupy a hyper-volatile world where violence is omnipresent and can, and does, explode for relatively mundane reasons. This is also a world where violence, once unleashed, tends to escalate randomly and rapidly. Life 'on road' is volatile because it is frequently populated

by unpredictable young men from chaotic backgrounds whose psychological instability is often compounded by long histories of violent victimization. Such young
men certainly face threats from territorial groups but that is only part of a more
complex picture. Many struggle to make a living at the retail end of crack-cocaine
and heroin markets; a trading place comprising incredibly violent space. Indeed,
as research from the USA and the UK attests (Jacobs, 1999 and 2000; Lupton
et al., 2002; Wilson et al., 2002), this is probably the most violent arena in the
criminal underworld. Violence is, as such, a competence that has to be learnt and
mastered in a world where street survival is literally the name of the game. While
'gang talkers' imagine that the problem of violence emanates from the presence
of organized 'gangs' (the *core*), the reality implies that it is the social disorganization of the street *periphery* and the self-destructive ways of 'on road' life
that prevail within it, that is the principal problem.

Violence may be ritualized and, as such, regulated by normative street codes (at
least in part) or, alternatively, it may be anomic, unregulated and normless where
the absence, not presence, of a clear social structure (which many 'gangs' provide)
creates the preconditions for violence to occur. For this reason it is difficult to
equate life 'on road' with 'subculture' in recognizable sociological terms (Hall and
Jefferson, 1976). Rather, 'on road' might be conceptualized as a way of life
predicated precisely on the social demolition of its inhabitants. In a social world
where capitalism is destructively reproducing itself from above, 'on road'
represents one of its concomitant effects, destructive self-reproduction from
below:

> Here a small number of socially marginalized men have come to respond to
> their predicament destructively in what becomes, at times, close to what
> Thomas Hobbes described as 'a state of nature', what he termed a 'war of all
> against all'. Life 'on road', is not a world where the social contract has much
> salience or purchase. This is the zone of the outlaw. This is a zone where
> deeply internalized anger and rage among depoliticized and deeply alienated
> young men finds violent expression. The tragedy here is that the rage and
> anger they feel is not directed outwards and towards the world that
> marginalizes them. Instead it is directed inward and against each other. Guns
> have become a part of this logic of self-destruction as young men pointlessly
> die at each other's hands.
>
> (Hallsworth and Silverstone, 2009: 373)

A moral panic?

If the violence of the street is not reducible to a question of 'gangs', how has the
problem of the street come to be constructed as a problem of 'gangs'? Or to
rephrase the question, how and why has the 'gangland Britain' thesis become
dominant to a point where it is seemingly taken to provide the accepted hegemonic interpretation of violent street worlds? One way of understanding this

phenomenon is to invoke the familiar sociological concept of 'moral panic' and to situate the emergence of the 'gang' as 'public enemy' as the latest in a long line of 'folk devils'. In this way, the rise of the 'gang' might be interpreted as a classic case of deviancy amplification.

In *Moral Panics and the Media* Critcher (2003) – following Cohen (1972; 2002) and Hall et al. (1977) – presents a processional model by way of explaining the stages through which moral panics evolve and develop:

- *Emergence.* This is the process, according to Cohen (1972: 9), whereby a 'condition, episode, person or group of persons emerges to become defined as a threat to societal values and interests'.
- *The media inventory.* Here the threat is articulated specifically through the mass media. An 'enemy' is identified and presented through processes of exaggeration, distortion, prediction and symbolization (Cohen, 2002: 16–34).
- *Moral entrepreneurs.* 'Various groups and organizations then take it upon themselves to pronounce upon the nature of the problem', and identify appropriate responses. For Cohen (2002: 1) the 'moral barricades are manned by editors, politicians, bishops and other right-thinking people'.
- *Experts.* Socially accredited experts then pronounce their diagnoses and solutions.
- *Coping and resolution.* Experts and moral entrepreneurs translate ideas into practice. Control initiatives are exploited and if – as is often the case – they are found lacking, they are expanded.
- *Fade away.* Moral panics rarely last long. The moral panic ends when the condition disappears, submerges or deteriorates.

The rise of the 'gang' within public consciousness appears to 'fit' with the moral panic model well. Up to 2002 there was limited media interest in 'gangs'. The focus of media reporting was, as stated, fixed upon the spectre of the 'mugger'. This radically changed in tandem with widespread media reporting of a series of violent episodes that came to be defined as 'gang'-related. It began in 2000 with the death of 10-year-old Damilola Taylor in South London,[1] but it was the apparently random murder of two girls in Birmingham, in 2003,[2] that cemented the arrival of the 'gang'. With a small but steady stream of fatal shootings, often involving young black males, the 'evidential basis' of a society facing new and alarming threats – posed by armed 'gangs' – evolved. Street crime effectively disappeared as a news story as the 'gang' steadily and incrementally came to replace the 'mugger' as the new public enemy.

There is little doubt that the media reporting surrounding the 'gang' had all the hallmarks of 'exaggeration', 'distortion', 'prediction' and 'symbolization' that Cohen (2002: 16–34) terms the 'media inventory'. Cases of violence reported as 'gang-related' were, on closer inspection, not 'gang-related' at all (including, interestingly, the death of Damilola Taylor, whose murder provoked the original 'discovery' of the 'gang' but who was actually killed by two brothers (see

Hallsworth and Young, 2008). Despite this, having 'discovered' 'gangs' the media has since applied the term permissively to include seemingly all and every group of (working-class) young people with any street presence. It is not only the media who apply the term 'gang' indiscriminately; Ofsted (school) inspectors, not normally recognized for their criminological expertise, felt qualified to identify a burgeoning 'gang culture' in British schools (Ofsted, 2005). Not only have 'gangs' arrived, according to such accounts, they have been ascribed organizational capacities that they cannot possibly possess, as was the case with the sensational reporting of a group termed the Muslim Boys in London. This 'gang', it was claimed by the *Independent* newspaper, had Al Qaeda connections and their stock in trade was (allegedly) forcibly converting their 'victims' to Islam (Malik, 2005). Add to this a rash of ill thought out 'gang' documentaries – most of which have relied upon treating exceptional cases as the norm, asking leading questions and often treating unsubstantiated (not to say frequently absurd) testimony as gospel truth – and the 'gangland Britain' thesis assuredly came to establish itself as 'the changing face of youth crime' (Pitts, 2008).

To sensational media reporting must be added the contribution of a range of other dubious moral entrepreneurs within the burgeoning 'gang control industry'. Lee Jasper – the then Mayor of London's principal adviser on 'race', youth and crime – proclaimed, in the *Independent* article on the Muslim Boys that they represented nothing less than the 'single greatest criminal threat' he had ever witnessed (Malik, 2005). And even more absurdly, when the Mayor of London, Boris Johnson, subsequently held a press conference – to publicize his anti-gang and anti-violence credentials – he was flanked by the actor Ross Kemp, whose 'expertise' on 'gangs' (and thus his credibility to pronounce 'solutions') amounted to no more than being cast as a gangster in a popular soap opera (*EastEnders*) and, on the back of that, fronting a 'documentary' series on 'gangs'. The Mayor's 'informed prognosis', for what it is worth: 'gang' members had bad role models and needed better ones (the military) (Crerar, 2008).

The emerging 'gang-control industry' – the presence of which has, para-doxically, fuelled moral panic – is nothing if not eclectic. To help develop its anti-gang strategy, the Home Office commissioned private consultants. At a seminar convened at 10 Downing Street – co-chaired by the Prime Minister and the Home Secretary – a representative of the Wave Trust (a proselytizing organization steeped in biologically reductionist theories of crime) argued, in part, that the problem of 'gangs' arose from the fact that the average 'gang' member had an atrophied brain by the age of 3 (Wave Trust, 2007). In a subsequent conference on 'gangs' – attended by the Mayor of London – an image of an atrophied brain appeared as part of a PowerPoint presentation provided by the Wave Trust (by now apparently accorded the status of experts). Truth to tell it looked rather like a walnut (see Figure 10.2).[3]

The head of the British Race Equalities Council at the time, Trevor Phillips, also attended the Downing Street seminar. He was subsequently quoted by the *Guardian* newspaper as a leading player in the development of the government's

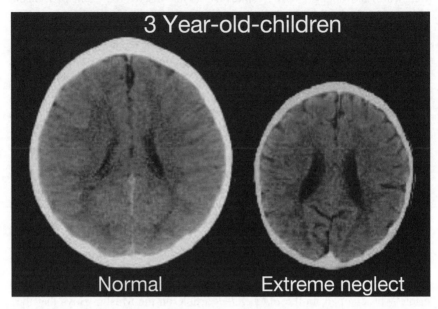

Figure 10.2 Fantasies of the street (2): the brain of a 'gang member'?
Source: Wave Trust (2007: 14)

anti-gang strategy (Muir, 2007) (although quite where his supposed 'expertise' on 'gangs' came from is unknown). Phillips' 'expert' solution was similar to (and as idiotic as) Ross Kemp's: gang members need military role models don't they?

Perhaps most problematic of all, academics have also played a significant role in helping cement the dystopian vision of a society plagued by 'gangs'. Notwithstanding the more nuanced attempts to understand 'gangs' – which have cast considerable doubt on any notion of an organized counter-force confronting the 'good society' (Aldridge and Medina-Ariza, 2005; Alexander, 2008) – the problem is that more accurate, but less sensational terms, like 'messy networks' (Aldridge et al., this volume) rarely appeal in quite the same way as sensationalized constructions of 'gangs' and, as such, are easily ignored by the media and political elites with an interest in having their fantasies of the street confirmed rather than challenged. An associated problem with academic 'gang talkers' actively searching for 'gangs' and deploying surveys to help them 'find' them, is that such fixed determination is almost certainly going to yield 'results'. More than that, given the fluidity and elasticity of 'gang' definitions, the 'researcher' can find as many or as few 'gangs' as their methodological variables – to measure 'gang' prevalence – allow. While the interventions of identifiable academic 'experts' into this policy arena might be expected to dispel some of the more grotesque media distortions, paradoxically it has acted to reinforce moral panic and to escalate processes of deviance amplification further.

Politicians comprise an additional constituency to have found considerable mileage in the 'gang'. New Labour ministers were quick to seize and pronounce on the 'gangland menace'. Tony Blair, when Prime Minister, was quick off the mark in pledging a crackdown on 'gangs' and actively promoting the implementation of anti-gang legislation. Similarly, Iain Duncan Smith, representing the new face of 'compassionate conservatism' (sic), produced a report on 'gangs' entitled *Dying to Belong* that presents yet another vision of the 'gangland Britain' thesis, offered this time as confirmation that Britain is indeed 'broken' (Centre for Social Justice, 2009).

At the practitioner end, a range of personnel have emerged from the woodwork in recent years, seemingly reinventing and presenting themselves as self-professed 'gang' experts and serving to front a disturbing proliferation of anti-gang policy and practice initiatives. As an example, at a conference run by the National Probation Service in 2008 ('Steps 4 Change: Addressing Serious Violence'), one practitioner presented a paper on the rise of girl 'gangs' flanked by two 'gang girls' whose voices were never heard (as the male practitioner did the talking for them). According to this 'expert', girl 'gang' members are far more dangerous than people imagine. Scarily the conference delegates were busy noting down this nonsense as if it was the gospel truth. The 'expert' concluded his presentation by drawing the audience's attention to the dedicated programme his organization now provides to tackle the 'disturbing' rise of 'gang girls'. As he noted (without irony), he had identified an 'important' gap in the market!

What moral panic and the work of the media – alongside an army of other 'right thinking people' (Cohen, 2002: 1) who should know better – have managed to cement, and quite successfully, is the fundamental notion that the UK is facing an unprecedented threat from organized criminal (youth) 'gangs'. The underpinning control fantasy provides that such 'gangs' are on the rise, they are large and organized, they are more dangerous than they used to be and they have to be stopped. All of this is said to necessitate the delegation of more and wider powers to the control apparatus. Perhaps inevitably, without any meaningful 'gang' intervention programme of its own, the UK government has looked for guidance to the USA, where the 'gang control industry' has tangibly failed but where such failure has not prevented its widespread implementation closer to home.

The industrial logic of 'gang' production

Moral panics tend by nature to be relatively intense but short in duration. Eventually they fade away as 'solutions' are developed by control agencies and/or the media lose interest and an alternative 'folk devil' is discovered to fill the void. While the 'discovery' of the 'gang' certainly fits with the developmental cycle of moral panic discussed by Cohen (1972; 2002) and Critcher (2003), its demise is less certain in the short term. Indeed, it is more likely that violent street life – engendered by multiple forms of marginality in polarized cities – will continue to feed the 'gangland Britain' thesis. Nor is it only 'gangland killings' that sustain this fantasy. The term 'gang' is now so nebulous, fluid and elastic that it can be randomly applied to just about any group of young people 'hanging around'. The fundamental idea that society is facing an organized counter-force – as distinct from a disorganized mess – ensures that the focus of attention remains on the 'gang' rather than the social and economic conditions that tend to produce violent street worlds. In this sense the 'gang' provides us with what Christie (2001) terms a 'suitable enemy', upon which an insecure society can vent its rage and indignation.

The continued rediscovery of the 'gang' also meshes well with the needs of the emerging post welfare security state that requires a tangible object on which to focus. Conceptualizing the street as an amorphous messy reality is too complex, fuzzy and uncomfortable for most control agents. It unsettles and challenges their explanatory universe that is typically constructed in arboreal terms. If the street world can be reduced down to readily defined 'offices' and neatly organized divisions of labour – 'lieutenants', 'soldiers', 'aspirants' and 'wannabees' – to particular group identities allocated 'risk' scores and, ultimately, to coercive control, it lends itself to convenience whereby multiple, intersecting and extra-ordinarily complex phenomena are simplistically encapsulated by the problem of the 'gang'. The term 'gang' will also remain popular because of its intrinsic growth potential. As noted, it is an elastic construct that can be mutated, blurred and hybridized at will. The term is pregnant with possibility. New 'gang' typologies are readily created – including 'girl gangs' – and blended with other reifications such as 'knife crime' and 'gun crime'.

Following Christie (2000), there is also an industrial logic to the reproduction of the 'gang menace'. Until recently the UK had no established 'gang' experts and certainly little by way of a developed 'gang control' apparatus. But this has all changed and there is now a burgeoning industry that, on the one hand, claims to suppress the 'gang', whilst on the other hand paradoxically feeds from it and, accordingly, has a vested interest in discovering and maintaining precisely that which it ostensibly aims to expunge. Ultimately, a stage has been reached where too many people have too great a vested interest in the 'gang' to surrender the gangland fantasy.

At the general level, 'gang talk' operates like a lubricant oiling the control apparatus in ways that allows its constituent cogs to turn and mesh together. 'Gang talk', in this sense, animates the system. It provides a clear and common focus around which the control apparatus – and its various vested interests – works. Take, for example, the research community who have had a field day: discovering 'gangs', defining 'gangs', producing 'gang' typologies and, not least, proffering views and informing 'action plans' pertaining to what needs to be done. This is now big business. Whereas, until recently, few academics were researching this issue, 'gang' research has now mushroomed. The political community is equally, if not more implicated. 'Gang talk' provides politicians with the ammunition they need in order to demonstrate governing competence within the emerging security state.

Where, until recently, there were few 'gang' experts and few 'gang' suppression programmes, these are now proliferating like weeds. One of the core beneficiaries is the practitioner community that has found common purpose in 'gang' suppression. By becoming 'gang' experts and – in some cases – chairing various anti-'gang' committees and task forces, many practitioners' career prospects have prospered. Others, particularly in the private sector, have created 'anti-gang programmes' attracting generous funding from central and local government. John Pitts (2008) refers to 'reluctant gangsters' but there is also a constituency of reluctant practitioners who have found that unless they also do 'gang talk', they are unlikely to receive the necessary resources needed to sustain services for the troubled young people with whom they work. Indeed, as an indication of such absurdity youth workers have been known to attempt to have their young people identified as 'gang' members precisely so they can access services and support that would otherwise not be available.

What is to be done?

From the perspective of the control imaginary the solution is clear. A new 'public enemy' has emerged and it must be suppressed. Inspired by the USA, 'solutions' are now being borrowed and are currently being rolled out across the UK. Many problems of the street certainly derive from the behaviours and actions of violent men operating within the volatile world that is the retail end of the illegal drug economy. This is a world where violence is produced by messy, amorphous and profoundly disorganized processes as distinct from organized and regimented divisions of labour. But because many 'gang talkers' occupy the space of the control imaginary this is not the street reality they typically want to see. It's simply not convenient: it collides with and unsettles not only their explanatory universe but also, in many cases, their vested interests in the industry that is keeping 'gang' mythology alive.

Real solutions cannot be found from within the control imaginary and others must be sought out. If the problem of the street is its social disorganization then, in part, a solution lies in creating a more organized street world. The way forward is not to confront this volatile reality by suppressing the 'gang', but by radicalizing and politicizing the often deeply alienated and marginalized young people who live amongst it. Far from looking at the emerging 'gang' suppression industry as the solution to the problem of street violence, it must itself be conceptualized as part of the problem. To build a better society, therefore, it is ultimately necessary to eliminate the 'gang' control industry.

Notes

1 In November 2000, Damilola Taylor, a 10-year-old schoolboy, was killed on a council estate in Peckham, south London, after being stabbed in the leg. Two brothers aged 12 and 13 were subsequently convicted of manslaughter.
2 Charlene Ellis aged 18 and Latisha Shakespear aged 17 both died outside a New Year's party in 2003 in Aston, Birmingham, after being hit by a hail of bullets dispensed from an automatic weapon in a 'drive-by' shooting.

3   This image was subsequently used by a senior Metropolitan Police Officer to illustrate
    the 'reality' of British 'gangs' at an international conference convened in Rome by the
    European Council in 2007. Sections of the audience were, to say the least, somewhat
    incredulous. On being asked where the neglected brain originated from, the officer had
    to concede that it belonged to a 3-year-old Romanian orphan subject to extreme
    neglect and abuse.

References

Aldridge, J. and Medina-Ariza, J. (2005) *Youth Gangs in an English City: Social Exclusion, Drugs and Violence*. Swindon: ESRC. Retrieved 30 August 2010 (http://www.esrc societytoday.ac.uk/esrcinfocentre/viewawardpage.aspx?awardnumber=RES-000-23-0615).

Alexander, C. (2008) *(Re)Thinking 'Gangs'*. London: The Runnymede Trust.

Bean, J.P. (1981) *The Sheffield Gang Wars*. Sheffield: D & D Publications.

Bennet, T. and Holloway, K. (2004) 'Gang Membership, Drugs and Crime in the UK', *British Journal of Criminology*, 44(3): 305–23.

Castells, M. (1996) *The Rise of the Network Society*. Cambridge, MA: Blackwell.

Centre for Social Justice (2009) *Dying to Belong: An In-Depth Review of Street Gangs in Britain*. London: Centre for Social Justice.

Christie, N. (2000) *Crime Control as Industry: Towards Gulags, Western Style*. London, Routledge.

—— (2001) 'Det idealiska offret' [The Ideal Victim], in M. Akerstrom and I. Sahlin (eds) *Det motspanstiga offret* [The Defiant Victim]. Lund: Studentlitteratur, pp. 46–60.

Cohen, S. (1972). *Folk Devils and Moral Panics: The Creation of the Mods and Rockers*. London: MacGibbon & Kee.

—— (2002) *Folk Devils and Moral Panics*, third edition. London: Routledge.

Crerar, P. (2008) 'Unruly Teenagers Need Tough Love says Boris', *Evening Standard*, 26 June.

Critcher, C. (2003) *Moral Panics and the Media*. Buckingham: Open University Press.

Hall, S. and Jefferson, T. (eds) (1976) *Resistance Through Rituals: Youth Subcultures in Post-war Britain*. London: Hutchinson for The Centre for Contemporary Cultural Studies, University of Birmingham.

Hall, S., Critcher, C., Jefferson, T., Clarke, J. and Roberts, B. (1977) *Policing the Crisis: Mugging, the State and Law and Order*. London: Macmillan.

Hallsworth, S. (2005) *Street Crime*. Cullompton: Willan.

Hallsworth, S. and Silverstone, D. (2009). '"That's Life Innit": A British Perspective on Guns, Crime and Social Order', *Criminology and Criminal Justice*, 9(3): 359–77.

Hallsworth, S. and Young, T. (2008) 'Gang Talk and Gang Talkers: A Critique', *Crime Media Culture*, 4(2): 175–95.

Home Office (2008) *Saving Lives, Reducing Harm, Protecting the Public: An Action Plan for Tackling Violence 2008–11*. London: Home Office.

Jacobs, B.A. (1999) *Dealing Crack: The Social World of Streetcorner Selling*. Boston, MA: Northeastern University Press.

—— (2000) *Robbing Drug Dealers: Violence Beyond the Law*. New York: Aldine de Gruyter.

Katz, J. and Jackson-Jacobs, C. (2004) 'The Criminologists Gang', in C. Sumner (ed.) *The Blackwell Companion to Criminology*. Oxford: Blackwell.

Lupton, R., Wilson, A., May, T., Warburton, H. and Turnbull, P.J. (2002) *A Rock and a*

Hard Place: Drug Markets in Deprived Neighbourhoods. Home Office Research Study 240. London: Home Office. Retrieved 30 August 2010 (www.kcl.ac.uk/depsta/law/ research/icpr/publications/drugs%20and%20dep.pdf).

Malik, S. (2005) 'Are "Muslim Boys" Using Profits of Crime to Fund Terrorist Attacks?', *Independent on Sunday*, 14 August.

Moshmus, G. (2005) 'Migrant Users of Heroin in Oslo', unpublished PhD thesis, University of Oslo.

Muir, H. (2007) 'Black Army Officers Recruited to Help Stop Gang Violence', *Guardian*, 4 September.

Office for Standards in Eductaion (Ofsted) (2005) *The Annual Report of Her Majesty's Chief Inspector of Schools 2004/05*. London: Ofsted.

Patrick, J. (1973) *A Glasgow Gang Observed*. London: Eyre Methuen.

Pearson, G. (1983) *Hooligan: A History of Respectable Fears*. London: Macmillan.

Pitts, J. (2008) *Reluctant Gangsters: The Changing Face of Youth Crime*. Cullompton: Willan.

Sharp, C., Aldridge, J. and Medina, J. (2006) *Delinquent Youth Groups and Offending Behaviour: Findings from the 2004 Offending Crime and Justice Survey*. London: Home Office.

Toy, J. (2008) *Die Another Day: A Practitioner's Review with Recommendations for Confronting Gang and Weapon Violence in London in 2008*. Available at: http://www. csas.org.uk/upload/documents/webpage/webpage/Practitioners%20.pdf

Wave Trust (2007) *Working Together to Reduce Serious Youth Violence: WAVE Conference for the 33 London Boroughs, Summary of Key Themes and Main Messages*. London: The Wave Trust. Retrieved 30 August 2010 (http://www.wavetrust.org/).

Wilson, A., May, T., Warburton, H., Lupton, R. and Turnbull, P.J. (2002) *Heroin and Crack Cocaine Markets in Deprived Areas: Seven Local Case Studies*, CASE report 19, Centre for the Analysis of Social Exclusion. London: London School of Economics and Political Science. Retrieved 30 August 2010 (http://eprints.lse.ac.uk/27367/).

Young, T., Fitzgerald, M., Hallsworth, S. and Joseph, I. (2007) *Groups, Gangs and Weapons*. London: Youth Justice Board.

Chapter 11

Gangs and transnationalisation

Rob White

Introduction

The issue of youth gangs has received considerable media, political and police attention in many different countries around the world in recent years. The aim of this chapter is to consider the gang phenomenon in an international context and, specifically, to discuss the nature of gangs through the analytical lens of transnationalisation. The term 'transnationalisation', as used here, refers to an approach that attempts to distil common and convergent elements among gangs from many national contexts, as well as identifying points of difference and divergence. The chapter begins with a brief overview of the burgeoning literature on youth gangs, particularly in Europe, and of the key propositions, tensions and disagreements that have emerged among those engaged in the study of youth group formations. A more extended discussion of key themes that may help us to understand the similarities and differences in gang formation around the world is then presented.

The chapter is necessarily speculative and exploratory in nature due, in no small part, to the breadth and diversity of gang formations (and gang research) and the complexity of the phenomenon at hand. Although generalisation is complicated, and in some senses inadequate, it is important to recognise broad international themes that constantly appear and reappear in the research literature as they provide the conceptual platform upon which our understanding of youth gangs might be enhanced.

Transnational analyses: debates and controversies

The concept of the 'gang' is highly contentious and controversial and, to put it simply, the research community is divided. On the one hand, it is claimed that gangs comprise a very specific type of social problem that must be studied in detail if prevention strategies are to be successfully employed. From this perspective, an effective and appropriate response to gangs and gang issues requires a thorough assessment of local communities and careful appraisal of what is happening at neighbourhood level (Howell, 2000). Intervention is generally directed at the gang itself, since this is seen as, in essence, the key problem. For other researchers, however, the complexities of gang life and gang formation preclude a traditional criminological analysis or criminal justice response.

Institutionally, the growing importance attached to the study of gangs is reflected in the formation of the Eurogang Research Network, with participation from over 20 different countries, including leading gang researchers from the United States (see Aldridge et al., Pitts and Squires, all this volume). Similarly, the number of publications deriving from gang research in recent years attest to the continuing and consolidating interest in youth gangs in various countries and continental regions, for example: the USA (Huff, 2002; Venkatesh, 2008); the UK (Pitts, 2008); Australia (White, 2006); Europe (Decker and Weerman, 2005); Africa (Matusitz and Repass, 2009) and, more generally, on the global stage (Duffy and Gillig, 2004; Hagedorn, 2007a; 2007b; 2008). A number of key themes and contentions typify the research literature including: gangs exist in many different forms; gangs constitute a problem that is growing (although to whom they are a problem is subject to debate); gangs are spreading across regions (both urban and rural) and across nation-state borders; gangs stem from, and represent, significant social changes within different national contexts (particularly shifting economic regimes and changing immigration patterns); gangs demand varying but integrated responses from both national and local state agencies and related authorities (although whether they are, or should be, the targets or the beneficiaries of state intervention is also open to debate).

Notwithstanding the increasing interest in the study of gangs, however, not everyone is convinced that the actual term 'gang' is appropriate or that gang research is necessarily desirable or socially progressive. Critical commentators in the USA and the UK, for example, have questioned both the 'gang' concept and the tendency to base research on mainstream (even populist) conceptualisations and constructions of the 'gang' (for example: Hagedorn, 2007a; Alexander, 2008; Hallsworth and Young, 2008; Hallsworth, this volume). A key criticism is that contemporary gang analysis or, as Hallsworth and Young (2008) put it, 'gang talk', blurs the complex and nuanced distinctions between youth groups, street gangs and organised crime (see also Aldridge et al., this volume; Hallsworth, this volume). In so doing, such approaches typically serve to entrench racialised connotations (wittingly or otherwise), whereby the 'gang' becomes a coded reference to black, minority ethnic and immigrant youth. Gang analysis and intervention is thus seen to apply to, and problematise, particular minority ethnic groups in ways and forms that ultimately invoke police attention and coercive interventions. Thus individual pathology – rather than systemic marginalisation and structural shifts in political economy – is emphasised which, in turn, feeds processes of criminalisation and the moral panics that accompany them.

There are also fundamental differences and debates concerning research methodologies and forms of data collection pertaining to gangs. A key example of this relates to the development and use of gang databases in the USA that, according to some, allow modes of legislated data collection that are over-inclusive and stigmatising of young people. The operational definitions of 'gangs' are thus highly politicised when linked to the question of government intervention, policy and social control and here too academics are implicated (Spergel, 2009). Indeed, US-style gang research – which heavily influences the methods presently being adopted as part of the Eurogang Research Network agenda – tends to be strongly positivist in orientation, whereby quantitative investigation is favoured, databases are established and particular political 'understandings' and interventions flow from them.

Meanwhile, some social scientists prefer to actually engage in close-up, firsthand observation of where people live in order to discern what they actually do with their time and to understand the values and meanings that they attribute to their complex social realities (Wacquant, 2007). The core argument here is that the 'social problem' of gangs is structurally generated, but dominant conceptualisations erroneously see it in terms of criminogenic tendencies, individual pathology, moral breakdown and/or crude positivist demographic causation. This denies dynamic social processes that also implicate power, for example, police discretion, brutality and neoliberal economics. Those who do get close to the complex realities, and who critique conventional understandings and associated criminal justice interventions, are often considered to be 'rogue sociologists' (Venkatesh, 2008), who are viewed with suspicion if not outright hostility by those with a stake in maintaining the (academic as well as political) status quo (Hagedorn, 2008; Hallsworth, this volume).

If attention is focused uncritically on a 'problem', then the 'problem' will more often than not appear to be real. This is one of the core dilemmas of gang research. For those who see gangs as a *bona fide* area of public concern, the recognition of gangs is a basic starting point for intervention and crime prevention. For others, who view gang discourse itself as part of the 'problem', the agenda becomes very different. In particular, the stigmatising impact of gang labels (Alexander, 2008) and the potential for unwarranted group profiling on the part of justice authorities (White, 2008a) are seen to be especially questionable. In sum, both gang as concept and gang research as social process, continue to be the subject of major ongoing debates. The doing of gang research is thus fraught with a number of ethical, political, methodological and conceptual controversies.

Gangs and transnational propositions

The lived realities of young people who identify with gangs are invariably complicated, ambiguous and complex and, as such, gang research and the development of appropriate anti-gang (or pro-youth) strategies are beset by persistent problems and definitional disputes. Despite this, key issues surrounding analyses of gangs can be summarised in the form of a series of core propositions (White, 2008a) based upon American, Canadian, European, British, Australian and South African studies and international research reviews including: Miller (1992); Decker (1996); Howell (1998); Gordon (2000); Klein et al. (2001); Esbensen et al. (2001); Klein (2002) and Standing (2005).

Proposition 1

International research has increasingly emphasised that gang formation is a *social process* involving complex forms of membership, transformation and disintegration.

Proposition 2

The composition of youth gangs is ever-changing and there are significant differences both in how such groups are structured and organised and in how different organisations, agencies and researchers describe them. As stated, the very term 'gang' – and the means by which its identity/ies is/are defined, framed and understood internally and externally – is complicated and pitted with *ambiguity*.

Proposition 3

Gangs are primarily expressions of *identity*, and identity itself is shaped by multiple intersecting factors including: community recognition of the group as a gang; the group's recognition of itself as a distinct gang; and the group's involvement in sufficient illegal activities to attract consistent negative responses from law enforcement officials and local people.

Proposition 4

Just as there are problems in defining what a gang is, so too there are major difficulties in attempting to establish who a gang member is. *Group membership is a fluid process* and, over time, specific individuals have varying degrees and types of association with groups and/or gangs.

Proposition 5

Even when a gang can be determined to actually exist, gang membership is rarely absolute or fixed, since *gang membership is highly variable and changing*, and there is often no clear dividing line between those who are in a gang and those who are not – there are layers of belonging and connection that vary according to circumstance and activities.

Proposition 6

Many young people who do not identify with gangs may nevertheless engage in gang-like behaviour, such as criminal activity, street fights, drug use and wearing of gang-type clothing. *Gang-related behaviour is not the same as gang membership*. Nor do all gangs engage in the full range of gang-like behaviour.

Proposition 7

Not all gang behaviour is necessarily criminal, illegal or 'bad' since a lot of what young people do is simply to hang out together. *Much of the time the gang is not a problem* for nearby residents, for other young people or for themselves.

Proposition 8

Where young people themselves claim gang membership, they tend to engage in substantially more antisocial and criminal behaviour than those who do not profess to be gang members. Thus *who young people say they are has implications for what they do and who they do it with*. Group identification is intertwined with group activity.

Proposition 9

Gang membership is heavily tied in with group violence. However, this violence is manifest within a wider *context of social marginalisation and exclusion* invariably based upon ethnicity. Antagonisms on the street – between groups of minority ethnic youth and authority figures such as the police, and between diverse groups of young people – are constantly reinforced by negative stereotyping, media moral panics and the day-to-day racism experienced by such young people.

Transnational gangs as a specific phenomenon

Hagedorn (2007b: 2) identifies three key differences between 'traditional' (American) criminology and a more global and alternative form of social analysis. Specifically, he argues that traditional criminology views gangs as temporary adolescent departures from the mainstream – deviant byproducts of industrial-isation, urbanisation and concomitant social disorganisation. By contrast – and based upon ethnographies and case studies from many different parts of the world – an alternative vision of gangs is based upon three key observations (Hagedorn, 2007b: 2):

- While most gangs are unsupervised teenage peer groups, many others have become institutionalised within ghettos, barrios and favelas across the world.
- Gangs are found all over the world, responding to and reflecting the changing socio-economic and political conditions of globalising cities.
- Gangs are 'social actors' whose identities are often formed by ethnic, racial, and/or religious oppression, through participation in the underground economy and through particular constructions of gender.

So, global analyses of gangs might reveal identifiable common features regardless of locality, but there remains an important distinction between the local gang and the transnational gang:

Various definitions have cited one or more of the following characteristics in defining a transnational gang: (1) such gangs are criminally active and operational in more than one country; (2) criminal activities committed by gang members in one country are planned, directed and controlled by gang leaders in another country; (3) such gangs tend to be mobile and adapt to new areas; and (4) the criminal activities of such gangs tend to be sophisticated and transcend borders (Franco, 2008: 3).

In essence, the transnational gang operates *across* boundaries and borders and not simply *within* them.

The transnational gang has been characterised as representing a different stage of gang development, far removed from street-level youth groups. So-called *first generation gangs* are seen to be turf-oriented and localised while *second generation gangs* are underpinned by a market, tending to be drug-centred rather than having a specific turf orientation. The *third generation gangs* are said to be driven by ambitious goals of power and/or major financial acquisition, to embrace a set of fully evolved political aims and a willingness to resort to terrorism in order to achieve such objectives (Franco, 2008). Not surprisingly, this type of analysis stems from, and is closely linked to, national security imperatives and the burgeoning conceptual conflation of 'criminal' and 'national security' issues and responses (Short, 2007; Hagedorn, 2008).

To conflate fundamentally different forms and modes of organisation into a unitary category of the 'gang' is clearly problematic, however. Rather, the actual world of gangs is marked by multiple and widely divergent forms, associations and operational dynamics. This makes the question of definition even more problematic:

> As today's gangs proliferate, they often morph into ethnic militias, drug posses, vigilantes, mercenaries, political parties or even religious police. Gangs and similar alienated and angry groups are a fundamental and long-term characteristic of the global era.
>
> (Hagedorn, 2008: xxiv)

There is no set structure, no predictable or evolutionary stage. Indeed, whilst gangs are ubiquitous, they are simultaneously local and unique. Each has to be understood in its own terms and in its own 'backyard'.

Having said this, it remains the case that transnational gangs exist, the origins and development of which are also highly contentious. Perhaps the most notorious of the transnational gangs in the world today stem from a period of forced deportations from the United States whereby street gang members in Los Angeles and elsewhere were arrested and deported to El Salvador, from where their families originated. Back 'home' (even though many had never lived there), such gang members associated with ex-guerrilla fighters and ex-soliders who had turned to crime in the absence of employment (Johnson and Muhlhausen, 2005). The net result has been the emergence and consolidation of the MS-13 and 18th Street Gangs in a revolving-door movement of people between parts of Latin America (particularly El Salvador and Mexico) and the USA. The transnational gang has, in effect, been made in the crucible of restrictive immigration policy and punitive criminal justice regimes.

What global gang study demonstrates is the methodological significance of historical appreciation, the importance of place and socio-economic contextual-isation. Specific historical and material conditions – including: shifting migration patterns; economic polarisation and social inequality; war and drought; varying capacities and willingness of nation-states to provide essential services and entrenched racism – shape how particular groups form and develop. Similarly, the threat (or opportunities for social change) posed by gangs is differentially con-ceptualised and portrayed depending upon local political context; from an emphasis on perceived criminality and threats to national security, through to their potential to stand at the forefront of significant societal reform. It is through global, comparative and historical analyses, therefore, that differences in the origin, formation and development of gangs on the one hand, and state and civil society responses to gangs on the other, are best understood.

The following discussion elaborates on some of these observations by con-sidering how they relate to *broad processes of social change*. In essence, the analytical gaze turns from discrete factors and specific trends to more general patterns that underpin the formation of, and responses to, youth gangs.

Commonalities and differences

While considerable variation in gang formation exists – type, size, structure and composition – important points of both commonality and difference warrant further explication.

Commonalities

As noted by many gang and youth studies researchers, the phenomenon of gangs is closely linked to *social exclusion*. The systemic and structural exclusion of identifiable categories and classes of young people from the mainstream institu-tions of society – most notably the institutions of formal paid work and education – is linked to wider processes of social change. In particular, globalisation has directly impacted upon, and fed into, the manner in which many young people are being re-positioned in their respective societies (Hagedorn, 2007a; 2007b; 2008). Fundamental shifts in the international political economy (in the form of the activities, and dominance, of transnational corporations), combined with the pervasive influence of microchip technologies (in the form of new communi-cations, especially the Internet), underpin profound social, economic and cultural changes across the globe. Increased urbanisation, social inequality and con-centrations of poverty are creating major hardships for young people in cities, particularly when labour markets fail to accommodate and absorb the movement of people into urban centres or provide employment for those who remain living in rural areas. Meanwhile, the free flow of images of material consumption, opportunity, wealth and street culture impact on those subject to the pressures and deprivations of modern life.

Social exclusion – particularly as it applies to the gang phenomenon – is manifest in three general tendencies:

- *Marginalisation* – whereby identifiable constituencies of young people are systematically excluded from mainstream institutions and are compelled to seek forms of social capital (social networks, friendship groups, institutional links) and engage in alternative means of gaining access to vital resources (money, food and shelter).
- *Criminalisation* – whereby the same young people become targets for concerted and systematic state intervention of a coercive nature. They are constructed in both the public eye and within the state apparatus as inherently and exclusively problematic to the social order, thus necessitating determined and forceful modes of intervention.
- *Racialisation* – whereby, in many countries, the processes of marginalisation and criminalisation are imbued with a distinctive 'racial' or 'ethnic' character, such that ethnic minorities, people of colour and immigrants become defined essentially as 'gangs', and thereby subject to coercive and corrective, rather than enabling and supportive, forms of state intervention.

These are by no means startling revelations. Critical criminology has long observed that class division and social inequality are fundamental to understanding the nature of particular forms of 'criminality' and the criminalising responses of the state (White and Cunneen, 2006; White, 2008b). The processes of marginal-isation are related to the presence of reserve armies of labour (particularly women and migrants and especially guest workers), the creation of surplus populations (for example, the long-term unemployed), and the pauperisation of both the working poor and the welfare poor. All of these are systemic social processes, as Wacquant (2007: 36) observes: 'a ghetto is not simply a topographic entity or an aggregation of poor families and individuals but an institutional form, a histori-cally determinate, spatially based concatenation of mechanisms of ethnoracial closure and control'. In other words, constructions of racialisation and the impact of racism are particularly salient.

Present conflicts and societal disjunctures – depending upon country and region – also have to be historically contextualised and understood with reference to imperialist traditions. Consider for a moment the implications of the colonial era for understanding contemporary Europe:

Due to the special relationship between the colonizers and the colonized, citizens were often free to travel between the European nation and the ex-colony. Many of these groups stayed in the colony nation, for example, England (e.g., India, Pakistan, and West-Indies), France (e.g., Algeria, Morocco, and Senegal), Portugal (e.g., Brazil and Angola), and The Netherlands (e.g., Indonesia and Surinam) have a large – and growing – number of inhabitants with roots in their former colonies.

(Decker et al., 2009: 395)

Colonialism is at one and the same time the maker of both difference and of deviance. The ethnic presence is both numerical minority and 'other' – the colonial subject. Racism is built into the fabric of much European tradition, history and citizenship, just as slavery is ingrained within American traditions. It follows that gang formations across different national contexts are historically embedded within long and complex legacies of colonial relations.

Differences

While general similarities are apparent across the many and diverse gang formations worldwide, there are, nevertheless, also important differences. At a systems level, this is perhaps best explained in terms of differences in the institutionalisation of welfare. The means by which societal resources are communally shared, or not shared, has a major impact on human behaviour, including the behaviour of identifiable groups of young people.

In countries that have a well-developed welfare state apparatus – universal provision of education, welfare, child care, income support, parenting benefits and so on – levels of social solidarity and social trust tend to be high. Conversely, for countries with less developed or poorly structured welfare systems, the opposite normally applies. Here the emphasis on individualism – and associated concepts related to individual responsibility and personal accountability – translates into lower levels of trust and less concern for the welfare of others (Paul, 2009). Fewer welfare safeguards and more tightly rationed (or denied) access to economic and social support, together with greater reliance upon individual initiative, enterprise and free markets, makes life and the competition for resources more demanding and altogether more difficult.

The general global trend vis-à-vis welfare provision, has signalled the steady retreat, if not erosion, of the agencies and benefits of the welfare state per se. This has occurred under the cover of neo-liberal reform, the ideological emphasis on individual rather than collective responsibility for welfare and the institutionalisation of cuts in welfare spending, user-pays schemes and a 'mixed economy' approach within which the free market expands and state provision contracts. As Hagedorn (2008) also points out, in many nation-states there is no universal welfare to cut in the first place, since the social and economic infrastructure is historically chronically weak.

With regard to gang formations and associated phenomena, the provision of state welfare, or not, impacts upon and shapes core social relations and conditions including:

- *Levels of violence* – in the most social democratic societies, where welfare provision is freely available, gang violence tends to be less intense, less deadly and less severe than elsewhere where welfare entitlements are more limited or simply not available (Medina, 2010). Institutional welfare provision moderates violence to the extent that extremes of poverty are mediated by some form of material support. Life often remains hard, but it is less desperate when such support is available.

- *Motivation for gang membership* – while all gangs involve some sense of identity and identification, often associated with ethnicity, the rationales underpinning gang membership vary (at least in part) due to economic (read welfare) circumstances. The *raison d'être* for becoming part of a gang often includes an accumulation logic (gaining access to economic resources) and/or it might rest on affiliation (being part of a group and engaging in processes of social belonging). Each is influenced, to a greater or lesser extent, by the nature of wider educational and employment opportunities and welfare settlements.

- *Evolving community–gang relationships* – gangs evolve, form, dissolve and reform over time. Some are embedded in local communities and have intergenerational roots, others are more transient and fluid. The precise function, role and/or place of a gang within a community is partly a reflection of what it signifies over time and the kinds of everyday relationships gang members have with the wider community (including non-gang-related activity). Pressures bearing down on gang members due to the impact of neo-liberal ideology, policy and practice will change the character of the gang–community relationship.

There are many additional differences between gangs, including the role and engagement of young women in gang affairs (see Batchelor and Young, both this volume), and gang structure and organisation (embracing entry and exit rituals and processes). Such differences require further detailed exploration taking account of cultural, local, regional, national and international patterns and the nature and impact of global trends in specific places and on particular demographic groups.

Transferences and identities

A core aspect of gang discourse that traverses borders and boundaries is moral panic. In many countries moral outrage is frequently created and/or stoked by the media in ways that both demonise particular groups of young people and/or brand them as 'gangs' (Cohen, 1973; Poynting and Morgan, 2007; Hallsworth, this volume). In turn, youth 'gangs' are frequently portrayed as 'dangerous', 'deviant' and 'destructive' and such media-constructed images are intertwined with political and public responses that call forth repressive measures and collective revulsion.

Transferences from place to place

Media negativity towards (and fascination with) 'gangs' involves the international circulation of particular ideas and images. Moral panic is not exclusively limited to a discrete one-off episode, nor are specific events necessarily separated from each other in mass media discourse. Indeed, as Poynting et al. (2004) convincingly argue, the means by which any identifiable group is persistently presented and conceptualised as a 'folk devil' stems from the ways in which discourses are assembled over time and serve to reinforce key messages and stereotypes.

In this way, the mass media are key to social constructions of ethnicity and social difference that transcend national borders. As stated, much popular understanding of youth gangs in North America, Europe and Australia is heavily racialised. In large part this stems from how the media presents and reports particular ethnic groups, with contemporary media images of minority communities in different national contexts being generally negative (for example, the Lebanese in Australia, north Africans in Italy, West Indians in England). This is especially the case with regard to recent immigrants and people of colour. Equally, particular events are often seized upon by the media to reinforce the 'ethnic' character of deviancy and criminality in ways that stigmatise whole communities (Collins et al., 2000; Poynting et al. 2004; Poynting and Morgan, 2007). As the experience in the United States indicates, immigration is frequently associated with the gang phenomenon. For example, the four major periods of gang presence in the USA – the 1890s, 1920s, 1960s and 1990s – were all linked to significant social changes including increased immigration (Decker et al., 2009; Johnson and Muhlhausen, 2005).

Beyond moral panic, however, not all groups respond in the same way to similar material pressures and popular media images. There are two key issues here that are of particular interest. The first relates to how certain ethnic and cultural groups are more likely to form gangs than others, and why this might be so. For example, van Gemert's (2005) research on Moroccan and Turkish immigrant youth in Amsterdam found that, compared to Turkish youth, Moroccan boys and young men are significantly over-represented in police statistics, and the majority of gang members are reported to be Moroccan. Here are two identifiable groups of immigrants with significant differences in how they appear to be settling into the host country. Explaining this difference requires a nuanced community studies rather than an homogenised 'gang approach'. A second issue pertains to how gang style and gang images are localised in their re-representation and reconstruction. To put it differently, young people might appropriate 'universal' images and yet transform them into unique forms and practices within their immediate milieu:

> Despite the similarity in names and gang style, there are important differences between Crips in the USA and Crips in the Netherlands. The latter are far less organized, are not organized around drug sales, are not territorial, and engage in much lower levels of violence. In other words, European Crips have

more in common with Crips gang style and affectation than organization or behavior.

(Decker et al., 2009: 401)

Here we have a case of ostensibly similar gang images, symbols and culture that in reality are quite different.

Continuing along the same lines, the terms 'Bloods' and 'Crips' are also used in New Zealand and Australia, where they essentially comprise ethnic markers: the Bloods refer to Samoan young people, the Crips to Tongan young people (White, 2008c). The colours each group wears (Bloods, red, Samoan; Crips, blue, Tongan) are immediate and striking signs of ethnic and, indeed, original island, origin. The relationship to US Bloods and Crips is tenuous, and the terms have basically been appropriated less as a gang identifier and more as local descriptions of ethnicity. Gang styles and associated cultural forms (such as Hip Hop), therefore, are culturally transmitted, but not necessarily culturally emulated. For example, the Australian Hip Hop scene is dominated by minority ethnic young people whose voices are distinctly (immigrant) Australian and whose cultural content/message is likewise unique to their circumstances (see White, 1999). Similarly, indigenous rappers in Australia have appropriated the form, but use different language (sometimes literally a different language) to express what matters to them in their particular cultural universe (White and Wyn, 2008).

Whatever the similarities and differences, the uniformly problematic images associated with gangs tend to impose and impact negatively. In other words, the social consequences of moral panics typically include ostracising and penalising identifiable youth groups – especially migrant or ethnic minority youth – on the basis of their presumed immoral and threatening behaviour, often by implementing legislation and stepped-up police interventions to prevent or prohibit street presence and certain types of activity. In this sense, the notion of 'transference' refers to the way in which certain people, ideas and images are conveyed from one place to another. From the point of view of moral panics over gangs, this usually includes popular representations of stereotypical gang characteristics that frequently fail to capture and/or accurately represent nuanced differences. The dissemination of such matter has been enhanced by the advent of the Internet and associated technologies such as Facebook and YouTube. Often what is conveyed is simply wrong or just plain racist. At the sharp end of this phenomenon, linkages between social identity and national security are forged, such as the recent case involving images of 'Muslim gangs in Australia' being posted on the Internet by a private US national security activist group. Furthermore, myths and images of this kind may also be picked up and perpetuated via 'legitimate' or 'respectable' Internet exchanges, such as the email information list of the Eurogang Research Network, which reproduced this particular 'story' without any analytical or critical comment.

Such representations tend not only to induce panic, fear and anxiety but they also impact worldwide on the ways in which young people see themselves and their activities; how they behave and how they make sense of their lives. Paradoxically, at this level, the gang image is not necessarily seen as 'bad' but rather as something to aspire to or emulate; the 'gangs' moral panic can thus serve to amplify the excitement attached to the label. For marginalised and often criminalised young people, transgression can be very appealing, especially as it both inverts the negativity of the label (being instead a sought-after status) and reinforces notoriety (since it feeds back into the very thing that is popularly detested). Street credibility and peer respect is fashioned out of precisely the process that most turns the state against the young people in question – the appearance of gang affiliation. Ironically, depending upon the jurisdiction, anti-gang strategies can materially feed processes of identity formation and group consolidation. As stated, this is most evident in the United States, where gang members in Los Angeles have been deported to El Salvador. The result of this has been the formation of US-style gangs in El Salvador and the subsequent flow back into the United States of gang members returning to their original 'home' (Zilberg, 2004). Thus coercive interventions can sustain and provide a feedback loop into the very problems presumably activating state action in the first place.

Globalisation and identity

Social identity forms a key aspect to understanding gang formation, gang activity and gang membership. Identity is multilayered and complex. For present purposes, it is important to note that much gang identification is forged through international as well as local contexts. All young people today are growing up in a world characterised by phenomena such as globalisation, neo-liberal political economy, war and consumerism. The specificity of personal being, however, is shaped not only by epochal and global features, but also by the mundane experiences of family, friends, neighbourhood, school and community (White and Wyn, 2008). The global may shape the local, but it is on the streets and in the suburbs that the particularities of social life are constructed and made manifest. This is why gang formations take on such different substantive shapes and characters.

Several recent edited volumes (see Short and Hughes, 2006; Hagedorn, 2007a; van Gemert et al., 2008) have each in their own way affirmed the complicated intersections between the ongoing projects of the 'self' (constructions of personal identity), the importance of specific local contexts (material resources and social histories), and wider global social, economic, political and cultural processes (globalisation) as they pertain to youth gangs. Group formations such as gangs are located in particular spaces at particular times and are engaged in particular kinds of activities. The collective and the personal – in terms of identities and wellbeing – are fused in the praxis of group formation and group dynamics. Furthermore, research has demonstrated that the complexities of social life frequently pivot around ethnicity and ethnic identity which, as stated, is itself dynamic, historical and multidimensional.

To understand both the fluidity and solidity of identity we need to comprehend actual migrations and migration processes, including ongoing links to historical homelands and ethnic traditions among certain migrant and established groups. But we also need to grasp both general ethnic identifications and the importance of territorial cross-ethnic alliances at the local level. This has been described by reference to the notion of 'defensive localism' (Adamson, 2000), in which gangs fight to protect territory. In protecting territory, however, ethnicity and locality combine in ways that sometimes privilege ethnicity, and sometimes territory – depending upon who the protagonists are, and who is defined as an 'outsider' at any given moment (White, 2008c). In analysing gang formation and gang activities, therefore, we need to appreciate the complex nature of group dynamics. Young people might simultaneously be members of particular gangs and of diverse social groups, and there is overlap between the two.

Conclusion

This chapter has provided a broad overview of what can be described as the transnational nature of youth gangs. Such transnationalisation incorporates several key elements. Analytically, processes of social exclusion, welfare institution-alisation and moral panic – and the particular concepts and social processes that pertain to each – are vital. There are various commonalities and differences in gang formation that flow from, and are a consequence of, the social positioning of young people in any particular society. Equally, within the global political economy transference processes – which in this instance includes the movement of images, ideas and people from one place to another – are also key. Such processes enable members of youth groups to develop and inhabit different symbolic and cultural universes at the same time through the magic of modern communications systems and technologies. Yet, when all is said and done, gangs are ultimately defined by, and tied to, localised material conditions and welfare settlements.

Social, economic and political exclusion, with consequently severely retarded life chances (vis-à-vis the mainstream), propels many young people into gang activ-ity. Globally, it is structural issues relating to inequality, poverty, unemployment and injustice that are at the heart of gang formation and gang activity. That said, as with the case of specific gang formations, the 'gang problem' will vary greatly from location to location. There are profound dangers in treating all such groups in the same way, particularly where this leads to social (and frequently racist) profiling, stigmatisation and pathologisation, and opens the door to criminalisation and inappropriate coercive state interventions. As Hagedorn (2008: 132) emphasises:

> The complex world we live in is not made up of neatly defined groups, some criminal, some political, some cultural. The world of gangs comprises flexible forms of armed groups, some changing from gang to militia to criminal syndicate to political party, or some existing as all types simultaneously.

Gang life is inherently changeable and complex.

References

Adamson, C. (2000) 'Defensive Localism in White and Black: A Comparative History of European-American and African-American Youth Gangs', *Ethnic and Racial Studies*, 23(2): 272–98.

Alexander, C. (2008) *(Re)thinking 'Gangs'*. London: Runnymede Trust.

Cohen, S. (1973) *Folk Devils and Moral Panics*. London: Paladin.

Collins, J., Noble, G., Poynting, S. and Tabar, P. (2000) *Kebabs, Kids, Cops and Crime: Youth, Ethnicity and Crime*. Sydney: Pluto Press.

Decker, S.H. (1996) 'Collective and Normative Features of Gang Violence', *Justice Quarterly*, 13: 243–64.

Decker, S. and Weerman, F. (eds) (2005) *European Street Gangs and Troublesome Youth Groups*. Lanham, MD: AltaMira Press.

Decker, S., van Gemert, F. and Pyrooz, D. (2009) 'Gangs, Migration, and Crime: The Changing Landscape in Europe and the USA', *International Migration and Integration*, 10: 393–408.

Duffy, M. and Gillig, S. (eds) (2004) *Teen Gangs: A Global View*. Westport: Greenwood.

Esbensen, F-A., Winfree Jr., L., He, N. and Taylor, T. (2001) 'Youth Gangs and Definitional Issues: When is a Gang a Gang and Why Does it Matter?', *Crime and Delinquency*, 47: 105–30.

Franco, C. (2008) *The MS-13 and 18th Street Gangs: Emerging Transnational Gang Threats? CRS Report for Congress*. Washington, DC: Congressional Research Service.

Gordon, R. (2000) 'Criminal Business Organizations, Street Gangs and "Wanna-be" Groups: A Vancouver Perspective', *Canadian Journal of Criminology*, January: 39–60.

Hagedorn, J. (ed.) (2007a) *Gangs in the Global City: Alternatives to Traditional Criminology*. Urbana and Chicago: University of Illinois Press.

—— (2007b) 'Introduction: Globalization, Gangs, and Traditional Criminology', in J. Hagedorn (ed.) *Gangs in the Global City: Alternatives to Traditional Criminology*. Urbana and Chicago: University of Illinois Press.

—— (2008) *A World of Gangs: Armed Young Men and Gangsta Culture*. Minneapolis: University of Minnesota Press.

Hallsworth, S. and Young, T. (2008) 'Gang Talk and Gang Talkers: A Critique', *Crime, Media, Culture*, 4(2): 175–95.

Howell, J.C. (1998) *Youth Gangs: An Overview*. Washington DC: U.S. Department of Justice, Office of Justice Programs, Office of Juvenile Justice and Delinquency Prevention.

—— (2000) *Youth Gang Programs and Strategies: Summary*. Washington, DC: U.S. Department of Justice, Office of Justice Programs, Office of Juvenile Justice and Delinquency Prevention.

Huff, R. (ed.) (2002) *Gangs in America*. Third edition. Thousand Oaks, California: Sage.

Johnson, S. and Muhlhausen, D. (2005) *North American Transnational Youth Gangs: Breaking the Chain of Violence*. Washington, DC: The Heritage Foundation.

Klein, M.W. (2002) 'Street Gangs: A Cross-National Perspective', in R. Huff (ed.) *Gangs in America*, third edition. Thousand Oaks, California: Sage.

Klein, M., Kerner, H-J., Maxon, C. and Weitekamp, E. (eds) (2001) *The Eurogang Paradox: Street Gangs and Youth Groups in the U.S. and Europe*. Dordrecht: Kluwer Academic Publishers.

Matusitz, J. and Repass, M. (2009) 'Gangs in Nigeria: An Updated Examination', *Crime, Law and Social Change*, 52(4): 495–511.

Medina, J. (2010) 'Youth Gangs in a Global Context', in S. Shoham, P. Knepper and M. Kett (eds) *International Handbook of Criminology*. New York: Taylor & Francis.

Miller, W.B. (1992) *Crime by Youth Gangs and Groups in the United States*. Washington, DC: US Department of Justice, Office of Justice Programs, Office of Juvenile Justice and Delinquency Prevention.

Paul, E. (2009) 'The Political Economy of Violence in Australia', *Journal of Australian Political Economy*, 63: 80–107.

Pitts, J. (2008) *Reluctant Gangsters: The Changing Face of Youth Crime*. Cullompton: Willan.

Poynting, S. and Morgan, G. (eds) (2007) *Outrageous! Moral Panics in Australia*. Hobart: ACYS Publishing.

Poynting, S., Noble, G., Tabar, P. and Collins, J. (2004) *Bin Laden in the Suburbs: Criminalising the Arab Other*. Sydney: Sydney Institute of Criminology, University of Sydney.

Short, J. (2007) 'The Challenges of Gangs in Global Contexts', in J. Hagedorn (ed.) *Gangs in the Global City: Alternatives to Traditional Criminology*. Urbana and Chicago: University of Illinois Press.

Short, J. and Hughes, L. (eds) (2006) *Studying Youth Gangs*. Walnut Creek, CA: AltaMira Press.

Spergel, I. (2009) 'Gang Databases: To Be or Not to Be', *Criminology and Public Policy*, 8(4): 667–74.

Standing, A. (2005) *The Threat of Gangs and Anti-Gangs Policy*, ISS Occasional Paper 116. South Africa: Institute for Security Studies.

van Gemert, F. (2005) 'Youth Groups and Gangs in Amsterdam: A Pretest of the Eurogang Expert Survey', in S. Decker and F. Weerman (eds) *European Street Gangs and Troublesome Youth Groups*. Lanham: AltaMira Press.

van Gemert, F., Peterson, D. and Lien, I-L. (eds) (2008) *Youth Gangs, Migration, and Ethnicity*. Cullompton: Willan.

Venkatesh, S. (2008) *Gang Leader for a Day*. New York: Penguin Press.

Wacquant, L. (2007) 'Three Pernicious Premises in the Study of the American Ghetto', in J. Hagedorn (ed.) *Gangs in the Global City: Alternatives to Traditional Criminology*. Urbana and Chicago: University of Illinois Press.

White, R. (ed.) (1999) *Australian Youth Subcultures: On the Margins and in the Mainstream*. Hobart: Australian Clearinghouse for Youth Studies.

White, R. (2006) 'Youth Gang Research in Australia', in J. Short and L. Hughes (eds) *Studying Youth Gangs*. Walnut Creek, CA: AltaMira Press.

—— (2008a) 'Disputed Definitions and Fluid Identities: The Limitations of Social Profiling in Relation to Ethnic Youth Gangs', *Youth Justice: An International Journal*, 8(2): 149–61.

—— (2008b) 'Class Analysis and the Crime Problem', in T. Anthony and C. Cunneen (eds) *The Critical Criminology Companion*. Sydney: Federation Press.

—— (2008c) 'Australian Youth Gangs and the Social Dynamics of Ethnicity', in F. van Gemert, D. Peterson and I-L. Lien (eds) *Youth Gangs, Migration, and Ethnicity*. Cullompton: Willan.

White, R. and Cunneen, C. (2006) 'Social Class, Youth Crime and Justice', in B. Goldson and J. Muncie (eds) *Youth Crime and Justice: Critical Issues*. London: Sage.

White, R. and Wyn, J. (2008) *Youth and Society: Exploring the Social Dynamics of Youth Experience*. Melbourne: Oxford University Press.

Zilberg, E. (2004) 'Fools Banished from the Kingdom: Remapping Geographies of Gang Violence Between the Americas (Los Angeles and San Salvador)', *American Quarterly*, 56(3): 759–80.

Index